Birds of Lake, Pond and Marsh

Water and Wetland Birds of Eastern North America

D0905876

John Eastman

Illustrated by Amelia Hansen

STACKPOLE BOOKS

0 11557 02681 8

Published by
STACKPOLE BOOKS
5067 Ritter Road
Mechanicsburg, PA 17055
www.stackpolebooks.com

Printed in the United States of America

Cover design by Wendy A. Reynolds

10 9 8 7 6 5 4 3 2 1

First edition

Library of Congress Cataloging-in-Publication Data

Eastman, John (John Andrew)
    Birds of lake, pond and marsh / by John Eastman;
  illustrated by Amelia Hansen.
       p.   cm.
    Includes bibliographical references (p.) and index.
    ISBN 0-8117-2681-9 (alk. paper)
    1. Water birds—East (U.S.)   I. Title.
  QL683.E27E35   1999   98-43576
  598.176'0974—dc21   CIP

To
Jacqueline Ladwein

How long may we have gazed on a particular scenery and think that we have seen and known it, when, at length, some bird or quadruped comes and takes possession of it before our eyes, and imparts to it a wholly new character.

Henry D. Thoreau

They are not brethren, they are not underlings; they are other nations, caught with ourselves in the net of life and time, fellow prisoners of the splendour and travail of the earth.

Henry Beston

Contents

Acknowledgments

Again I thank my friend and collaborator, illustrator Amelia Hansen, for dedicating her energies and superb artistic gifts to this project, as she has in three previous books. Making sense of some of my vague, conflicting, and disorganized ideas and requests is not the least of her contributions to these efforts.

I appreciate the time and critical talents of several readers of the manuscript in whole or in part. Dr. Richard Brewer, professor emeritus of biology at Western Michigan University, is a well-known ecologist and ornithologist, now active in the land conservancy movement. James Granlund, author, teacher, and ornithologist, has introduced many aspiring naturalists to the pleasures of birding and butterflying. And W. C. Joe Johnson, noted waterfowl biologist at Michigan State University's Kellogg Bird Sanctuary in Augusta, Michigan, has been active in reintroducing trumpeter swans to the wild. Each of these gentlemen has offered useful comments and suggestions, for which I am deeply grateful. I alone, however, remain solely responsible for the final text.

My friend and longtime field collaborator Jacqueline Ladwein, to whom this book is dedicated, has provided invaluable observations and efforts, as always. My thanks also go to Stephen Allen, Jane E. Barrick, Calvin J. Everly, Richard Johnson, and John and Dodie Ruiter for various favors extended. Dr. Michael B. Stuart kindly provided access to specimen collections at the University of North Carolina–Asheville. Dr. Richard Brewer granted permission for use of several Hansen illustrations from *The Atlas of Breeding Birds of Michigan*, by Brewer, McPeek, and Adams (East Lansing:

Michigan State University Press, 1991); and I thank Russell Schipper for his loan of Hansen's original drawing of the American bittern for this book.

Curtis and Shirley McComis and Eric Mills have provided me frequent occupancy and use of their northern Michigan property, an action that swamps all definitions of generosity.

I thank the countless bird researchers whose fieldwork, discoveries, and writings not only enable books like this to be written, but so enhance our perceptions, knowledge, and enjoyment of the life around us.

One prominent life around me is Susan Woolley Stoddard, my loving companion, who has done most of the necesary drudge work—typing, retyping, running off draft copies—for all my books. She has numerous better things to do as well and does them. Her generosity and efforts, though unseen, form a major part of all my endeavors.

Introduction

This book is the second of a 3-volume series on the most common and familiar bird species of eastern North America—birds that most of us can see in the appropriate season without traveling too far from home. First in the series was *Birds of Forest, Yard, and Thicket* (1997); completing the series will be *Birds of Field and Shore*. A primary aim of this series is to bring news about these birds up to date—to convey the results and discoveries of recent research, especially findings of the past 2 decades. My foremost sources, listed in the Selected Bibliography, include records of my own bird observations plus much shared knowledge and opinion from respected birding colleagues. Accounts treat each species from an ecological perspective—that is, as community dwellers coequal with their plant and animal associates in the total complex of their habitats and environment.

The 41 species of water and wetland birds presented in this volume range across the spectrum of bird families from waterfowl to finches. Many of them show distinctive adaptations for living in wet habitats. Most occur outside as well as within the regional focus of this book (that is, east of the Mississippi and north of the Ohio rivers). Most also occur in this region for only part of the year owing to the physical fact that snow falls and water freezes, rendering food inaccessible or absent throughout most of this region in winter. The evolutionary solution to this problem is, of course, escape and departure—in a word, migration. Most birds that nest exclusively in northern regions of the continent can be best observed in lower latitudes during these periods of travel to and from their breeding and winter ranges.

Forty-one species represent only a fraction of the water and wetland birds that occur in North America. Rather than strive for total inclusiveness, giving perfunctory accounts of *all* such birds— a job already accomplished by many excellent state and regional bird guides—I have opted for closer looks at some of the so-called core species of these habitats. My particular selection of these is arbitrary; I readily grant that other valid options may exist.

Taxonomic sequencing of birds follows the recent DNA classification scheme advanced by Burt L. Monroe, Jr., and Charles G. Sibley in *A World Checklist of Birds* (New Haven: Yale University Press, 1993). The present state of bird taxonomy and nomenclature is chaotic; one of the least stable items of a bird's biography these days is its name and relationship slot. Family and subfamily designations, as in finches, swing back and forth—and American and European namers and classifiers are often at odds over the same bird. The Monroe-Sibley system used in this book and by increasing numbers of ornithologists worldwide at least offers a uniform set of criteria (DNA relationships) by which to classify birds; this cannot be said of most other systems. Fashions and fierce partisanships change in taxonomy as in everything else. Today "splitters" have gained the upper hand over "lumpers." The recent tendency has been to "promote" or upgrade many formerly subordinate races or subspecies to mint-fresh bird species. One result has been massive disparities among the various classification systems in the total number of species they include in their world checklists.

Such matters only peripherally concern this series. Each species account herein is divided into several sections. Each begins with the bird's English and Latin **names,** as given in *A World Checklist of Birds;* family and order designations follow. Where 2 or more species of a single family are given accounts, an introductory paragraph on the family precedes the accounts. A brief description of the bird's appearance and sounds follows its names. Section headings are as follows:

Close relatives identifies the bird's nearest kin.

Behaviors describes the bird's characteristic actions, focusing on what an observer may actually see. Included here are the bird's breeding distribution and migrational habits. Descriptions of specific seasonal behaviors and activities follow under seasonal subheadings:

Spring is when migrants arrive, singing or other vocal sounds peak, and most North American birds form pair bonds and begin nesting. Many yearling birds return in spring to areas near their birth sites, and most previously mated adult birds return to their previous breeding territories (such homing behavior is called *philopatry*). Many birds remain monogamous breeders throughout a season and some throughout their lives. Seasonal monogamy most often "comes with the territory"—that is, a female bird selects a desirable territory and almost incidentally accepts the male that "owns" it. Yet some 60 species (at last count) of North American songbirds are known to engage in at least occasional breeding, or extrapair copulations, outside the primary nuptial bond; the total swells even further when nonsongbird species are included. Nesting data are presented in a boxed paragraph at the end of this seasonal section.

In *summer,* most birds complete nesting activities; song diminishes and juvenile birds disperse. Feathers litter the ground in late summer, when annual plumage molts occur in most species, and many migrant birds assemble in premigratory flocks (often called *staging*).

Fall is another highly stressful season of migration. Some species migrate only to the southern United States; others move much farther, to Central and South America. Some of the Neotropical migrants that travel farthest move from North American fall to South American spring, but they do not renew breeding activities at their destinations.

Winter for most birds is a season of feeding, either in flocks or solitarily, depending on the species. For certain species that winter in the North, this may be a season of great hardship and mortality if food becomes scarce, as it often does. Winter distribution of migrants is also described in this section.

Ecology focuses on specific details of the bird's relationships to other organisms and to its seasonal environments. Sequenced paragraphs discuss the bird's habitats, nesting, food, competitors, and predators. Not detailed in most accounts are the bird's external and internal parasites, mainly protozoans, worms, mites, and insects. Almost all birds carry them, and many bird species carry the same genera or species of parasites. The most common skin and feather parasites include fowl mites (*Ornithonyssus*), bird lice (Philopteridae), larval louse or hippoboscid flies (*Lynchia*), and larval blowflies (*Protocalliphora*). Many birds also carry internal parasites, such as roundworms, tapeworms, and flukes. Avian pox, a common viral disease, results from *Poxvirus avium* infection. "I suspect that parasites have been very influential in the evolution of birds," wrote ecologist Richard Brewer.

Focus, a catchall section, presents information on origins of the bird's name, the bird's place in native or cultural history, details of certain adaptations it may show, elaborations on previous sections—anything interesting that fits nowhere else.

Latin names of plant and animal organisms other than birds are kept to a minimum; I include them only for specific organisms that bear special ecological relevance to the bird.

Several recurrent terms may need defining:

Birding is the methodical field activity of observing birds; *birders* are people who engage in this activity, either as a pastime or for data collection.

Incubation is egg heating by a parent bird, accomplished by sitting on the eggs for long intervals over days or weeks; in most (though not all) North American species, incubation is done exclusively by females. Incubating females usually develop brood patches, temporarily bare areas of abdominal skin by which they transfer body heat to the eggs. Some species begin incubation when the first egg is laid, resulting in differential hatching times (*asynchronous hatching*). In many species, however, incubation starts after the laying of the last egg in a set, or *clutch,* and hatching occurs more or less simultaneously (*synchronous hatching*).

Altricial young are nestlings that remain in the nest for an extended helpless period and require much parental feeding and brooding, as in most songbirds. *Precocial young* are chicks that leave the nest soon after hatching, follow the parent, and immediately begin feeding themselves, as in most gamebirds and waterfowl.

Fledging refers to an altricial nestling's development of feathers and its act of leaving the nest, thereby becoming a *fledgling* until it can feed independently. For precocial chicks, fledging is the act of first flight. Used as a subhead in the boxed paragraph in the *Spring* section of accounts, *fledging* refers to the number of days between hatching and nest departure for altricial young and to the number of days between hatching and first flight for precocial young.

A *juvenile*, or immature, bird feeds independently but has not yet developed its first winter (usually adultlike) plumage, a molt that occurs concurrently with the feather molt of adult birds in late summer or fall.

Territory is, in broadest definition, the area defended by a singing male or bonded pair of birds. Territories vary in size among species and also among members of the same species. Territory size often depends on abundance of the species and quality of habitat in a given area. Birds establish their territories by singing and by defensive behaviors against intruders of the same or competing species. Most songbird breeding territories enclose both nesting and feeding sites. Many birds, however, must leave their territories to feed, drink, or bathe; a loose designation for these extraterritorial areas is *home range*. Colonial pairs usually defend much smaller territories than solitary nesters, though some of the latter (such as many ducks) also maintain extremely small territories. Nonbreeding territories in some species may include defended food sources, night roosts, and winter foraging sites.

A resident bird's *home range* is the total space it inhabits in a given area; home range encloses the territory but is not defended. Home ranges of separate pairs of a species often overlap.

An *area-sensitive* or *area-dependent* species is a species that favors, or thrives best in, large, unfragmented habitat areas.

It's no news that North American wetlands are in trouble. Most alarming is the fact that far fewer of these unique repositories exist now than when many of us were born; thousands of acres have disappeared from our environmental legacy. And too many of those that remain survive in threatened or degraded condition. As a direct reflection of these events, many water and wetland organisms of North America have undergone conspicuous—in some cases precipitous—declines during the past half century. Birds, existing near the top of the food chain, represent only a single conspicuous item in the spectra of creatures affected by human activities and attempts to improve matters.

Changes in water and wetland bird life have resulted from three main causes. Probably the most important one is the outright loss of wetland habitats owing to drainage, diversion, and landfills for agricultural and suburban development purposes. Before about 1940, wetland loss occurred mainly by ditching and drainage, after that by filling. To a certain type of myopic vision in our society, a swamp or marsh is viewed as an obstacle or challenge to progress, a candidate for "reclamation" so that it too can be "used" according to the prevailing gospel of economic growth. The nonhuman dwellers in such areas must either retreat to still-extant wetland habitats, in which they must compete with already resident populations, or be consigned to death and disappearance as the living space to which their evolution has adapted them ceases to exist.

The second threat to water and wetland wildlife results from the physical fact that lakes and wetlands form natural sinks and repositories for the environmental chemistry—including contaminants. Each fertilizer, toxic spray, chemical residue, or metallic pollutant sooner or later ends up in the water, where it immediately enters the food chain and often becomes further concentrated in plant or animal tissues. Ultimately such contamination may affect the physiology, reproduction, even genetics of the resident organisms.

A third threat, often an aspect of the first, is fragmentation—divisions and subdivisions of large wetland tracts into patchy swales, dikes, mazes of ditches and canals, or small pocket marshes. Certain area-sensitive species, including some frogs and birds such as American bitterns and swamp sparrows, seem to thrive best in spacious, extensive marshlands or other large, uniform wetland habitats unbroken by the partitions of agriculture or land development.

Reciting the litany of environmental problems sometimes becomes onerous, tiresome, especially to those of us not constitutionally inclined to evangelism or Viewing With Alarm. Many naturalists wear negativity like a hair-shirt uniform these days. Rather than cite records of failure and reveal What Needs To Be Done, I much prefer to climb into my hip waders, travel out to a swamp or marsh, and see what is there. For me, the pursuit of perceiving what is there—ignoring for this instant what was, might be, or could be there—comes down where "all the ladders start," to paraphrase Yeats. Simply seeing what emerges to be seen has in itself become project enough for my own life, at least. And while I recognize that such an effort of consciousness provides hardly a spark of the energy needed to "fix" the Earth and render it hospitable to all its creatures, I remain convinced that all of one's best efforts—Thoreau called it philanthropy and took a dim view of it—can finally go nowhere without initial donning of the waders, as it were.

So that's what we do in this book and this series—don waders, see some sights, hear some sounds.

Come along.

1

WATERFOWL FAMILY (Anatidae),
order Anseriformes

This family (called wildfowl in England) includes the ducks, geese, and swans, almost 150 species worldwide. Forty-three species breed in North America. All are aquatic, swimming birds; are strong, swift fliers; and are gregarious, feeding and migrating in flocks. The 3 front toes are webbed, an adaptation for swimming. Short legs, relatively long necks, and broad, flat *(lamellate)* bills also characterize the waterfowl. Many ducks have a colored wing patch, most easily seen in flight, called the *speculum.* Most waterfowl migrate at night, sometimes along *migration corridors,* often in broad fronts between breeding and wintering areas. Migration corridors in the eastern United States exist within the geographic designations of Atlantic and Mississippi flyways. The flyway concept is useful for biologists in plotting general movements of waterfowl but does not pretend accurate definition of the actual routes flown.

Many ducks, geese, and swans fly in V- or wedge-shaped formations (or variations thereof); other birds that do so include some species of gulls, cormorants, pelicans, ibises, cranes, herons, and storks, among others. Nobody really knows why such flight formations are advantageous to these birds, though guesses are rife. A favored theory for many years was that wing-tip vortices (wind eddies) of the bird in front help produce lift for the bird behind, thus increasing flight efficiency for all but the leader bird; motion picture analyses have largely demolished that theory. Other not-quite-convincing theories suggest that V-shaped formations result from the bird's angle of vision, enabling it to maintain optimal visual contact with the bird ahead and behind, thus providing more accurate orientation for a flock. Since leaders at the apex of a V often change position with other birds in the flock, the role of dominance in the flock hierarchy appears discounted. Better understanding of this common but still puzzling social behavior is obviously needed.

Most North American waterfowl form pair bonds on their winter ranges, a system that profoundly affects their breeding distribution. It works this way: Most waterfowl species exhibit an unbalanced sex ratio, tipped in favor of males; females select their mates from this surplus. Thus a female on the winter range often pairs with a male that hatched far from her own natal site. During spring migration, the pair homes to *her* natal or previous nesting site, not his. Thus it is primarily the female birds—in addition to habitat conditions—that control the continental distribution of waterfowl. This system also works against inbreeding, mixing the gene pool. All waterfowl eggs hatch synchronously (within a few hours of each other), and all hatch precocial young, ready to leave the nest soon after hatching. Most waterfowl do not feed their young but lead them to water areas where the young can immediately begin feeding themselves. In summer, waterfowl undergo their annual plumage molt, which involves a flightless period of several weeks as they replace wing and tail feathers. Most waterfowl typically secrete themselves in dense, marshy areas during this vulnerable period.

Until recent years, many waterfowl species continued a long trend of population declines, mainly owing to loss of wetland habitats. Waterfowl numbers bottomed out during the late 1980s and early 1990s owing mainly to extended drought conditions in the "waterfowl factory" of the prairie states and provinces. From 1994 to date, however, duck populations have shown notable increases each year, a situation that waterfowl biologists hope may reflect efforts to restore and reclaim wetlands in that region, most notably by the organization Ducks Unlimited. Even before this recent trend, a few species (such as mute swans, snow geese, and Canada geese) were already increasing their numbers in some areas to the point of nuisance, crowding out other waterbirds, and in some cases, degrading their own habitats. Long-term overpopulation signifies as serious an ecological problem as long-term decline. To address them effectively, both problems require ecologically holistic frames of reference beyond the capacities of ornithology alone to provide.

WATERFOWL FAMILY (Anatidae)

Ruddy Duck *(Oxyura jamaicensis)*

This chunky little duck measures slightly more than a foot long. Drakes often swim with tail cocked erect. In the breeding season, drakes show rusty-red body plumage plus black cap, bright white cheeks, and blue bills. Hens are grayish with light brown cheeks crossed by a dark line beneath the eye. In winter plumage, males are also gray but white cheeked. Ruddies usually remain silent, but drakes voice sputtering notes during courtship.

Close relatives. Ruddies belong to a small subfamily (Oxyurinae) of waterfowl called stiff-tailed ducks. Seven *Oxyura* species exist worldwide, but only the ruddy and the masked duck *(O. dominica)* of the Gulf area and southward reside in North America.

Behaviors. Its name refers only to the drake, and even then it is accurate only 4 or 5 months of the year. The rest of the time, these are drab,

Ruddy ducks, especially drakes with their cocked tails and white chins, are most distinctive in breeding plumage; hen is at top, drake below.

gray-brown little divers, males distinguished from afar by only the white cheek patch. People in the Northeast usually see ruddies only during migration seasons, usually in flocks of 5 to 15 on the water. Their large, dark feet are set so far back that on land, where ruddies rarely venture, the bird's posture is erect, like a penguin's, but it can hardly walk. On water, it must run across the surface into the wind for some distance before its short, rounded wings lift it. Ruddies often skim low over the water in characteristic rapid, jerky flight, "like large bumblebees," as an observer wrote. Usually, though, they dive rather than fly when escaping danger. The fan-shaped tail of short, spiny feathers, unlike any other nonrelated duck's, functions as a rudder for the big foot-paddles when the duck swims beneath the surface. Ruddies can also sink without a ripple, like pied-billed grebes. They typically dive 2 to 10 feet for food, a dive usually lasting about 20 seconds. Occasionally ruddies also feed on the surface or immerse only their heads.

Ruddies occasionally mingle with American coots, rarely with other waterfowl. They usually feed singly, in pairs, or in small groups by themselves. Reproduction in this species seems much less behaviorally structured and predictable than in most ducks. Monogamy, nest-site fidelity, and the drake's parental role often appear variable and ill defined when extant at all.

This migrant duck's breeding range centers in the northern prairie states and provinces of the Great Plains. Smaller breeding colonies extend discontinuously across the continent both east and west; subspecies also breed in the Andes of South America and, recently, in Europe. Ruddies and cinnamon teals are the only waterfowl that breed on both American continents.

Spring. April is the peak migration month for ruddies. The birds travel almost entirely at night, and pairing apparently occurs both during migration and upon arrival. Although migration in small groups is typical, large flocks of ruddies, numbering several thousand, may sometimes be seen during migration stops on large lakes. Drakes molt gradually into their ruddy plumage, mainly during April, and attain their bright blue bills.

The pair bond in this species appears exceedingly loose and variable—usually brief, temporary, and sometimes *polygynous* (1 drake simultaneously pairing with 2 or more hens). Some ruddies apparently breed as yearlings, most not until their second or third year. The major display exhibited by drakes toward hens is *bubbling*. The drake cocks his tail vertically and erects his small feathered "horns," barely discernible on the crown. He inflates his neck and beats his lower bill 5 to 9 times against it, all within a second or so, producing tapping sounds and a ring of bubbles in the water as the bill motions force air from the breast feathers. Other displays include the ringing rush (a headlong dash across the water), head dips, wing shakes, and others. Drake territoriality is likewise flexible and ill defined. In pairs that remain together for any duration, drakes defend areas of about 10 feet surrounding the mate ("mobile territory"), and both sexes defend the nest site. Hens select the nest sites, but both sexes often build several nestlike platforms before actual nesting begins, probably using some of them later for brooding or resting places. Many drakes desert their mates as incubation begins or even before; others remain attentive longer into the season.

Ruddy ducks are noted for brood parasitism, laying eggs in nests of other ruddy hens as well as of other species, including redheads, northern pintails, cinnamon teals, canvasbacks, grebes, rails, and American bitterns. Dump nests, in which several hens may lay 17 to 60 eggs, are not incubated. Even in otherwise successful nests, 2 or 3 eggs often fail to hatch, indicating deposition by an intruding hen in a nest already being incubated. (About 6 ducklings hatch per nesting hen.)

Nesting occurs mainly in May and June. Many drakes form nonbreeding flocks in spring and remain together through summer. As in most ducks, the sex ratio in this species is unbalanced toward drakes, which compose about 60 percent of most ruddy populations.

EGGS AND YOUNG: 6 to 8; eggs cream-white, nest-stained, rough-surfaced, very large (comparable in size to great blue heron or wild turkey eggs). INCUBATION: by hen; about 25 days. FLEDGING: 6 to 7 weeks.

Summer. As relatively late-season nesters, ruddies produce only a single brood per year. Nesting often continues into July. In contrast to seasonal procedure in most ducks, drake ruddies frequently accompany hens and broods in summer. Most researchers have assumed that such drakes are parent birds; more probable, perhaps (given the tendency of many drakes to form only loose pair bonds), is the more recent theory that these drakes may simply be males that socially attach themselves for various durations to any hen present.

Ruddies in most areas show high rates of nesting success (some 70 percent) despite relatively high levels of nest desertion due to flooding, predation, and perhaps brood parasitism. Hens brood their young for several days, at least, but many desert their broods at age 4 to 6 weeks when the adult birds begin their annual molt. This is also the period of greatest duckling loss, in contrast to most duck species, which show highest mortality within the first few days of life. Also unlike most ducks, ruddies have no intermediate eclipse plumage; by late July or early August, they disappear into the marshes, replacing their wing and tail feathers—then, more gradually, head and body plumage. No longer colorful (their bills also darken to gray-black), ruddy drakes are now grayish and white. Juveniles resemble adult hens in plumage.

Fall, Winter. Night migration from the northern breeding range begins in September, slightly earlier than in most other diving ducks. Ruddies are as unpredictable in migration as in breeding behaviors, and their numbers widely fluctuate from year to year along their migration corridors, which mainly trend east-west toward the seacoasts rather than north-south. Many ruddies apparently shift corridors and stopover sites in successive years, perhaps reflecting water level changes on breeding areas. When small flocks land after a night's flight, wrote waterfowl biologist Frank C. Bellrose, "I have observed them countless times in compact rosette-like clusters" on the water. More than half the ruddy population travels to Pacific coast wintering areas (mainly California) and western Mexico. Atlantic coast migrants concentrate in brackish estuaries of Chesapeake Bay and North Carolina. Smaller populations winter along the Gulf coast and, inland, as far north as they can find open water.

Ecology. Ruddies favor prairie marsh habitat, both large and small ponds with dense emergent vegetation, for nesting areas. In nonprairie areas, ruddies have also adapted to marshy lakes and sewage lagoons, where nonbreeding flocks often feed through summer. During migrations, they can often be seen on open lakes, but they also feed in smaller bodies of water than most diving ducks, often in gravel-pit and excavation ponds. Winter habitats are mainly coastal inlets and estuaries that provide rich aquatic vegetation. Common nesting cover includes tall, dense stands of hardstem-bulrushes, *juncus* rushes, sedges, and cattails growing in 10 to 12 inches of water, usually within 100 feet or less of open water. In some areas, muskrats appear to be important ruddy duck associates; these mammals create open swimming lanes and channels in marsh vegetation, allowing access to the ducks for nesting. Some nests are attached to stems about 7 or 8 inches above water level, others are built up from the marsh bottom, and still others are floating. The ducks often arch surrounding plants over the nest, forming a concealing canopy. The basketlike nests consisting of plant materials, often skimpy constructions when eggs are laid, become sturdier as incubation begins and hens add materials to the rims. Nests average about a foot in diameter. Some hens add large amounts of down to the inner nest, some none at all. Ruddies occasionally adopt vacated nests of redheads or American coots.

Ruddies are mainly vegetarians (about 72 percent of diet); pondweed seeds, tubers, and leaves are favored items, as are stoneworts, wild celery, and seeds of bulrushes and ditch-grass. Animal foods consist mainly of midge and other insect larvae, amphipods, and small snails. Ducklings feed heavily on midge larvae.

Brood parasitism occurs fairly often. Ruddies often parasitize nests of canvasbacks and redheads, especially; those species also deposit eggs in ruddy duck nests on occasion. Competition seems generally insignificant, however, despite the ruddy's tendency toward brood parasitism of its own and other waterfowl species. Dietary overlap occurs, especially among lesser scaups, canvasbacks, and redheads, but in one notable study, "each species tended to forage in a particular part of shared ponds and was more often found alone than with another species." Such habits apparently reduce occasions for competitive interactions.

Egg predators include gulls, crows, and northern ravens. Foxes, skunks, and raccoons prey on both eggs and ducklings, and pike, bass, black-crowned night herons, gulls, and minks capture the latter. Predation seems a relatively unimportant influence in ruddy duck populations, however, perhaps because of this bird's high nesting success and effective escape behaviors.

Focus. During the 1890s, before hunting regulations existed, redheads and canvasbacks were the market hunter's favorites. Overhunting depleted their abundance, and the still-numerous ruddy duck replaced them as tasty bird of choice. Ruddies in turn fell to perilously low levels by the 1920s, about the time that federal laws began to control hunting. Numbers have since increased, but the data conflict regarding long-term population trends. Oil spills have caused major kills of ruddies in winter concentration areas (such as San Francisco Bay), where large percentages of the continental population remain vulnerable to such catastrophes. Today's hunters prefer to aim at ducks that fly rather than dive to escape, and most researchers believe the ruddy's abundant status in North America is currently secure. Elsewhere it is more than that; ruddies are called "flying rats" in England, where the late prominent ornithologist Sir Peter Scott is widely blamed for its growing presence (increasing by about 10 percent per year). Some of Scott's captive ruddies escaped from the Wildfowl Trust in Gloucestershire in 1952, began breeding in the wild, and have since expanded their range throughout much of Europe. In Spain, where ruddies first appeared in 1982, the birds have alarmed conservationists by competing and breeding with a globally threatened species, the native, closely related white-headed duck *(O. leucocephala),* producing an aggressive hybrid population that threatens to replace the latter species. The occurrence reminds us that the harmful ecological effects of species introductions flow in both directions across the seas, that America is not the exclusive victim of such attempts or accidents. In England, control efforts have become highly controversial, with most experts ruefully agreeing that "the flying rat is here to stay."

Longevity of this species remains unknown.

SWANS (TRIBE ANSERINI)

Largest of the waterfowl, swans also have the longest necks, with 25 cervical (neck) vertebrae—more than any other warm-blooded animal, including giraffes—and relatively the shortest legs. Males are called *cobs;* females are *pens,* and first-year young are *cygnets.* Adult sexes look alike except that cobs are usually somewhat larger than pens. Most adult swans of both sexes wear all-white plumage.

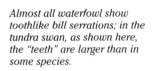

To become airborne, swans must launch from a running start of 15 to 20 feet over the water surface. They seldom dive, feeding on bottom vegetation by stretching their *Almost all waterfowl show toothlike bill serrations; in the tundra swan, as shown here, the "teeth" are larger than in some species.*

necks beneath the surface, sometimes uptilting like mallards. Although swan bills have sharp cutting edges along the sides, food plants are more often torn than cut.

Swans begin breeding at age two or three, usually mating for life. Three of the world's 7 swan species breed in North America; in addition to the 2 species accounts that follow, the trumpeter swan *(Cygnus buccinator),* a once-rare species, breeds in scattered locations. The whooper swan *(C. cygnus),* native of Eurasia, regularly visits Alaska during migrations.

WATERFOWL FAMILY (Anatidae) - SWANS

Mute Swan *(Cygnus olor)*

The full length of this swan is about 5 feet, its wingspan about 7 feet. When swimming, its S-curved neck and orange, black-knobbed, downward-pointed bill are characteristic. The wings in flight produce a distinctive, musical whistling sound. Flocks fly in irregular lines or V formations with deep, powerful wingbeats. Mute swans utter occasional hisses and snorts when disturbed but are usually silent.

Close relatives. The tundra swan *(C. columbianus)* and the trumpeter *(C. buccinator)* are the mute's nearest North American kin. The black swan *(C. atratus)* is native to Australia and the black-necked swan *(C. melanocorypha)* to South America.

Behaviors. This bird, the typical park swan, is a native of Eurasia. Long semidomesticated in England, it was introduced to

America about 1910 as an ornament to country estates and city parks. Many North American populations stemming from these imports now exist, located mainly in Atlantic coastal bays and estuaries and in the Great Lakes region. Slow and stately as it cruises, the mute swan looks beetle-browed with its knobbed bill (the knobby protrusion appears in the bird's second year). When threatened or aggressively displaying, the bird characteristically raises its wing feathers, creating a hooded arch over its back. Swans spend much time grooming and preening. This bird is among the few species of nonmigrating North American waterfowl; mute swans may, however, travel 100 miles or more to find open-water sites in winter. In their native Eurasia, they migrate to north Africa, India, and Korea.

This head-on view of an immature mute swan shows its grayish neck plus the beginnings of a knob at the base of its bill.

Spring. Mute swans, having usually paired the previous fall, begin nesting activities in early spring, often as ice begins receding from lakes and ponds. The family of the previous year now splits as the parents turn belligerent, usually reclaiming the previous year's territory of some 5 to 10 acres. (Two-year-old swans may also pair and establish territories, but mutes seldom actually nest until age three.) Mute swans tolerate few trespassers on their territories, vigorously attacking other swans and waterfowl, dogs, even humans that venture too close. Their beating wings can inflict bruises, sometimes real injury to a child; the main weapon is the large wrist, or *manus,* joint of the wing. Conspicuous courtship displays include head dipping, mutual head turning, and (after copulation) rearing up breast-to-breast in the water, necks outstretched, heads wagging. Displays between cobs on adjacent territories include body rotation movements with feathers fluffed out. The alighting display, in which both members of a pair land from flight with great splashing and commotion, is also common.

Both sexes construct the nest. Nesting usually begins in early April, hatching in mid-May. Although most mute swans maintain pair bonds for life, instances of polygamy occur as does re-pairing if one mate dies. Incestuous matings are common in captive flocks and occur at least occasionally in the wild. The cob often cares for the first-hatched cygnets while the pen continues to incubate unhatched eggs, all of which normally hatch within 24 hours. Cygnets often ride on a parent's back.

EGGS AND YOUNG: usually 4 or 5; eggs pale gray to bluish green. INCUBATION: mainly by female; 4 or 5 weeks. FLEDGING: cygnets fly in about 4 months.

Summer. The family group remains together, and the territory often expands as feeding areas enlarge. Parents provide food for cygnets by pulling up vegetation, to which insects are often attached, and dropping it on the surface; the adults also foot-trample in shallow water, dislodging bits of debris and subsurface invertebrates. The nest often remains the primary site for loafing, preening, and brooding of cygnets. Pens begin their annual feather molt in mid-July, some 25 days before the cobs. This staggered molt ensures that one parent remains able to fly while the other replaces its flight and body feathers, an important timing sequence for defense of the still-flightless cygnets. Unmated adults often move to large, open waters, flocking together during the molting period *(molt migrations)*. First-year juveniles, flocked together throughout the breeding season, wear dingy brownish plumage and have pinkish bills and gray feet. During their second summer, mute swans molt into white, adultlike plumage, also developing dull orange bills and small forehead knobs.

Fall. As territorialism diminishes, family groups still remain together, even within the larger grouping of flocks. Transition from family to flock society, as in many waterfowl, is often marked by brief, hostile exchanges between individual birds before things settle down and general tolerance reigns. Many researchers believe that lifelong pair formation between young swans occurs at this season.

Winter. Mute swans need open water for feeding, and they move as they must to find it. They travel from frozen inland lakes to ice-free coastal bays and river mouths, gathering in large flocks at these sites but with family groups remaining more or less intact. Winter on the Great Lakes is often a season of hardship and reduced food availability for mute swans, a situation that limits their North American distribution. In early March, as soon as open water begins to appear in the ice-locked lakes and ponds, they hastily return to their inland breeding sites, often ravenous for food.

Ecology. Mute swans require shallow-water habitats; a depth of 18 inches to 2 feet is about maximal for feeding. For nesting, the birds favor marshy edges of lakes and ponds rimmed with thick cattail or other emergent growth.

The large, bulky nest mound consists of coarse plant materials—cattail stalks, bulrushes, reeds—lined with feathers and down from the swan's breast. Often the entire structure measures 5 or 6 feet across, with an inside diameter of 15 inches or more. Sometimes the nest is built on floating mats of vegetation, frequently atop a muskrat lodge, which provides a firm base. Swans on the nest are usually easily seen from afar, owing to their white plumage and the relative openness of early-spring marsh growth.

The mute's diet consists of about 95 percent aquatic vegetation, much of it submerged plants that it pulls loose from the bottom. An adult mute probably consumes about 8 pounds of aquatic vegetation daily. Pondweed leaves are favored items, as are stoneworts, water milfoils, and eelgrasses. Floating plant foods include duckweeds and filamentous algae. Seeds of aquatic plants are also consumed, as are small numbers of snails, insect larvae, and frogs (cygnets feed mainly on such high-protein matter for their first month). Swans also become omnivorous scavengers in park and zoo settings. Mutes sometimes destroy Canada goose nests, but such aggressiveness is probably more of a territorial than predatory behavior as such.

Competition from other waterfowl is negligible, though often a feeding mute swan attracts a train of smaller waterbirds such as dabbling ducks and American coots, which devour fragments of plant materials torn loose by the swans. American wigeons, especially, are frequent feeding associates of mute swans. "Swans usually do not respond aggressively to ducks because of the size difference," wrote biologist Roswell Van Deusen, "though swan feeding habits are more ducklike than goose-like." The relationship

The mute swan on its nest is usually very visible in the still-open marsh of early spring.

appears *commensal;* that is, the ducks benefit by the swans' actions in bringing food within surface reach, while the swans neither gain nor suffer. In another aspect, however, the mute swan ranks significantly as an aggressive food and space competitor. Its recent rate of increase (30 to 40 percent annually in some eastern states) threatens defoliation of subsurface vegetation in many water areas where mutes uproot plants quite indiscriminately, thus depleting the productive capacity of ponds for other food and feeding organisms. Their territorial aggressiveness often brings them into conflict with other waterfowl, especially other swan species, geese, and common loons, sometimes forcing these birds into marginal, less optimal sites for breeding and feeding.

Predation on swans is directed mainly at cygnets. Even with

parental protection, they sometimes fall prey to snapping turtles, minks, great horned owls, and other predators. In the mute swan population that nests near my home, I have often noted shrinkage of cygnet broods by about half from May to June. "Losses during the second week are particularly heavy," wrote biologist Peter Scott, "because by then the young birds have used up the reserves of yolk which sustain them through the first few days." Ingestion of lead shot pellets from pond bottoms kills many swans and other waterfowl, and bloodsucking leeches sometimes attach to the birds, especially cygnets. Many juvenile swans in urban areas collide with overhead wires during their first flights. Outbreaks of a tiny parasitic flatworm trematode *(Sphaeridiotrema globulus),* seedlike in appearance, often result in mute swan die-offs. The trematode passes through an intermediate snail host before becoming a threat to swans inside another snail host; the swans eat vegetation to which the latter snails are attached, and the eaten snails release the trematodes, which embed in the swan intestine and release toxins that kill the swan.

Focus. Ancient lore regarding swans (probably most often this species) reveals the hold of this bird upon human imagination. Through Norse, Egyptian, Greek, and Teutonic mythologies, among others, swans have symbolized the supernatural. This was the swan "responsible for the Trojan War," writes naturalist Janet Lembke, when Zeus transformed himself into a swan to seduce Leda, who thereupon gave birth to Helen and thence to the events recorded by Euripedes, Homer, and Virgil. The swan maiden figured in many legends. In heraldry, swans have signified wealth and royalty through the centuries.

Nobody knows whether mute swans are native to England or were introduced there from continental Europe—nor when the birds were first domesticated as park ornaments. Unlike other swan species, the mute thrives in close association with humans. Since medieval times, all mute swans in England have been considered royal property of the monarch, who grants charters for their ownership and care. To be thus favored by the Crown was a mark of high social standing and special distinction. Such birds were pinioned and branded with "swan marks," notches cut in the upper mandible of the bill, to identify the swan keeper. Some 900 swan marks were once catalogued, and an elaborate system of medieval red tape controlled every aspect of their breeding and culture. Royal distinction did not forgo the use of swans as table birds for banquets, however; until wild turkeys were introduced from America in the seventeenth century, a high-class Christmas dinner in England invariably centered around roast swan. Today, however, killing a swan in Britain amounts to an unpatriotic act, nigh unthinkable.

In America, the mute swan's increasing abundance gives it progressively less status. Waterfowl biologists condemn it for its aggressive competition with native waterfowl for food and space. Some New England cranberry farmers have witnessed virtual destruction of their cranberry bogs by invading mute swans, which devour the sprouts. Control efforts by state wildlife personnel have focused on locating nests and shaking the eggs to addle them, thus preventing hatching, but such methods remain highly controversial. The public, by and large, admires these spectacular birds for their appearance and sees little of the threat they pose to our native waterfowl.

Captive mute swans have survived up to 4 decades, but average longevity is probably less than 2.

WATERFOWL FAMILY (Anatidae) - SWANS

Tundra Swan *(Cygnus columbianus)*

Formerly known as the whistling swan, this North American native is our smallest swan, measuring over 4 feet long with a 6- or 7-foot wingspread. Its snowy plumage is set off by black feet and bill. Adult bills are often marked with a small yellow spot on each side of the bill base. Juvenile birds show dingy brown plumage and pinkish bills until their second year. Tundra swans carry their long necks straighter, with a much slighter S-curve, than mute swans. Their high-pitched, quavering, sometimes clarinetlike notes ("wow-HOW-oo") sound more gooselike than the trumpeter's bugling or the mute's subdued snort ("Its cry is more of a baying than a whistling," one swan observer wrote).

Close relatives. See Mute Swan. The Eurasian subspecies (recently upgraded to species status in Europe) is called the Bewick's swan *(C. bewickii).*

Behaviors. Tundra swans are much more abundant than our other native swan, the trumpeter; they are also much shyer and wilder than the mute swan. We in the East or Midwest see it mainly during its migrations to and from its arctic breeding range and during winter on the Atlantic coast.

Tundra swan wingbeats appear relatively slow and shallow. Top airspeed is probably about 50 miles per hour. The birds usually fly in high V-shaped formations when migrating, often in oblique lines at other times. Like all swans, tundras require a running start for takeoff and must face the wind in so doing.

Tundra swans reside during spring and summer in the high Arctic. The Bewick's swan breeds in northern Siberia, wintering primarily in the Netherlands, Great Britain, and eastern Asia.

Spring. North-migrating tundra swans congregate en route in huge flocks at traditional sites, which include western Lake Erie, Green Bay, Wisconsin, and the northern Mississippi River. Most arrive on their previous breeding areas by mid-April to mid-May, and nesting begins shortly thereafter. Cygnets of the previous year, which have accompanied their monogamous parents north, now separate from them. Probably few

Tundra swans lack the knobbed bill of mute swans and are smaller birds; note the distinctive bill spot near the eye.

tundra swans nest before their third spring, though information on this swan's breeding habits remains slim owing to its remote habitats. Some 40 to 60 percent of the population on the breeding range is paired and territorial; the nonbreeding birds (mainly 1- and 2-year-old juveniles) assemble in large or small flocks along northern coastal estuaries for the summer.

Courtship rituals include arching and bobbing of necks, bowing, and synchronous calling. In areas of abundant populations, 1 pair per square mile is about average density, but distribution is quite thinly scattered across the breeding range.

Cobs select the nest site, and both sexes build the platform nest. Pairs often repair and reuse nests of the previous year.

EGGS AND YOUNG: 4 or 5; eggs cream-white, often brown stained. INCUBATION: by both sexes (but mainly pen); about 5 weeks. FLEDGING: cygnets can fly in about 13 weeks.

Summer. Cygnets leave the nest with parents soon after hatching, but they cannot feed beneath the surface until about 2 weeks old because of their body buoyancy. Parent swans bring plant materials to the surface, but whether the cygnets' early foods mainly consist of small invertebrates (especially midge larvae) or plant fragments remains unknown. The family group remains together from hatching until the following spring. Some 3 weeks after cygnets hatch, the adult swans begin their annual feather molt. One sex starts molting days or weeks before the other, but sources conflict on whether pens or cobs are first. Broods usually remain within 400 yards of the nest, probably until they can fly in August or early September. At night and during rest periods, tundra swans usually roost on land at or near the nest, in contrast to water roosting at other seasons.

Fall. Tundra swans begin premigrational staging in large flocks by mid-September and start moving southward shortly thereafter. A flock, consisting of numerous family groups, may number 100 or so birds. Individual flocks may cover huge distances, flying day and night before descending for rest stops. Most fly at altitudes ranging from 3,000 to 5,000 feet, some even higher; aircraft have occasionally collided with high-flying swan flocks. Flocks travel along age-old skyways during the entire fall season, some congregating in traditional rest areas along the way, lingering for days or weeks, others leapfrogging past these places to land at others. The main migration corridor angles southeast across North Dakota and the Great Lakes states to Chesapeake Bay.

Many researchers believe that pair formation of first-time breeders occurs during fall migration or on the winter range.

Winter. "It is not cold weather that forces swans to travel," wrote one observer, "so much as it is the loss of food and water"—a statement that generally applies to all migrant birds. Two North American tundra swan populations exist, divided on the basis of their winter range locales. The eastern population (about 60 percent of the total) winters mainly in Chesapeake Bay and coastal estuaries of Virginia and North Carolina; most of these birds breed in the Northwest Territories, others above Hudson Bay. Much of the western population (about 40 percent), mainly from Alaska and northwestern Canada, winters in the San Francisco Bay area and at various inland sites. Family groups in winter remain intact but often assemble in large flocks for feeding and resting mainly on the water, where they also roost at night. During winter, white plumage replaces the gray body feathers of first-year swans; gray feathers remain on the head, neck, and wings until the annual molt in summer. Migrational movements, using the same corridors traveled in fall, commence in early March. Northbound tundra swans proceed slowly, stop frequently, and are often halted by stormy weather.

Ecology. Tundra—the treeless, waterlogged, permafrosted land lying above latitude 74 degrees N—is the tundra swan's chief breeding habitat. Dominant plants here include grasses, sedges, mosses, lichens, and heaths such as Labrador-tea and blueberries. This swan's favored winter habitat is food-rich coastal estuaries.

Tundra swans usually build their platform nests on elevated hummocks of vegetation in shallow tundra pools; such high spots are often the first snow-free sites of the tundra spring. The nest itself adds another 12 to 18 inches to the elevation. Mosses, grasses, and sedges, plucked from the immediate area, are the main materials used. Such digging and uprooting often create a moatlike circle of open water up to 15 feet in diameter around the nest. Nest diameter may measure 5 or 6 feet.

Food consists mainly of leaves, stems, and tubers of aquatic vegetation. The swans' rooting and yanking, some observers claim, seem to stimulate the subsurface growth of plants, resulting in more food production over subsequent years, for both the swans and other waterfowl. At migration stops and on the winter range, pondweeds (especially sago pondweed) are especially preferred, as are wild celery and smartweeds. Spike-rushes, arrowheads, and wid-geon-grass (ditch-grass), plus marginal grasses and sedges, also rank high. With shrinkage of wetland habitats, tundra swans have extensively adapted in many areas to feeding in fields, gleaning waste grains and seeds, including corn, rye, and soybeans, as well as plucking shoots of winter wheat. Sometimes the swans fly miles inland for such feeding. In Chesapeake Bay flocks, the diet turns largely to animal foods, mainly small clams.

Competitors are relatively few, though food-robbing ring-billed and herring gulls frequently attack clam-feeding swans in Chesa-peake Bay. Territorial tundra swans often chase other waterfowl—most notably Canada, white-fronted, and snow geese, and oldsquaw ducks—especially when the cygnets are small. Waterfowl that show some amount of white plumage seem to evoke more swan aggres-siveness than dark-plumaged waterfowl. Tundra swans, however, often associate with Canada geese in certain winter feeding areas. The geese often spot potential danger before the swans do, rousing a clamor and alerting the swans.

Tundra swan predators attack mainly eggs and cygnets. Snowy owls, gulls, jaegers, common ravens, and arctic foxes are the chief raiders. Other hazards occur during migration, the most perilous periods for migrant birds. Wings may ice up during stormy weather, forcing the swans down in areas far from water. One well-known tun-dra swan trap is the Niagara River, where entire flocks of disori-ented, fog-bound birds have been swept over the falls. Also, ingested lead shot pellets poison tundra swans on occasion.

Focus. This is one of the swans that, according to long-held folk myth dating back to Aristotle, voices the so-called "swan song" upon its demise—a soft, melodious series of notes quite unlike its usual sounds. The expression has become a metaphor for a final earthly act or creative impulse. Ornithologist H. Albert Hochbaum, among others, reported its actual occurrence, calling it one of the most beautiful utterances of any waterfowl. These notes are voiced, he said, when the swan is shot and falling crippled to the water. He likened it to the tundra swan's common "departure song," uttered just before it launches into flight but rarely heard unless one approaches much closer than these swans usually allow. To ornithologist Richard Brewer, "the talkativeness of these birds is one of their most striking traits—on water and also flying. A large flock up high sounds to me like a mob approaching the city gates or the castle."

Tundra swans have been long protected by law. They remain fairly secure on their breeding range, owing to early seasonal nesting in nigh-inaccessible tundra. Nest success is usually high, and annual survival rates for adults are about 92 percent, an amazingly high figure for waterfowl (or any bird). First- and second-year swans show lower survival rates, probably because of their greater vulnerability to predation and harsh weather. Since 1984, hunting has been permitted on the east-wintering population—currently 3 Atlantic seaboard states—plus the Dakotas and Alaska. Most are taken in North Carolina. The meat, by all accounts, is tough eating, more palatable in younger birds. Fur traders of the mid-1800s shot many for their skins. Inuit of the high Arctic and other northern tribes used swan eggs and flesh for food and swan's down for clothing; they probably still do in some areas. One argument for abolishing hunting seasons on this swan is that few gunners can distinguish it in flight from the at-risk trumpeter swan.

The oldest known wild tundra swan survived for 21 years, but most adults probably live half that long or less.

GEESE (TRIBE ANSERINI)

Geese, more closely related to swans than to ducks, are intermediate in shape and size between those two groups. Their bodies are less flattened than those of ducks, and they have shorter necks and longer legs than swans. Legs of geese are set farther forward than those of swans and ducks, enabling most geese to walk on land more easily than the other two groups. Both sexes wear identical plumage. Essentially vegetarian, geese not only feed in the water but, unlike most other waterfowl, also graze extensively on land, especially in fields. Males are slightly larger than females, and their calls are somewhat lower pitched. The name *goose,* once applied only to the female (males were *ganders*), now usually refers to both sexes; young geese are *goslings.* Strongly monogamous, geese require at least 2 years to become sexually mature and usually pair for life. In flocks, they exhibit strong dominance hierarchies and are usually led in flight by an old male. Twenty-four species range worldwide, mainly in temperate zones. Six species, including the following two, are North American natives.

WATERFOWL FAMILY (Anatidae) - GEESE

Snow Goose *(Anser caerulescens)*

Measuring about 30 inches long, the snow goose has all-white plumage except for strongly contrasting black outer wing tips, which become most visible in flight. Its bill and feet are pink, and its head profile is distinctively marked by the *rictal grin*—the bill's black cutting edges, which give the bill a grinlike appearance. The call, a high-pitched, resonant yelp (some observers liken it to the bark of a fox terrier), is usually heard in chorus as the birds flock or migrate. Two distinct races exist: the lesser snow goose *(A. c. caerulescens)* and the slightly larger greater snow goose *(A. c. atlantica).* Each occupies a separate breeding range, but the lesser is more abundant by far; this account deals mainly with that subspecies. Complicating matters is the fact that the lesser snow goose appears in two plumage variations *(morphs):* the all-white body with black wing primaries; and a dark-bodied form, slate gray with white head and neck, often called the *blue goose.* Both color morphs are almost equally abundant, and they often intermingle during migrations and on their winter range.

Lesser snow geese appear in two color morphs: the so-called blue goose (top), and the all-white form (bottom); both interbreed.

Close relatives. In North America, other *Anser* species include the greater white-fronted goose *(A. albifrons)*, Ross's goose *(A. rossii)*, and the rare emperor goose *(A. canagica)*. The common barnyard goose is a variety of the greylag goose *(A. anser)*, a European species.

Behaviors. Snow geese tend to fly in U- or J-shaped wedges, irregular groups, or oblique lines. Individual birds undulate in flight, accounting for their popular alias "wavies." At a distance, wrote ornithologist George Bird Grinnell, they "look like so many snowflakes being whirled hither and thither by the wind." Highly social at all seasons, snow geese—"the most vociferous of all waterfowl," wrote one researcher—yip incessantly in flight and when feeding. Their falsetto chorus often precedes the actual appearance of the high-flying birds during migrations.

Lesser snow goose breeding range spans the high Arctic from Wrangel Island in Siberia to Baffin Island (but few breed in Alaska) and south to James Bay. Greater snow geese, more restricted, nest even farther north on several arctic islands and in northwestern Greenland.

Spring. From their winter ranges in late March and early April, millions of snow geese wing northward day and night in large flocks, moving somewhat faster than in the fall. Most of the eastern population travels up the Mississippi flyway, angling abruptly eastward near Winnipeg to James Bay, thence northward along the west shore of Hudson Bay. Mating of bonded pairs apparently occurs during migration, especially at rest stops just preceding arrival on the nesting area, usually about mid-May. Adults usually arrive a week or so before the yearling geese, which do not return to their natal colony site but settle on nearby water areas. Snow still covers most of the colony sites. As bare ground appears, the flocks separate first into smaller groups, then into pairs. Two-year-old geese now form pair bonds for the first time, but most do not actually breed until their third year. In a new pairing, it is the female who "homes" to her native colony and is accompanied by her mate, who may have spent his first year in a far-distant colony. Older breeders return to the colony site of the previous year, sometimes even to the same nest. Nesting colonies in certain traditional sites number up to 500,000 birds or more, often in association with nesting Ross's geese.

The snow goose pair vigorously defends its territory, the size of which greatly depends on amounts of bare ground space exposed by snowmelt and on the abundance of birds. Eighteen to 40 square yards per pair was typical in one snow goose colony, but these geese can tolerate densities of up to 1 nest per 6 square yards, or up to 1,000 nests per square mile. Territories are smaller in colony interiors than in outer areas, and territories decrease in size as incubation proceeds. Nesting begins as soon as snow conditions permit, usually from early to mid-June, often extending into July. Late-melting snow causes many pairs to inhibit nesting; parent geese also desert many nests in late incubation stages, perhaps for stress-related reasons of crowding. Dump nesting, the depositing of eggs in the nest of another goose, also occurs, probably when a pair is evicted from its own territory by another pair. Up to 80 percent of nests receive dumped eggs during harsh-weather springs. As *determinate layers* (like all waterfowl), female snow geese cannot renest once the annual ovulation cycle has begun, so a nesting failure for whatever reason is irremediable for that year. Once incubation begins, females rarely leave their nests; males guard the nest and attack intruders. By not feeding, females may lose 25 percent or more of their spring weight, and starvation on or near the nest sometimes occurs.

EGGS AND YOUNG: average of 4; eggs dull white. INCUBATION: by female, about 24 days. FLEDGING: about 6 weeks.

Summer. Most nests are still being incubated as summer begins. Goslings begin feeding with their parents less than a day after hatching, but females brood their goslings for 2 or 3 weeks. Family groups wander widely on land and water, sometimes for 30 miles, in search of food. Weather and predators take a toll of goslings (probably some 15 percent), most during their first week of life.

Yearling snow geese begin their annual feather molt in early July; breeding adults begin about 2 weeks after goslings hatch. The adults remain flightless for about 3 weeks; they can fly again at about the same time the goslings begin flying. By mid-August to early September, snow geese begin to move from their northern ranges and mass in huge numbers at traditional staging areas, including southern James Bay.

Fall. Peak migration movements occur in October and November. Migration flocks of 100 to 1,000 geese, consisting of family groups, are common. Flying day and night, they typically travel at altitudes of 2,000 or 3,000 feet, sometimes much higher. Snow geese moving from James Bay to the Gulf fly almost nonstop. Unlike most migrators, their fall routes in midcontinent do not repeat their spring passageways; the fall corridors are more direct, running in parallel series over the western Great Lakes, then merging in the lower Mississippi flyway to the Gulf.

Winter. The historical snow goose wintering areas are coastal marshes of Louisiana and Texas, where hundreds of thousands of snow geese arrive each fall. Most of the eastern population has arrived on its winter range by December. The white morph predominates in western areas of this range; the blue morph is more frequent in the east. Until the 1930s, researchers believe, the two morphs were *allopatric* (geographically separated) on the winter range. Then coastal birds began moving inland into pastures and rice fields of the Gulf states, bringing both morphs together and resulting in increased pairing between them. Today much of the North American snow goose population remains heavily dependent upon coastal rice production areas. Since about 1970, however, snow goose migrational habits have dramatically changed, and the entire winter range has shifted northward. Most snow geese, both white and blue morphs, now winter in greatest density in the Midwest, especially along the Missouri River in northwestern Missouri. These patterns continue to shift. Some of the eastern population also winters along the Mexican Gulf coast, and most of the western migrants winter in California's Imperial and Central valleys and in Puget Sound. By late February, most wintering snow geese are beginning to migrate; much of the Gulf population stops in northwestern Missouri for several days or weeks before resuming northward flight.

Ecology. Snow goose habitat requirements include tundra coastal plains and islands for colonial nesting and coastal marshes for feeding. As wetland habitats decline, especially in snow goose migration corridors, the birds increasingly forage in upland fields.

The nest, which one observer described as "a built-up scrape" in moss or gravel, becomes enlarged with use over several years. Females add mosses and grasses to old nests, gradually building raised sides, also placing small amounts of down in the nest bowl. One study found that nests sheltered by willow shrubs standing over 16 inches tall (mainly Canada or barren-ground willow, *Salix brachycarpa*) proved more successful than nests sited near smaller willows or in areas without willows. Sites containing lyme grass, a wild-rye, were also favored.

The bill's sharp cutting edges make snow geese effective grazers, grubbers, and snippers of vegetation, which constitutes most of the diet. On the breeding range, they feed extensively on rhizomes and shoots of sedges (including bulrushes), marsh grasses, horsetails, cotton-grasses, and other marsh plants. Dominant winter range foods include rootstocks of bulrushes, cattails, salt-meadow cord-grass, and stems and seeds of spike-rushes, panic grasses, and wild rice. Snow goose food habits, however, "have become revolutionized in recent years by agriculture," notes waterfowl biologist Frank C. Bellrose, a change tied in with coastal wetland depletion. The shift began with the California wintering population and soon spread eastward. Snow geese began extending their winter range as rice-paddy cultivation developed, flocking inland up to 150 miles from the Gulf coast. Waste grain in cornfields, shoots of winter wheat and rice, and pasture grasses now widely supplement the marsh plant diet in snow goose migration corridors and winter range. Powerful attractants include marshland burns, which stimulate the growth of green shoots and facilitate goose access to roots and bulbs.

Snow goose competitors are relatively few and insignificant. In the past 2 decades, however, snow geese have become alarming competitors of other waterbird species—and, in a sense, with their own habitats. Continuing snow goose overpopulation of colonial breeding sites now exceeds, in many areas, the ability of tundra grass-sedge communities to support the geese. This situation has resulted in the widespread destruction of tundra habitat. Extensive foraging and grubbing for roots in thin tundra soil by dense hordes of geese strip the surface, causing the rise of inorganic salts from underlying marine sediments through increased evaporation. The resulting highly saline soils (3 or more times saltier than seawater) reduce plant and invertebrate food sources for many ducks and shorebirds, and also kill much shrub willow vegetation. "Up to a certain population density," wrote one researcher, "goose grazing triggers a positive feedback mechanism that enhances plant pro-ductivity"—but beyond that density, the mechanism breaks down, and the habitat becomes degraded in a cascading sequence of events. Ruined habitat forces the geese into marshlands they have not previously occupied. The entire sequence, researchers believe, results from the bountiful food supply provided by agriculture on the birds' winter range, indirectly promoting snow goose reproduc-tive success and population growth. Agricultural subsidies for rice growers in the Gulf marshland "eliminated a winter survival bottle-neck," according to waterfowl biologist Joe Johnson.

Egg and gosling predators include sandhill cranes, herring and glaucous gulls, parasitic jaegers, northern ravens, polar bears, wolves, and red and arctic foxes. The foxes often cache eggs by burying them. Caribou sometimes trample nests and eat damaged eggshells. Severe weather on the breeding range, however, probably kills many more snow geese than predators take. Thousands also die from fowl cholera.

Focus. Despite an annual mortality rate of about 30 percent for adult snow geese and the hazards of tundra nesting and semiannual migrations, the trend of snow goose increase continues at almost 5 percent annually. In 1996, the midcontinental population of snow geese was estimated at 3 to 5 million birds. Such expansion, endangering tundra habitats for other birds, worries Canadian and U.S. wildlife biologists. "At a time when many species are in decline and others are going extinct," one of them wrote, "this dramatic increase should be regarded as a great success. But in this case, a boom in one species' numbers has put other birds and plants at risk." Concerned scientists have formed the Goose Habitat Working Group, which proposes lengthened hunting seasons and other measures to reduce goose populations. Arctic Inuit peoples have long collected snow goose eggs for food, and the group wants to encourage this activity as well. But these are stopgap solutions at best. Probably the best hope for control lies in management efforts where the overpopulation problem began, on the winter range. Failing such efforts, North American snow goose populations are sooner or later headed for drastic declines as breeding habitat degrades.

Until 1973, the blue morph was listed as a separate goose species; evidence of interbreeding between blue and white morphs had preceded official "lumping" of both as the same species by about a decade. Both morphs remain in their distinctive plumages lifelong. Interbreeding between them may produce either morph or intermediate-colored offspring (usually birds with white breasts and dark backs), though each morph favors its own plumage type for pairing. In the midcontinental population, various shifts of proportion have occurred during the past 30 years. The blue morph has slightly predominated in abundance for much of that time, but no discernible long-term trends have become evident.

Snow goose lifespan averages about 8 years, but many live for 2 decades or longer.

Canada Goose *(Branta canadensis)*

The most abundant, widespread, and familiar goose in North America as well as the world, the Canada goose is readily identified by its white "chinstrap," its black head and neck contrasting with paler breast and brownish wings, and its resonant, honking calls. Sizes range from the almost swan-size giant Canada goose *(B. c. maxima)* to the mallard-size cackling goose *(B. c. minima)*. The giant race, one of the most common, often shows other markings: a white neck ring, a white forehead spot, and a distinctive "hawk's-head" pattern (facing rear) as part of the cheek-patch profile.

Waterfowl biologists have classified 11 distinct subspecies of Canada geese in North America, based on sizes, plumages, breeding range locales, migration routes, and wintering locales. (Some biologists believe there are many more, possibly up to 40.) Most of the medium to large subspecies migrate and reside east of the hundredth parallel of longitude; the smaller, darker races dominate west of that line. The 6 eastern populations, with their dominant races or subspecies, are as follows, from east to west: north Atlantic (Atlantic race), mid-Atlantic (interior race), Tennessee Valley (interior and giant races), Mississippi Valley (interior race), eastern prairie (interior race), and tallgrass prairie (Hutchins's, lesser race). The giant race is common in all areas. Each race breeds apart, and they seldom hybridize; in a practical sense, they are distinct species. Two or more races often mix together during migrations, however, and on the winter range. Size and plumage differences between giant and interior races of Canada geese (which commonly occur together) are obvious in the field. Male Canadas are slightly larger than females. The male's two-syllable honk, "ke-ronk," is lower toned than the female's "kink kink."

Close relatives. Five *Branta* species range worldwide. In North America, the only other resident *Branta* is the brent goose *(B.*

bernicla), often called brant. The barnacle goose *(B. leucopsis)* is a native of Greenland and arctic Europe. Another European species, the red-breasted goose *(B. ruficollis),* is the smallest goose of all. The endangered nene or Hawaiian goose *(B. sandvicensis)* is restricted to Hawaii.

Behaviors. The Canada goose is the bird most people think of as *the* wild goose or honker. Its high, migratory V formations and nasal, quavering chant from the sky herald the arrivals of spring and winter. Thoreau called Canada geese "grenadiers of the air . . . coming to unlock the fetters of northern rivers." Yet this creature that so conspicuously travels the continent twice a year, even occasionally competing with the airlines for high traffic lanes, nests in utter stealth. A goose spotting you from a pond thicket can freeze still as a rock, its head outstretched with not a feather ruffled by breeze, not a pond ripple set forth by slightest movement.

Canada geese have a large repertoire of display postures, a body language fairly easy to interpret once you learn its details. Many of these movements are easily seen in any flock year-round, and most of them involve motions of the head and neck. Threat or aggressive displays include folded-neck and extended-neck postures with head lowered and pointed at the opponent; vertical head pumping, often preceding a direct attack; and vigorous swinging of the outstretched neck, rotating the head. Geese convey other messages during courtship (see Spring). A flock of geese on water often signals its imminent takeoff by suddenly erupting into loud honking, head pumping, and facing into the wind. Landing seems trickier for them; they stretch their feet forward and their necks downward before splashing down, an awkward-appearing performance. Landing in strong wind, a goose may "whiffle" on its descent, turning on its side (or sometimes flipping completely over), stalling its airlift, and plummeting 5 or 10 feet before righting itself. These giddy acrobatics seem more characteristic of younger geese than older adults, which seem more inclined to sober landings.

Like most waterfowl, Canada geese mate for life. Should one partner die, the other usually bonds to a new mate within a year or less. Most large flocks consist of subflocks made up of individual family units. These smaller groupings are easily observed in any large flock on water. In the goose social hierarchy, large families dominate smaller ones. Families in turn dominate pairs, which dominate single geese. Males dominate family units.

Canada geese, native to North America, range from the high Arctic to the southern United States and northern Mexico. They have also been introduced into Europe and New Zealand.

Spring. "For the farmer, the rancher, the city dweller, and the Cree Indian," wrote biologist Frank Bellrose, "the northward flight of Canada geese symbolizes spring." Likewise, to Aldo Leopold, "one swallow does not make a summer, but one skein of geese, clearing the murk of a March thaw, is the spring." Observers have noted differential migrations in some areas, with two peak movements: March–April and May–June. Except for far-northern populations, however, most Canada geese have arrived on their breeding ranges by earliest spring. They usually return as family units to the previous year's nesting site, but yearling geese soon separate into flocks by themselves and depart their first home, often traveling up to several hundred miles (usually northward) from the natal area. Some yearlings may form lifelong pair bonds now, but their first nesting seldom occurs until their second or third year.

Within most of their breeding range, as snow and ice begin to retreat, Canada geese are among the first birds of the year to nest (great horned owls, crossbills, and a few others precede them). The female leads her mate on a search, often inspecting old nest sites, perhaps choosing one she has previously used or scraping a new hollow nearby. Now the pair, especially the male, becomes aggressively territorial, defending an area that may vary from a quarter acre to many acres in size, depending upon density of population and height of surrounding vegetation. Throughout the incubation period, males may readily attack any intruder, including other geese and humans. Following a successful challenge to an intruder, the pair typically performs a mutual action called the greeting or triumph ceremony. This consists of head shaking, neck stretching, male snoring notes, and strident honking in perfectly timed duet. Head and neck dipping precedes copulation. The female builds the nest, beginning with a slight scrape, then reaches from it to pluck adjacent vegetation. Gradually she forms a base and rim around herself, adding down from her breast after egg laying begins. The male stands guard near the nest as incubation begins. He accompanies his mate when she leaves the nest, usually twice daily (early morning and afternoon) for short periods of feeding and bathing.

After hatching, nest territorial bounds immediately dissolve, and the family moves about together in mobile territory, often in single file on water. Sources differ on whether the male or female usually leads or trails the family procession.

EGGS AND YOUNG: typically 5 or 6; eggs creamy white, becoming nest stained. INCUBATION: by female; about 4 weeks. FLEDGING: about 2 months, sometimes less.

Summer. After hatching, goslings leave the nest with parents in a day or less, but brooding continues for the first few days. An oft-noted occurrence is the *creche* or gang brood, a mixed brood of 10 to 20 goslings swimming and feeding under the care of a single pair of adults—a kind of day-care system also seen in flamingos, ostriches, penguins, and a few other species. Creching occurs mainly in densely occupied nesting areas, where many goslings hatch at once. Their imprinting on a single female parent may be incomplete or delayed for 2 or 3 weeks. Some studies suggest that such brood interchange results from a literal mix-up of abundant progeny. Other studies indicate that younger, inexperienced females may sometimes lose their goslings to the care of older adults, resulting in formation of large extended families.

Yearling and other nonbreeding adult geese begin their annual feather molt some 10 days after parent adults, usually in June. The birds remain flightless for 4 to 6 weeks. Family groups become secretive, moving to more secluded areas during this period. During this flightless period, the Inuit and other natives hunt Canada geese for food. By late summer, molting is completed, goslings are fledged, and family groups often join large multifamily flocks on open land and water areas.

Fall. Canada goose populations vary extensively in timing of fall migration. Many populations depart their breeding areas in early fall or before; others (such as the giant Canada goose), wrote Frank C. Bellrose, "are notorious for their late fall departures." Peak travel occurs in September and October, but thousands of geese *stage,* or gather, at large wildlife refuges in the northern tier of states. They often associate with snow goose or brant migrants on these areas. If open water is available and food is plentiful, many remain over winter in these areas or until harsh weather sends them farther south. Most eastern populations, however, winter inland from southern Illinois to Kentucky. Incoming migrants join resident year-round geese, swelling numbers to hundreds of thousands.

Flying both day and night, Canada geese travel in flocks that may number from 30 or less to 100 or more birds. Observer opinions differ on the gender and constancy of the lead bird in a flying flock. In a migrating flock, thinks Frank C. Bellrose, the leader "is probably the gander of the largest family." In a lifetime of observing geese, he never witnessed the point goose in a migratory flock changing positions, as has been reported. Most flocks travel about 40 miles per hour at an altitude around 2,000 feet, though occasionally much higher flocks are spotted by pilots. As they fly, they voice their constant contact calls—"goose music," as Aldo Leopold called it. Their voices precede their wedge formations, often drifting down from the night sky as you lie snug abed.

Winter. As on their breeding ranges, flocks *home* to particular wintering areas, resulting in highly localized populations, often of mixed races, that return year after year. Family groups remain together in subflocks and in large flocks on the winter range. Early morning and evening hours are preferred feeding times, but flocks may stay on feeding grounds all day if not disturbed. At night, they usually roost in open water. Winter storms or cold snaps may send resident flocks southward on minimigrations for brief periods, but the birds often bounce back when weather abates. Winter is barely half over when flocks in many locales begin restless behaviors. From their southernmost range, they may depart northward as early as mid-January. More northern wintering flocks begin moving about mid-February or early March. These early migrants often travel in 50- to 100-mile leaps, generally keeping apace with the 35-degree F. isotherm, where melting snow and ice expose food and patches of open water. Later migrants tend to move longer distances at once, thus making up in some measure for the time lapse.

Ecology. A variety of wetland habitats may host Canada geese. In the breeding range, a pair usually requires at least 5 acres of open water plus access, near or far, to upland fields or open land for grazing. Primary requirements on the winter range are grazing habitats for feeding and open water for drinking and resting sites. Canada geese, as we know, are exceedingly adaptable to human environs and readily become semidomesticated. Suburban parks, lawns, and golf courses provide ample grazing habitats.

Canada geese probably show greater diversity in nest sites than any other waterfowl. The site is usually located within 50 yards of water (often much closer), contains some amount of cover (usually emergent aquatic vegetation), and is on high enough ground to give the nesting goose a clear overview of the surroundings. Typically the birds nest atop muskrat and beaver lodges, bulrush mats, and marsh hummocks, and on dikes, ditch banks, and small islands. (In certain prairie and delta marshes, the presence of muskrat lodges may be chief attractants.) Occasionally the geese inhabit aboveground structures such as abandoned heron, hawk, and osprey nests, human-made tree platforms, or elevated washtubs. Nest

Small islands along shoreline marshes provide ideal nesting habitat for Canada geese.

materials consist of sticks, cattails, reeds, and grasses, all gathered from the immediate vicinity.

Canada geese are almost wholly vegetarian grazers. Their natural food consists mainly of shoots and seeds of grasses, legumes, and such aquatic vegetation as spike-rushes and bulrushes. They cannot digest cellulose well, however, and must consume large amounts of vegetation to satisfy their energy needs. The passage of food from gullet to excretion averages about 2 hours. (One researcher conducted a heroic quest for science: "I know from personal experience," wrote M. A. Ogilvie in his book *Wild Geese*, "that a fresh goose dropping from a bird feeding on grass has little or no taste, except perhaps that of chewed grass.") But Canada goose food habits, especially during migrations and winter, have changed extensively since presettlement times. Such changes reflect the country-wide expansion of agriculture; these changes also account in large part for the phenomenal increase of goose populations and shifts in their winter distribution over the past several decades. Wintering Canada geese show marked preference for farm-grown grains (especially corn) and grain shoots (such as winter wheat). Stubble fields with their waste grain are also favored feeding sites. Aldo Leopold pointed out the "prairie-bias" of feeding Canada geese, noting the "conspicuous fact that the corn stubbles selected by geese for feeding are usually those occupying former prairies. No man knows whether this bias for prairie corn reflects some superior nutritional value or some ancestral tradition" or merely "the simpler fact that prairie cornfields tend to be large." Today much of the forage grains and greens that migrant and wintering Canada geese consume is provided expressly for them in state and federal wildlife refuges. As a consequence, many formerly transient flocks have become permanent winter residents in these areas. The birds (mainly goslings) also consume small amounts of invertebrates.

Competition with other waterfowl is negligible in most areas. Canada geese seem highly tolerant of other species such as ducks and herons, often nesting in proximity to them. Canada geese do not regularly associate with other waterfowl. On upland feeding sites, however, other goose species plus grazing ducks such as mallards often mingle freely with them. The recent increase of mute swan populations in the eastern United States offers potentially competitive situations; conflicts often occur between these species in joint breeding areas (see Mute Swan).

Predators, which consume mainly eggs and goslings, include jaegers, gulls, common ravens, American crows, magpies, foxes, coyotes, minks, and (in some areas) dogs. Goslings, even when very young, are able to dive, thus avoiding the beaks or talons of predatory birds. Attacks by blackflies (Simuliidae) and snapping turtles sometimes kill goslings.

Focus. Trends of rapid increase in Canada goose populations over the past several decades continue. The spectacular comeback of this once-depleted species, especially in middle and eastern North America, is an oft-cited victory of wildlife conservation efforts. Overhunted to extirpation in many areas, most breeding Canada geese had vanished from the north-central states by 1900. Severe drought during the 1930s reduced many migratory populations as well. Since then, the growth of federal and state refuge systems has helped build eastern Canada goose populations to numbers that probably far exceed their presettlement abundance. Especially notable is the recovery of the giant Canada goose, the largest race, once believed to have become extinct by 1920. In 1962, however, a surviving population was identified in Minnesota, and subsequent management efforts have produced a success story that for waterfowl biologists "may well have become one of their greatest nightmares," as ornithologist James Granlund remarks. Today, as a consequence, 2 large populations of Canada geese reside in eastern North America: the wild migrants and the more or less permanent residential population of the suburbs, introduced since World War II. The latter population has become the larger by far.

The present overpopulation of Canada geese in open suburban areas—parks, airports, golf courses—has given the bird an increasingly negative image. From a bird of near-legendary status venerated by Aldo Leopold and other conservation pioneers when Canada geese were far fewer in number, its subsequent transformation into a "trash bird" of urban areas is a case of familiarity breeding contempt. Honkers defecate about once every 3 minutes—almost a pound per day per goose—wherever they graze, and lawns full of goose manure lose their appeal for human sunbathing and picnicking. Control of nuisance geese by removal, extended hunting seasons, and planting of distasteful grasses such as tall fescue has had little widespread success. The birds also trouble farmers at times, especially by ravaging soybean crops in some areas; most grain feeding, however, occurs during the postharvest season, and mainly on wildlife refuges planted for the purpose.

"Wawa," the Ojibwa word for the Canada goose, is perpetuated in the town name of Wawa, Ontario, where a large statue of the goose welcomes visitors. Fennville, Michigan, located near a large goose refuge, hosts an annual goose festival for hunters (motto: "Get your goose in Fennville"). Long a staple source of meat for Native Americans, Canada geese also provided flight feathers for arrow fletching and goosedown for bedding. Goose grease became a popular medicinal and cooking ingredient. And Canada goose migrations, which sky watchers invariably declare as happening earlier or later than usual, still provide an endless seasonal topic and bellwether.

Captive Canada geese may survive for several decades, but most wild geese probably live only 5 or 6 years. Annual mortality rates of fledged geese average less than 30 percent. Canadian naturalist Jack Miner, who established an Ontario migration refuge for Canada geese as early as 1904, was an early proponent of their conservation. Miner spread much information and folk wisdom (along with some notable misinformation) about the species in his many books. Most ornithologists discredit the widely reported "piggyback phenomenon"—tales of hummingbirds or sparrows hitching rides on Canada geese during migration. Such behavior involves too many anomalies to be true.

TYPICAL DUCKS (TRIBE ANATINI)

The smallest members of the waterfowl family, ducks are also the most diverse. Typical ducks number almost 90 species worldwide. Some 34 species breed in North America, inhabiting both freshwater and marine habitats, and most are migratory. Ducks differ from geese and swans in ways other than size and diversity: Male and female plumage in many species is different *(sexually dimorphic);*

most species molt twice a year, both times in summer; their courtship displays are much more intricate; most exhibit elaborate distraction displays when young are threatened; they do not mate for life but usually only for a single breeding season; and only the female is parental, rearing the young. Males are called *drakes*, females are *hens*, and the young are *ducklings*. Ducks are usually grouped by their feeding characteristics: *Dabbling ducks*, mainly vegetarian, feed from the water surface, tipping up to forage just beneath it and rarely diving. *Diving ducks* (also called *bay ducks*) plunge the entire body beneath the surface, feeding on vegetation, fish, and other animal matter. *Sea ducks*, many of which frequent freshwater areas as well, are also divers.

Dabbling Ducks

Dabblers, also called river, pond, or puddle ducks, feed primarily by tipping up to submerge head and neck or by dabbling from the water surface. In contrast to diving ducks, they can spring directly into flight without a running start, and their feet are set farther forward and to the sides, making them waddle when they walk. Dabblers also fly at a relatively higher altitude during nonmigratory flights. Most dabbler populations show an unbalanced sex ratio, with drakes predominating. The sexes are *dimorphic*, having different plumage. Most drake dabblers are brightly patterned. Both sexes show a white or colored *speculum*—a wing patch on the upper surface of the secondary feathers—useful for identifying the birds in flight. Fall and winter are the courtship and pairing seasons for dabbling ducks. Most dabblers undergo a double molt: the breeding plumage, acquired in late summer or fall and worn until the following summer, when the birds molt into a dull *eclipse* (nonbreeding or hiding) plumage. During eclipse molt, they lose their wing and tail feathers, becoming flightless for a period of days or weeks. They soon molt the eclipse plumage, replacing it with new breeding plumage. The brief eclipse period in ducks corresponds somewhat to the seasonal winter plumage of many songbirds.

Seven General Categories of Ducks in Spring and Early Summer (as paraphrased from H. Albert Hochbaum)

1. Unpaired birds not yet courting.
2. Unpaired birds in prenuptial courtship.
3. Mated pairs.
4. Unpaired sexually active drakes.
5. Unpaired novices (yearling drakes).
6. Postbreeding drakes that have begun molting.
7. Unpaired hens (yearlings and unsuccessful nesters).

Dabbling ducks frequent restricted or enclosed bodies of water—ponds, small lakes, riverine habitats—rather than large, open-water expanses. Some 40 species exist worldwide, 11 in North America. All of the latter except the wood duck nest on the ground and are of one genus, *Anas*. Northeastern species omitted from the following accounts include the gadwall *(A. strepera)* and the green-winged teal *(A. crecca)*.

As waterfowl biologist H. Albert Hochbaum wrote, "The mating displays of ducks, like the drumming of the Ruffed Grouse, may be observed through most of the year. . . . Courtship behavior is not completely seasonal, and is not confined entirely to the period of reproduction," even though seasonal peaks of courtship occur in all duck species. Yet ducks also undergo an annual period, usually during the summer molting periods and after, when they become, in Hochbaum's words, "as sexless as the Sultan's eunuch," owing to physical shrinkage of the gonads. Their behaviors at such times show no sexual discrimination.

WATERFOWL FAMILY (Anatidae) - TYPICAL DUCKS - Dabbling Ducks

Wood Duck *(Aix sponsa)*

About 20 inches long, both sexes of the wood duck show a sleek, swept-back head crest. The drake in breeding plumage is one of the most colorful, intricately patterned ducks in the world, a rich blend of reds, glossy iridescent greens and purples, and burgundy-brown—"as if constructed in an artist's studio," wrote ornithologist James Granlund. Two white, U-shaped "straps" on chin and throat, orange-red eyes, and predominantly red bill further decorate the head. Hens, dull gray-brown with subtle hues, show white eye-patches, chin, and throat. In flight, the wood duck's white belly, long rectangular tail, broad wings, bill angled downward, and habit of bobbing its head up and down identify it. The hen often utters a loud, squealing "hoo-eek" call as she launches into flight; drakes voice much softer, goldfinchlike "twee? twee?" notes.

Close relatives. The only other *Aix* species is the mandarin duck *(A. galericulata)* of Asia.

Behaviors. This "Beau Brummel among birds," as ornithologist Arthur C. Bent labeled it, is almost preternaturally spectacular. The wood duck differs from other dabblers in that its legs are farther forward and it has strong, sharp toenails, enabling it to perch in trees; some ornithologists prefer to classify the wood duck apart from the dabblers for that reason.

On land, woodies can run faster than any other duck, up to 7 miles per hour; on water, though they primarily feed from the surface, they occasionally dive several feet. Woodies have the largest eyes of any waterfowl, indicating visual acuity in low-light conditions, and they have larger odor-sensing organs than most birds. The large eyes, broader wings, and longer tail than most other dabblers "enable the wood duck to accommodate, with a minimum of injury, precarious flight through the tree mazes that dot its habitat," according to one research team. Not many birds turn their heads while flying; wood ducks can and do, another identifying feature.

A common behavior of pairs is *allopreening* or mutual preening, especially the head areas. Drakes do it more often to hens than vice versa. When a pair launches into flight, the hen takes off first, and the birds usually rise at a 45-degree angle. Loafing, usually from midmorning to late afternoon, is an important part of a duck's day, the time when it preens and naps, conserving energy. The loafing site, often a log at the water's edge, is commonly used as a daily gathering place by several wood ducks (usually drakes) at once.

Three distinct wood duck populations—the Atlantic, interior, and Pacific—range in North America, absent only from the Rockies and Great Plains. The 2 eastern populations breed from southern

Canada to the Gulf. The largest abundance is concentrated between latitudes 30 and 43 degrees N.

Spring. About a third of all wood ducks breed where they winter, and southeastern resident wood ducks do not migrate. Northern wood ducks, however, are early migrators, traveling at night and arriving on their breeding range in mid-March and April. Hens return to their natal areas year after year, and unpaired yearling drakes also return to their birth sites. Most wood ducks begin breeding as yearlings. Some 90 percent of the hens have already paired with mates on the winter range, but the pair bond usually lasts for only a single nesting season. Ritualized displays and call notes (see Fall) continue, leading to copulation, which is often signaled by repeated bill jerking with head thrust upward and wing and tail markings displayed. Commonly seen flying and swimming together at this prenesting stage are wood duck trios consisting of two drakes and a hen. Bonded pairs seem to tolerate the presence of third-party bachelor attendants, sometimes through the entire breeding season, but usually only until incubation begins. "This association," speculates biologist Frank C. Bellrose, "may ensure that a female acquires a new mate if the paired male dies or prematurely terminates the pair bond."

Wood ducks do not establish or defend territories as such. The paired hen's presence, however, constitutes a "moving territory," and she is rigorously guarded by the drake. The home range, in which feeding and loafing occur, is variable in size, spanning a half mile to several miles, depending on habitat, and often overlapping with home ranges of other pairs. Unless the hen returns to a nest cavity she has previously occupied, she searches out suitable nest sites for several days, the drake (or drakes) accompanying her. Aggressive encounters with other wood duck pairs sometimes occur near erected wood duck nest boxes as the birds compete for cavities. Adult pairs typically begin nesting about 2 weeks sooner than yearlings. Drakes usually remain attentive to hens until just before hatching—a longer period than for most ducks. Incubating hens tend to leave the nest twice a day—early morning and afternoon or evening. Occasionally, according to Bellrose, 2 or 3 pairs "remain associated into the early stages of incubation in what I believe is an attachment between mother and daughter(s)." He suggests that this attachment is the means by which yearlings find the nesting areas where they hatched the previous year. As drakes abandon their mates, they often join other drakes in small communal roosts, which gradually increase in size and number as spring advances. Unmated drakes often remain in small, loose flocks through the breeding season.

Dump nesting, in which two or more hens deposit eggs in a single nest, is common among wood ducks. Any nest containing more than 15 eggs is probably a dump nest, and instances of 40 or more eggs in a nest have been documented. An intruding hen (often a yearling) arrives at an occupied nest during the morning when the host hen is away. Some of the intruders have nests of their own, some do not. Sometimes the resulting egg collections are never incubated, but often the nest's original proprietor does incubate them and raises the large brood as her own. This intraspecific parasitism occurs more frequently where nesting densities are high and nest cavities are in short supply.

EGGS AND YOUNG: typically 10 to 15; eggs pale olive green or brownish. INCUBATION: by hen; about 4 weeks. FLEDGING: 8 to 10 weeks.

Summer. Broods typically hatch in spring and early summer; hens brood their ducklings for about 24 hours, then lead them to water. The often observed departure of flightless wood ducklings from the nest is one of the more dramatic episodes of nature. The ducklings must somehow get from cavity nests, often high up, to the ground, where the hen waits, "coaching" their exodus with soft, repeated notes. One after another, the ducklings climb to the cavity exit with sharp-clawed feet, then spring with fluttering wings from the hole into space, sometimes free-falling as much as 60 feet. They may bounce once or twice on the ground, but being composed mainly of fluff and cartilage, they are seldom hurt. Because wood ducks often nest away from water, the trek to the nearest pond or creek is a journey that may last several hours and span a mile or more through dense vegetation. The hen moves fairly fast, her brood trailing behind her; often the weakest ducklings lag and get left behind. Predators sometimes kill entire broods during this exodus. Once on water, the day-old ducklings begin to feed, instinctively seeking overhead cover along shorelines. They can also dive, using feet and wings to propel themselves underwater for distances up to 15 feet. For brood rearing, hens typically seek wetland or pond areas 10 acres or more in size, often leading their ducklings through a succession of wetlands before settling in an area that contains ample food and cover. By the second week, the new home range, small or large, is relatively stable, and all hen and brood activities—feeding, loafing, concealment—occur here. Brood bonds begin to break up after the fifth week, just before the juveniles start to fly. An average of only 25 to 50 percent of ducklings survive to the flight stage. Unlike many other waterfowl, wood ducks sometimes raise 2 broods in a season, especially in their southern range; they also renest if the original nest fails or is destroyed by predators. Late broods are usually hatched by late July.

As pair bonds dissolve, drakes and nonbreeding wood ducks begin to establish communal roosts at night, flying to them around sunset. Later, juveniles and hens also flock together in the evening. Most roosting is on water beneath overhanging shoreline cover; buttonbush is a frequent cover shrub in numerous wood duck roosting sites, many of which have been used year after year by the ducks. The birds disperse at daybreak.

In July, as molting time approaches, many drakes depart the nesting areas and move northward to lake and marsh feeding areas. Most of these *molt migrations* extend no farther than 35 miles from the nesting area. Here the drakes begin molting their colorful breeding plumage, replacing it with a drab brown *eclipse* plumage; only the white chin, eye area, and throat remain distinctive. Hens and juveniles tend to remain on or near the brooding area through summer. Brood rearing may delay onset of the hen molt for a week or more after the male's. Juveniles also molt into their first adult plumage. The molting birds remain flightless from 3 weeks to a month, concealing themselves in dense marsh cover.

When the birds regain the ability to fly in late summer, the drakes, wearing resplendent new breeding plumage, often return to breeding areas. *Fall.* This season of migrations from the northern breeding range is also the foremost period of wood duck courtship and pairing, which occur mainly at transient and winter roost sites. Most of the birds depart from late September through October, flying at night; adult birds precede most juveniles by about 10 days, though enough age-class overlap occurs that plenty of adults remain to guide the younger birds south (if in fact they do). Northeastern migrants join year-round resident woodies in the southeastern states, west to central Texas.

The end of the breeding season signals the end of monogamy in wood ducks. Pair formation begins when 10 or so drakes congregate around a hen on water and perform *display bouts* lasting up to 20 minutes, separated by intervals of preening and feeding. A variety of notes and whistles are sounded, the only time wood ducks are vocal to any large extent. Woodies have some 21 ritualized courtship displays, complex movements that include head and bill jerks, wing and tail flashing, chin lifting, rearing up, and other stylized motions. Such displays, accompanied by much chasing and splashing, may also establish a dominance hierarchy among the courting drakes, one of which the hen allows near her. This initial pairing, however, may last only briefly; the hens are coquettes, and ritualized competition may resume for days or weeks. Stable pairing is the eventual result. Few if any wood ducks re-pair with their previous mates. Many are already paired, at least temporarily, by the time they reach the winter range, and pairing continues through fall and winter. An indication of pairing status may be seen in the number of 2-bird flocks flying.

Winter. Latitude 35 degrees N is about the northern limit of the winter range, though small numbers occasionally linger farther north. Paired and unpaired birds disperse during the daytime from nocturnal roosts that may number several thousand wood ducks. By late February, most of the migrants are beginning to move gradually northward, arriving at northern breeding sites as the ice retreats.

Forest ponds and floodings provide optimal wood duck habitat.

Ecology. On both summer and winter ranges, wood ducks primarily inhabit forested wetlands. A mixture of water, timber, and marsh provides optimal habitat for these birds. For nesting habitat, river bottomlands with mature hardwoods standing within a mile of wetland areas that meet food and cover requirements are ideal. For feeding and brood rearing, the birds favor shrub swamps, streams, overflows, and shallow ponds with an abundance of wet thickets and emergent and overhanging vegetation for cover. "The lower the stream banks, the clearer the water and the greater abundance of oxbows, cut-off channels and islands," assessed one wood duck expert, "the better the stream for breeding wood ducks." Where farm or suburban areas contain the elements of their basic habitat needs, wood ducks often reside close to people as well. Beavers frequently create desirable wood duck habitat by impounding streams and flooding timber. Wetland areas that wood ducks do *not* typically inhabit include bogs, fast streams, and salt and brackish marshes.

For nesting, wood ducks seek tree cavities, usually in living to avoid apparent contradiction with trees that stand in or adjacent to wetlands. Important cavity tree species used by wood ducks include silver and red maples, American elm, sweet gum, American basswood, American be-ech, and white and red oaks. Usually the tree selected has a breast-height diameter of at least 12 inches; the higher the cavity, the more attractive it seems to wood ducks. Most wood duck nest cavities average about 25 feet high. The birds favor rel-atively small entrance holes—4- to 8-inch open-ings—over larger ones, and a cavity depth of 6

Wood duck hens make frequent use of nest boxes placed for them, as seen in this cutaway view; wooden "steps" on the entrance-hole side (left) enable ducklings to climb out.

to 20 inches. Abandoned nesting or roosting holes of pileated wood-peckers are sometimes claimed (one researcher speculates that once-abundant pileated woodpecker cavities may have guided the evolution of hen wood duck size and shape). Placement of nesting boxes of specified size in trees or on posts above water has become an important and successful wood duck management procedure. Hen wood ducks bring no materials into the cavity; wood debris inside the natural cavity and shavings placed in nest boxes form the basic nest, and the hen adds tufts of down shed from her breast.

The wood duck's omnivorous food habits, wrote Frank Bellrose, "are one of several factors that enable the species to occupy an extensive breeding range." Most of the food consumed by woodies occurs on or near the water surface and on shorelines. Although plant materials provide about 90 percent of the diet, important sources of protein for breeding hens and ducklings include aquatic beetles and bugs, emergent mayflies, ants, spiders, tadpoles, and small frogs and fish. Duckweeds and pondweeds are favored plant foods, but seeds and fruits, both aquatic and land-based, make up the year-round basic diet. One authority states that no other water-fowl species eats more seeds of water-lilies and water-shield. Cone scales of bald cypress are an important food on the winter range.

Also high in usage are seeds of wild rice, pondweeds, bur reeds, smartweeds, and arrow-arum. Waste corn, flowering dogwood and winterberry holly fruits, wild grapes, and (especially) acorns, swallowed whole, are also widely consumed; according to Bellrose, "acorns [mainly of the red oak group] are the favored foods of more wood ducks in more places than any other plant food." Thus the birds feed in woodlots and harvested fields as well as in wetlands, especially when wetland habitat foods are in short supply.

Wood duck competitors—especially for tree cavity nest sites—are numerous. Raccoons and gray and fox squirrels are probably the foremost contenders, as are opossums, flying squirrels, screech-owls, and barred owls. Woodies evict squirrels at times and at other times are evicted by them. Squirrels also create and maintain cavities that wood ducks later use. European starlings are not serious competitors in most areas, since they favor entrance holes of about 3 inches. In erected wood duck houses, however, starlings often harass and invade, puncturing wood duck eggs and building bulky nests over them. Wood duck boxes also attract hooded mergansers, American kestrels, screech-owls, northern flickers, tree swallows, great crested flycatchers, house wrens, eastern bluebirds, common grackles, squirrels, raccoons, opossums, deer mice, honeybees, and wasps.

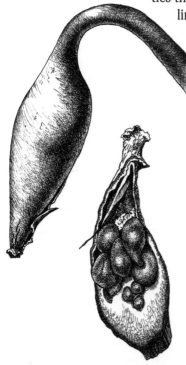

Arrow-arum, growing in pond margins, produces pods full of black berries relished by wood ducks.

Predators on incubating hens and eggs are also numerous. In natural cavity nests, losses may amount to half or two-thirds of all wood duck nests. Raccoons, gray and fox squirrels, northern flickers, black and gray rat snakes, and bull snakes are the foremost egg raiders. With their surface feeding habits, wood ducks consume less toxic lead shot than many other waterfowl species.

Focus. Wood ducks do not closely associate with most other waterfowl, probably because of their distinctive habitat requirements. They do, however, frequently join mallards at loafing sites. Though the wood duck's presettlement numbers are uncertain, many researchers believe that it was the most abundant duck of the eastern United States during the nineteenth century. We know that earlier it was at least fairly abundant because of its wide representation in prehistoric Indian cultures. Wood duck effigies on pottery bowls and ceremonial pipes of Mississippi Valley cultures are outnumbered only by owl effigies. Natives also trapped the ducks for food and used the colorful drake plumage for decoration. That plumage is still valued by fly-tying fishermen, who create both wet and dry artificial trout flies from the bronze-barred side feathers, known in the trade as "fly tier's gold."

Because of widespread market hunting and 8-month open seasons, wood duck populations plummeted from about 1890 to 1920; some observers believed them on the edge of extinction. The Federal Migratory Bird Treaty Act of 1918, credited in large part with saving this species, completely outlawed open seasons on the woodie, the only game duck thus singled out. The ban lasted until 1941, when 14 states in the Atlantic and Mississippi flyways were allowed to resume restricted hunting. Conservation programs, plus the bird's high breeding potential and adaptability to various foods and wetland habitats, enabled its dramatic recovery by the 1960s. Today in several states it has resumed first place in duck abundance; it ranks second only to the mallard in most states of the 2 eastern flyways. Some 800,000 wood ducks are taken annually by hunters.

Audubon and Thoreau knew the woodie as the "summer duck," a name that stuck until about 1900. "Goodwin shot them," journalized Thoreau in 1858, "and Mrs. ____, who never sailed on the river, ate them. Of course she knows not what she did. What if I should eat her canary?" Thoreau questioned why it was more important that "Mrs. ____ should taste the flavor of them dead than that I should enjoy the beauty of them alive."

Widespread clearing of bottomland nesting habitats in many

areas has been somewhat offset by the increasing use of wood duck nest boxes, which may contribute some 5 percent of the annual recruitment (increase in autumn populations). Correct specifications and placement of nest boxes are important; random erection of nest boxes in wetlands seldom succeeds and may even create death traps. As one biologist writes, "Unless nest houses are safer from predation than natural cavities, they contribute little or nothing to the benefit of the bird."

Few wood ducks survive longer than 7 years; the mean lifespan is less than 2.

WATERFOWL FAMILY (Anatidae) - TYPICAL DUCKS - Dabbling Ducks

American Wigeon *(Anas americana)*

Measuring about 20 inches long, the wigeon, also called baldpate, is distinctively marked. Drakes show a white forehead and crown with a shiny green band sweeping back from the eye. The light brown body plumage has a distinctly pinkish cast in profile; white rear flank feathers and black undertail coverts are also highly visible. Hens are brownish with contrasting grayish heads and necks. Both sexes have pale blue bills tipped with black. In flight, they show wedge-shaped tails; white, sharply demarcated bellies; and large white patches on the forewing (the hen's is less distinct). Drakes utter a piping, 3-note call in flight ("whee *whee* whew"); hens voice a loud "kaow" and infrequent low quacking notes.

Close relatives. The Eurasian wigeon *(A. penelope)* resides in Eurasia and Iceland, regularly visiting both Atlantic and Pacific coasts of North America. The Chiloe wigeon *(A. sibilatrix)* is a South American species. Closely related are all other *Anas* species (see Dabbling Ducks).

Behaviors. Seen in profile from a distance, the drake is probably best identified by the pinkish hue of its body plumage. The hens, which closely resemble the females of some other duck species, can be trickier to identify. Wigeons ride high in the water, grazing from the surface somewhat like coots, sometimes tipping up to feed in shallow water, pivoting quickly, rarely diving. In flight, wigeons usually move in bunched, irregular flocks rather than Vs, erratically turning, twisting, and changing positions. Ordinarily, like most dabblers, they fly quite high even when not on migration, most active in early morning and evening hours. Wigeons are noted for their frequent association with gadwalls and with diving ducks, swans, and coots when feeding. They often seize bits of food brought up by the divers, sometimes aggressively grabbing food from them as they surface.

American wigeons are seen in pairs like this only in spring; the drake stands behind the sitting hen.

American wigeons nest farther north than any other dabbler except northern pintails. They range across North America from arctic tundra south into the Dakotas and mountain states. Prairie Canada—mainly Alberta and Saskatchewan—hosts the largest abundance of breeding wigeons. In the northeastern United States, we see these ducks commonly during their migrations and sometimes during winter, rarely in summer.

Spring. Among waterfowl, wigeons are not among the early-spring migrants. Peak travel occurs in April, with most birds arriving on their breeding range in late April and early May. Some are paired by this time, but the pair bonds are tenuous, and many begin or renew courtship after arrival. Northward movement is usually in small flocks of 10 or fewer ducks. Groups of drakes compete for the attentions of single hens with much splashing, flight chasing, and ruckus. As in most dabbling duck species, the sex ratio favors drakes—about 3:2 in this species. Ritualized aggression includes gaping, turning the back of the head to hens, preening behind the wing, and raising tips of folded wings. Unpaired ducks probably home to their natal sites; paired drakes accompany their mates to the latter's home areas. Most hens first mate as yearlings, and nesting usually begins in late May or June. Size of territory and home range remain unknown in this species. One study recorded a nesting density of 5 pairs per square mile.

EGGS AND YOUNG: 8 or 9; eggs white. INCUBATION: by hen; about 24 days. FLEDGING: 40 to 50 days.

Summer. Hens lead ducklings soon after hatching to water, where they chase and consume insects. Wigeon broods seem more sedentary than other duckling broods, remaining close to the nest site. A brooding wigeon hen is among the loudest of all ducks, quacking incessantly when disturbed and sometimes performing distraction displays. Some broods apparently combine with others. Probably many hens renest in case of nest failure or predation.

Drakes abandon the hens in June soon after incubation begins, moving to the concealing cover of large marshes. Here they begin their annual molt, remaining largely flightless in henlike eclipse plumage through July (about 35 days). Hens molt in August after the broods are almost full grown. Many drakes and unmated wigeons, now in full breeding plumage, begin southward migratory movement as early as mid-August; next to blue-winged teals and northern pintails, wigeons are the earliest ducks to migrate south.

Fall. Wigeon migration peaks in September and October, often in large flocks, in contrast to their spring migration. Most wigeons breeding in the central Canadian provinces pass down the Central flyway to the Gulf coast, eastern Mexican coast, and the Yucatan peninsula. Large numbers also angle to the Pacific flyway, flying to Oregon and California's Central Valley; and to the Atlantic coast, traveling in slanted migration corridors across the eastern United States.

Winter. The main wintering areas for large wigeon populations in the eastern United States are Louisiana and South Carolina coastal marshes. Some courtship and pairing evidently begin soon after the ducks arrive in November and December, the rate of which increases through winter. Most juvenile wigeons acquire their first adult breeding plumage on the winter range. By early March, when northward movement begins, about 80 percent of the hens in some wintering populations are already paired.

Ecology. Habitat needs include open water that offers submersed or floating vegetation, located near densely vegetated upland sites for nesting. Prairie potholes and small islands in large lakes are often favored, as are large ponds over small ones. Wigeons also need marshland areas for summer molting and winter cover.

The ground nest is a slight depression matted with dry grass and weed stems, thickly lined with feather down. Most are built on dry ground within clumps of concealing vegetation, usually located some 20 to 50 yards from water. Common nesting habitats include stands of coralberry (buckbrush), greasewood, rushes, goldenrods, nettles, and tall grasses. Some nests, however, are barely concealed.

In contrast to most dabbling ducks, which are primarily seedeaters, wigeons favor the leaf and stem parts of aquatic plants. Pondweeds, coontail, wild celery, and filamentous algae constitute much of their diet on the breeding range. In coastal estuaries of the winter range, their main foods are eelgrass, ditch-grass (widgeongrass), bushy pondweed, and muskgrass (stoneworts). Lacking submersed vegetation, wigeons turn to seeds of such wetland plants as rice cut-grass, wild millets, smartweeds, and buttonbush. They also opportunistically feed on pasture grasses, clovers, and waste grain in sorghum and corn fields, and eat some aquatic invertebrates, mainly snails and insects. Wigeons sometimes form feeding associations with diving waterbirds, especially redhead and canvasback ducks and American coots, and rob them of food morsels. "It is amazing how tolerant coots and redheads are to this thievery," remarked one observer.

Except for such feeding interactions, competition in this species seems negligible.

The foremost nest predators are American crows, ground squirrels, and skunks.

Focus. The name *wigeon* (formerly spelled *widgeon*) comes from the French word *vigeon,* "whistling duck," which in turn may have developed from the Latin *vipio,* "small crane."

Though not as spectacular as wood ducks or as common as mallards, American wigeons merit much more study than they have received. Many details of their breeding biology remain unknown or, at best, are inferred. One study calculated an average 54 percent annual mortality for all age classes. The longevity record is about 9 years, but most wigeons probably live less than half that. Because of their diets, these ducks are less vulnerable to lead shot poisoning than most others; they ingest fewer seeds, thus fewer deadly pellets.

Since the 1930s, wigeon populations have been gradually expanding eastward from their historic central-prairie breeding range. Today small breeding populations continue to build in eastern Canada and New England. Creation of new habitats, such as sewage lagoons, coupled with loss of prairie wetland probably account, at least partially, for this shift in distribution.

WATERFOWL FAMILY (Anatidae) - TYPICAL DUCKS - Dabbling Ducks

American Black Duck *(Anas rubripes)*

Dark, sooty brown plumage with a paler brown head marks both sexes of the black duck, the only North American dabbler in which drake and hen are almost identical in appearance. In flight, the flashing white underwings and purplish *speculum* (upper wing patch) are distinctive. Visible sexual differences appear in bill color (adult drakes show bright yellow, hens olive green saddled or mottled with black) and leg and foot color (coral red in drakes, dull red in hens). Hens are loud, resonant quackers; drakes utter low-toned croaks. Blacks measure about 22 inches long.

Close relatives. The mallard *(A. platyrhynchos),* with which black ducks extensively hybridize, and the mottled duck *(A. fulvigula),* a Gulf coast species, are genetically very similar to the black; relatives also include most other dabbling ducks *(Anas* spp.).

Behaviors. Two distinct populations of this eastern North American duck exist: the northeastern maritime group and the interior population that resides in regions drained by the Great Lakes and James Bay.

Black ducks utilize only Atlantic and Mississippi flyways. Black ducks usually fly swiftly in small flocks (5 to 25 birds), either in Vs or angular lines and often quite high. Like most dabblers, they can spring instantly into flight, rising straight up for 8 or 10 feet. Before alighting in a pond, they often circle it several times before coasting down on stiff wings downturned like ailerons, tipping slightly from side to side. On water, they tip up to feed beneath the surface; they can also dive but rarely do so except to escape danger. They also walk fairly rapidly on land.

A loud, quacking decrescendo heard from a woodland pool is the hen of either this species or the mallard. This railing, angry-sounding yammer of about 7 quacks is the hail call, often given when she is apprehensive or separated from the drake. Usually a drake is somewhere nearby; the only time the hen is not paired or being courted is during incubation, brood rearing, and molting, a period of only a few weeks during the year (a statement that generally applies to most North American ducks).

Black ducks associate with mallards on much of their range where both species coincide. In many instances, judging from the high occurrence of hybrid offspring, the two species apparently do not distinguish between each other. The fall population sex ratio is about 55 percent drakes.

Black duck range lies mainly east of the Great Plains, from the northern treeline to the Gulf. Blacks are hardy and winter tolerant;

The black duck's purple speculum, unlike the mallard's bluer patch, has a top border of black feathers; the mallard's border is white.

though many migrate to the central tier of states, many others winter on the breeding range, mainly in coastal maritime and southern Great Lakes sites where open water abounds.

Spring. Black ducks are early migrators, gradually moving from southern or coastal areas to the breeding range, often arriving concurrently with icemelt from early February through mid-April. Almost all the hens are paired by this time; most probably return to their natal or previous nesting areas accompanied by their new mates. Both sexes usually begin pairing as yearlings, though up to 10 percent of hens do not breed during their first year. Nesting often

commences only a few days after spring arrival, usually in late March or April. Timing the dates of arrival and onset of nesting, "it seems very likely," wrote researcher Bruce Wright, that copulation occurs and many eggs are fertilized during migration. Three-bird flights and other defensive behaviors by drakes result from attempted intrusion of a single drake on a paired hen.

Centering a pair's home range, which may span up to 5 square miles, is the *activity center,* averaging an acre or so in size. Here the pair feeds and loafs before incubation, and here the drake settles in a nearby *waiting site* (a sort of territory) during the early stages of

The black duck drake (top) and hen mallard (bottom) look much alike; mallard hens, however, are lighter brown in color and have whitish tail feathers.

female incubation. The hen joins him here when she leaves the nest to feed and bathe. Waiting sites are usually areas of open water or shoreline backed by dense vegetation. Drakes remain at close hand for about 2 weeks after incubation begins, then abandon their mates. Occasionally hens remain paired through summer and fall, probably because of nest failure and consequent renesting (predation and flooding destroy many initial nests). By late May, drakes begin to assemble in large marshes and tidal estuaries. Broods are seen by mid-May in southern portions of the breeding range.

EGGS AND YOUNG: 8 to 10; eggs dull white or pale buff-green. INCUBATION: by hen; about 26 days, but variable. FLEDGING: about 10 weeks.

Summer. Sometimes black duck hens nest a mile or more from water, and the first excursion from the nest may be a long overland trek, with the hen trailed by her brood. Such a journey, often begun several hours after hatching and sometimes over rough terrain, quickly eliminates the weaklings that can't keep up, providing the first test of survival fitness. Hens remain with their broods until fledging, but before this, the brood often splits into smaller groups that range and feed more or less independently for long intervals. After desertion of the hens, the broods often mix with other broods, forming groups of 10 to 20 juveniles. They soon join the flocks of molting drakes in deep marsh cover. The hens begin their annual molt somewhat later than the drakes but tend to remain solitary until they gain their new flight feathers.

Unlike most dabblers, black ducks apparently develop no interim eclipse plumage before acquiring new flight feathers. Some researchers suggest that this dark-plumaged duck has no need of a different plumage for concealment during the flightless stage, a situation that generally applies to all ducks in which sexes are similar. In August, the fresh-plumaged adult ducks wander widely, especially northward and westward, sometimes for hundreds of miles. This is the only time of year when blacks abundantly appear in subarctic regions and the Canadian prairieland into Alberta. Drakes soon begin to congregate in traditional staging areas—large inland marshes and tidal flats of Hudson Bay and the Atlantic coast, among others—and here, in late summer, juveniles and hens flock in to join them.

Fall. Some southward migrational movements begin along the east coast in September, but black ducks often linger late on their staging areas and summer range, vacating only when marshes and pools freeze over in November and December. Most blacks migrate only as far as marsh freeze-up occurs, homing for the winter at traditional sites along the Ohio, Tennessee, and Mississippi river valleys and the Atlantic coast. All ducks tend to travel via specific migration corridors and return to the same winter sites, but "this trait appears most pronounced in the black duck," wrote waterfowl specialist Frank C. Bellrose. Relatively small populations travel as far as the Gulf states. Courtship displays reach peak intensity in October, and pairing continues through winter. Even the juveniles pair, at least temporarily, at this time. Displays, almost identical to those of mallards, include head and tail shakes, head bobbing, water flicking, neck arching, and wing spreading, exposing the colorful speculum. Copulations occur in the fall, diminish during winter, intensify in the spring.

Winter. During fall and winter flocking, black ducks often feed at night, spending the daylight hours in large, offshore *rafts,* compact flocks that seemingly remain motionless, like a raft. ("Perhaps their feet work automatically," wrote ornithologist Arthur C. Bent, "for they never seem to drift much.") In the Northeast, rafts inhabit coastal waters and marshes through winter. Inland, the ducks often gather and loaf on the ice of frozen lakes and ponds. According to Bellrose, "their attachment to a particular winter ground is so strong that when tidal feeding grounds have become frozen in New England, some black ducks have starved rather than migrate farther southward." Courtship behaviors and pairing continue in the social context of the large winter flocks. Black ducks in the southern winter range begin moving northward in February.

Ecology. Often called the "forest duck" because of its breeding habitat preferences, the black duck favors shrub and forest wetlands for nesting. Its subhabitats, however, are diverse. This duck's basic needs include open, shallow water for feeding; logs, hummocks, or beaches for loafing bars; relatively dry, often forested areas for nesting; and dense marsh or streamwide cover for brood raising. Beaver ponds often provide optimal habitats for black ducks. But cover usage varies widely, as blacks show wide tolerance for territorial sites ranging from dense vegetation to almost open or flooded conditions.

This wide adaptability extends to nesting sites. Black ducks usually nest on the ground in fairly dry upland thickets or woods, or on a slightly raised hummock in tall grass or marsh vegetation, especially near woodland edges. Forested islands, sedge meadows, and dikes are also favored sites. Occasionally I have found black duck nests in sphagnum bogs, usually on hummocks sheltered by leatherleaf shrubs. Especially in flooded woodlands, blacks also may nest in tree crotches and cavities, stumps and dead snags, sometimes in vacated hawk or crow nests. A ground-nesting hen scrapes a shallow basin with feet and bill, adding dry grasses, plant stems, pine needles, or woodland debris. As incubation proceeds, she adds down from her breast. Cavity-nesting blacks usually occupy larger, shallower, more bucketlike (roofless) holes than wood ducks and American goldeneyes, also cavity nesters.

Because of its variety of habitats, including salt, brackish, and freshwater marshes, the black duck's food habits are almost omnivorous. Animal food forms a larger proportion of the diet than in most dabblers. During the breeding season, the black duck consumes about 80 percent vegetable foods and 20 percent animal foods. During winter, the diet becomes about 85 percent animal—snails and other mollusks, amphipods, even small fishes. Ducklings feed exclusively on water invertebrates for their first 12 days, especially aquatic sowbugs, snails, mayfly and dragonfly nymphs, and beetle, fly, and caddisfly larvae, then shift to seeds and other plant food. Predominant plant foods in coastal marshes include eelgrass, widgeon-grass, and seeds of sedges, bulrushes, wild rice, bur reeds, and pickerelweed. Interior swamps and marshes provide seed foods from pondweeds, water lilies, smartweeds, cordgrasses, wild millet, buttonbush, bald cypress, and black tupelo (gum). In some areas, acorns and waste corn in fields are important fall and winter foods.

The black's chief competitor is the mallard, whose increase and range expansion over the past several decades have, in some areas, threatened black duck breeding populations (see Mallard). Yet competition may not be the right word for birds that treat each other as *conspecifics*—the same species. Once geographically separated, blacks and mallards are ecological equivalents in many respects, and genetically they are almost identical. Hybrids are common, occurring at a rate of about 4 percent where the species coexist, and show various intermediate plumages. Many of these hybrids can and do reproduce. Mallards seem to be either more adaptive or more aggressive than black ducks in areas where they overlap, though the jury is still out on this. In any case, the long-term effects of such mixtures appear more influential on black duck than on mallard populations, as judged by the black's concurrent decline over the past decades (see Focus).

Foremost nest predators include gulls, American crows, and (especially in tree nests) raccoons. Snapping turtles and bullfrogs take many ducklings. Great horned owls are probably the major predators of adult blacks. Ducklings often succumb to disease caused by the protozoan blood parasite *Leucocytozoon simondi,* transmitted from bird to bird by bites of the parasite's alternate host, the blackfly *(Simulium rugglesi).* Bottom-foraging food habits make black ducks among the species most vulnerable to lead shot poisoning, known as *plumbism,* especially along heavily hunted Atlantic flyway marshes and estuaries. Muskrat traps also take a high toll.

Focus. This duck's name is a misnomer, as is true of so many birds, for no part of its plumage is truly black; yet it is much darker brown than the hen mallard, with which it is sometimes confused. "Dusky duck" and "black mallard" are two of its common names.

Black ducks, historically not only the most abundant northeastern dabbler but the most numerous breeding duck east of the Mississippi, have undergone a 60 percent decline in numbers since about 1950 (about 3 percent per year). Various causes are postulated, but loss of breeding habitat is apparently not one of them; acid precipitation, eliminating many invertebrate food species, may be. Black duck decline parallels the increase and range expansion (since about 1900) of mallards, perhaps brought about by deforestation and other land-use changes that have eliminated the natural barriers once separating these species. Wherever mallards are, black ducks decrease, and many researchers believe that hybridization between them has been mostly to the competitive and genetic detriment of the black duck.

The black duck–mallard relationship remains a puzzler, and much more research is needed to clarify it. An epochal 1986 study found that as much genetic difference often exists within the species as between them; that both should actually be classified as a single species, the black duck being no more than a melanistic (dark) color morph of the mallard; that the black duck is a relatively recent evolutionary derivative, owing to former geographical isolation, of a mallard ancestor; and that continual interbreeding is slowly restoring the ancestral mallard dominance while fostering continued decline of the black duck. Other studies find that black duck hens, when courted by both black and mallard drakes, usually choose the mallard for mates; that drake mallards are competitively superior to black duck drakes in claiming optimal breeding sites as well as in effective courtship behaviors; and that these behavioral relationships, rather than ancestral gene dominance, are the keys to black duck decrease. And still other studies seem to show that the matter of behavioral dominance is more variable and complex. As research sorts out these matters, some revision in classification will probably result. The entire problem serves to remind us that categorizing biological species is a human endeavor designed for our own convenience of understanding, not necessarily reflecting nature's reality.

One study estimated that 65 percent of young black ducks die from various causes during their first year and that the annual mortality rate is about 40 percent for immatures and 20 percent for adults. Longevity records of almost 20 years have been recorded, but probably few black ducks survive anywhere near that age.

Some of the late-fall migrants in the Atlantic flyway from northern breeding areas are large old drakes with brighter bill and foot colors than more southern populations. So different do they appear that until 1943 they were considered a subspecies called red-legged black ducks; age differences probably account for the variation.

The black duck is the foremost game duck of the Atlantic flyway, and hunters shoot many thousands of migrants annually, For table fare, the maritime population is considered less tasty than the interior ducks, which have a more vegetarian diet.

WATERFOWL FAMILY (Anatidae) - TYPICAL DUCKS - Dabbling Ducks

Mallard *(Anas platyrhyncos)*

This most common North American duck is also among the easiest to identify. Drakes show a glossy green head separated from the chestnut brown breast by a white neck ring; grayish back and sides; black, upcurled feathers centering the white tail tip; and yellow bills. Hens are straw brown streaked with darker brown, have orange bills splotched with black, and have whitish tails (a useful identity mark in separating this species from black duck hens). Both sexes show a violet-blue speculum (wing patch) bordered by white bars, visible in flight, and orange feet. The hen's loud, decrescendo quacking is virtually identical to that of American black duck hens. Drakes utter low "reeb-reeb" and "kwek" notes. Average length is 2 feet or slightly less.

Close relatives. American black ducks *(A. rubripes)* are so closely related to mallards that hybrids commonly occur. The mottled duck *(A. fulvigula)* is genetically similar. Less commonly, mallards also hybridize with almost all the other 8 *Anas* species of North America.

Behaviors. Mallards are the most abundant ducks not only in North America but also globally in the Northern Hemisphere. In the eastern United States, along with mute swans, they are often the typical park waterfowl, associating comfortably with humans and easily becoming semidomesticated, sometimes to the point of being pigeonlike nuisances. Wild mallards, however, are a different story, seldom closely approachable by people. Though many mallards migrate, they may be seen year-round wherever open water exists

Mallards, among the most abundant ducks in North America, reside in many wetland habitats. The green-headed drake (foreground) shows distinctive curled tail feathers.

except in their farthest-north breeding range. They often fly in large flocks of 40 to 60, sometimes many more, with relatively slow wing-beats in Vs or U-shaped formations.

Many of their social behaviors, especially courtship, closely resemble those of American black ducks, with which they often associate, but the two species also exhibit subtle differences. Some-times, where they coexist (that is, almost everywhere in eastern North America except Atlantic coastal marshes), mallards seem to dominate interactions, but whether this is a simple reflection of larger mallard numbers or of innately greater mallard aggressive-ness remains largely unknown (see Ecology and American Black Duck). In other places, however, the two species seem behaviorally *conspecific* (as one species), and conflict is seldom observed. Soli-tary mallards are seldom seen; the birds are either paired, leading broods of young, or in flocks. Mallard range includes all of North America from the Arctic into central Mexico and almost the entire Northern Hemisphere worldwide. They have also been introduced into Hawaii, Australia, and New Zealand.

Spring. The mallard's North American breeding range encom-passes the northern third of the United States to the arctic treeline, reaching the greatest density in the Canadian prairie provinces—the so-called "waterfowl factory" for the Central flyway. Most mallards that have wintered in the southern United States migrate north in February and March, are already paired, and often begin to nest by late March. Travel to the northern range continues through April, most hens homing to their natal or previous nesting sites *(philopatry)*, their new mates accompanying them. Not all hens return to their previous breeding sites, however; food availability, habitat conditions, previous nesting success, and mate choice influence the rate of philopatry. Details of nesting chronology closely resemble those of black ducks (see American Black Duck).

April is the primary mallard nesting month throughout much of its range. The hen selects a nest site during evening reconnaissance flights, cruising low over marsh or field, followed closely by the drake. Paired drakes likewise establish one or more shoreline territories or waiting areas up to a quarter acre in size; these defended areas are separate from, but usually within 100 yards of, the nest, which is not defended. The hen joins the drake in these areas during intervals off the nest. Size of the home range varies greatly, depending upon habitat and mallard density. As in other dabbling ducks, the drakes abandon nesting hens several days after incubation begins—or is it the other way round? One study suggests that hens may initiate drake desertion by abandoning the drake waiting areas. Despite the oft-repeated assertion that drakes invariably desert the hens during incubation, my own observations convince me that split-up of the mallard pair often occurs much later or less regularly than the experts tell us; I have witnessed too many instances of wild pairs swimming with broods to account it a rare occurrence. Yet many, probably most, drakes do fly to large marshes during hen incubation. There they gather in large flocks and, from May into summer, enter henlike eclipse plumage and become flightless for 3 to 4 weeks or longer.

Many broods hatch in May. The nest is often placed far from suitable brood-raising habitat, and hen and brood must swim or walk for a mile or more over a period of days, even after reaching the nearest water. Relatively high occurrences of extrapair copulations and multiple paternity are seen in mallards; in one study, at least 48 percent of broods revealed, by genetic testing, the involvement of more than 1 drake. When a paired drake mates with a hen other than his mate, it is often a quick, aggressive action *(forced copulation)* not preceded by courtship displays. Some biologists suggest that this behavior is a secondary reproductive strategy for both drakes and hens, helping assure the likelihood of fertilized eggs. This behavior is now seen to be fairly common among many so-called "monogamous" birds.

EGGS AND YOUNG: 8 to 10; eggs greenish buff or whitish. INCUBATION: by hen; average of 28 days. FLEDGING: 50 to 60 days.

Summer. The hen broods her ducklings for about 12 hours before leading them to the nearest water. Nest failure or predation usually results in a renesting attempt by hens; this could explain why some drakes remain paired beyond the initial incubation period. Also, unpaired drakes remain in breeding condition longer into the summer than paired drakes. As soon as the juveniles fledge (July or later), hens gather on marshes or remain in the rearing area during their own molt and flightless period. Summer is a time of movement off the breeding area as the birds assemble in traditional gathering places, usually large marshes. Most drakes have attained their new flight feathers and breeding plumage by mid-August. Toward late summer, flocks may build to thousands in size as hens and juveniles join the drakes. Mallard families have by this time ceased to exist as individual members disperse to various flocks and assembly locales. Pairing often begins in late summer as courtship behaviors recommence.

Fall. Mallards are generally late migrators, moving southward no sooner than weather forces them and no farther than they must to obtain food. Consequently, their migration is often irregular and prolonged, sometimes not peaking until November or December. The largest numbers of mallards travel from the Canadian prairies down the Mississippi flyway, sometimes called the mallard flyway for the millions of ducks that travel through and winter in this river corridor. Courtship flights and displays intensify through fall and winter; most adult mallards are paired by late October. Average fall populations consist almost equally of adult mallards and young of the year.

Winter. Mallards winter most abundantly between latitudes 34 and 36 degrees N in eastern Arkansas and western Mississippi. In smaller numbers, wintering populations extend to the Gulf and central Mexico, and northward to the Great Lakes and New England. Sudden spells of snow and cold will often send them south from the northernmost regions in dead of winter; then, as a warm spell sets in, they may wing back to the recently vacated area. Many, if not most, wintering mallards in New England join park mallard flocks, probably decoyed by the resident ducks. Hen mallards begin their prebasic molt in late fall or winter, replacing all body plumage in a period of 6 weeks or so. By early January, at least 80 percent of mallards are paired, though typically a few hens remain unpaired until their return to the breeding range. The paired ducks tend to segregate from the unpaired by moving to smaller, more secluded wetland spaces. Unpaired drakes remain gregarious in flocks in the larger marshes. By February, many mallards are beginning to leave their wintering areas. They "race spring itself," wrote one observer, "often forging ahead to be forced into temporary retreat by late winter blizzards."

Ecology. Optimal mallard habitat consists of a permanent marsh surrounded by small, shallow ponds, but mallards also inhabit other wetland complexes—swamps, lakes, and streams. Marsh habitat is especially important for brood rearing and for cover during molting. In the Canadian prairie provinces, where mallard breeding density is greatest, spring ponds often dry up as the season advances to summer. Thus hens may find themselves far from water when broods hatch, necessitating long overland treks to water.

Most mallards nest on the ground within 100 yards of water, often in marsh growth. Not uncommonly, however, they also nest far from water in upland meadows and hayfields or on dikes, muskrat lodges, and small islands. One study found that nesting success in marsh sites was about 40 percent higher than in drier upland sites. Whatever cover type mallards choose, the nest is usually placed in dense plant growth about 2 feet high. The hen scrapes a nest bowl, rimming it with fragments of vegetation and adding down as incubation proceeds. Often the final structure is a bulky mass. Exceptions to the typical nest placement often occur, but as waterfowl biologist Joe Johnson states, "the ancestry of females choosing strange nesting sites

Mallard nests, frequently discovered in dense cover when the hen flushes off, are often thickly lined with feather down.

[such as forested areas, tree hollows, flower boxes, landscape plantings] is worth questioning, as many semidomestic [mallards] have been released."

Primarily seedeaters, mallards consume a large variety of wetland food items. Seeds of wild rice, pondweeds, and smartweeds are favored in the Northeast, as are wild celery, barnyard grass, corn, and acorns. Fields of wheat and barley stubble are frequently invaded by feeding flocks; mallards, more than any other duck, have adapted to agricultural land use and in some areas consume large amounts of spring-planted wheat and barley. Given a choice, the birds seem to prefer their native wetland foods, but this option appears increasingly limited in many areas. Mallards also eat aquatic insect larvae and mussels, which form about 10 percent of the spring and summer diet.

Mallard–black duck interactions have been discussed in the previous account. Mallards have been known to hybridize with some 40 other duck species, producing mostly sterile offspring. Many ducks, including mallards, occasionally lay eggs in nests of other birds of their own or other duck species. Mallards are often nest-parasitized by redhead ducks in areas where the two species overlap.

Mallard nest predators include American crows, skunks, foxes, coyotes, and ground squirrels. Hayfield mowing, trampling by cattle, and flooding also destroy many nests. Lead shot ingestion remains a toxic hazard for mallards. A blood parasite common to both mallards and black ducks, causing much duckling mortality, is the protozoan *Leucocytozoon simondi,* transmitted by blackflies. In some northeastern duck populations, 100 percent of the ducks may be infected.

Focus. Many mallard populations stem from propagation by game farms and pen-raised park flocks. Releases of these semidomesticated fowl have no doubt helped swell mallard range expansion throughout the Northeast. Until the twentieth century, mallards were mainly prairie ducks, rarely seen from the Great Lakes eastward. Before 1900, only occasional wanderers had been spotted in New England. Thoreau makes no mention of the bird in his journals; he apparently never saw one. Land clearing evidently encouraged the eastward spread of the species, bringing it into frequent contact with its conspecific, the American black duck, which occupied eastern woodland habitats.

Like black ducks, most breeds of farmyard ducks, including the white Pekin (but not the Muscovy), are basically mallards in genetic makeup. Individual mallards have survived for 3 decades and longer in the wild, but average longevity is much less owing to high annual mortality rates. Some 50 percent or more of the mallard population dies each year; hunting pressure plus natural losses account for this figure. Because it is the most numerous game duck, the mallard is also the most widely hunted. In most years, however, more than one offspring per adult survives, thus maintaining or increasing population levels. In years

Seeds of wild rice are highly favored by mallards, among many other bird species; unfortunately, this native plant has become scarce in much of its range.

when production falls below this ratio, as it did during the 1980s, the population declines.

The name *mallard* (from the French *maslard,* "wild duck") is actually a sexist label, stemming from the Latin root *masculus,* "male." In Old World lexicons, evidently, the entire species thus became identified with the gender.

WATERFOWL FAMILY (Anatidae) - TYPICAL DUCKS - Dabbling Ducks

Blue-winged Teal *(Anas discors)*

Recognize this marsh duck by its small size (about 15 inches long) and gray-blue patch on the forewing, best seen when the bird flies. A green *speculum* (wing patch), brighter in the drake, shows behind the forewing patch in flight. Drakes in breeding plumage are easily identified by a white facial crescent in front of the eye and by a conspicuous white flank patch at the rear. The brownish chest and sides look speckled brown from a distance. Hens, mottled brown, are difficult to distinguish from the hens of other teal species. Drakes voice high-pitched, lisping, peeping notes, usually in flight; hens quack like mallards but fainter and more rapidly.

Close relatives. Some 16 small dabbling ducks labeled teals exist worldwide. In eastern North America, the green-winged teal *(A. crecca)* is the only other common resident teal. Northern shovelers *(A. clypeata),* along with cinnamon teals *(A. cyanoptera),* a western species, and garganeys *(A. querquedula),* a Eurasian teal, are collectively known as blue-winged ducks because of their blue forewing patches. The Baikal teal *(A. formosa),* an Asian breeder, occasionally shows up in Alaska. All other *Anas* species also bear close kinship.

Behaviors. Blue-wings have a distinctive flight style. Usually flying in small, compact flocks of 8 to 12 birds, they twist and turn erratically, rolling from side to side, often low over water or marshland (a style copied, as one observer noted, by stealth bombers and F-16 fighter planes). Their small size and rapidly shifting movements often make them seem to be flying much faster than they actually do (about 30 to 50 miles per hour). When feeding, blue-wings usually graze the water surface or immerse only head and neck, tipping up less frequently than other dabblers. They often feed in company with other dabblers, including mallards and green-winged teals, and American coots. Usually the last migrant ducks to arrive in spring and the first to depart in the fall, blue-wings are, next to mallards, the most abundant breeding ducks in the great prairie "duck bowl" of the Dakotas and Canada. Two separate blue-wing races inhabit North America. East of the Appalachians, the Atlantic seaboard race *(A. d. orphna)* breeds from North Carolina to New Brunswick; the more numerous race *(A. d. discors)* breeds west of the Appalachians to the Rockies, and north-south from the Arctic to Texas.

Spring. April is the usual month of blue-wing arrival on the breeding range. On migration, blue-wings fly long distances between stops for feeding and rest, mainly at night. Migration sometimes "dams up" behind late-lingering ice in the North, proceeding again as the ponds and marshes open. Blue-wings exhibit much less homing behavior *(philopatry)* to previous nesting areas than most waterfowl species, thus are more likely to pioneer new habitats. This flexibility probably relates to the irregular occurrence and impermanence of prairie pond habitats, many of which either never develop during drought conditions or dry up in late spring. Most blue-wings are paired by the time they arrive—even most yearling blue-wings nest—but much courtship occurs at rest and feeding stops during spring migration. Bowing, head-bobbing, and chasing of hens by two or more drakes characterize these displays. Once the drake is paired, his mobile territory consists of the area around the hen, which he vigorously defends, rather than a specific land site. Nest-searching pairs fly low over the terrain, and hens usually begin egg laying in late April or May. In some marshes, teal nesting may be loosely colonial, with nests as close together as 30 feet. Size of the home range varies from 17 to 100 or more acres, apparently depending more upon habitat (access to water areas) than population density. Within this area, pairs establish loafing sites, to which the drakes retire when incubation begins.

EGGS AND YOUNG: usually 9 or 10; eggs dull white or tannish.
INCUBATION: by hen; about 24 days. FLEDGING: about 6 weeks.

Summer. Drakes remain companionable with their mates until the second or third week of incubation, then begin joining other deserting drakes. Many drake flocks concentrate in large, dense marshes as they begin their eclipse molt, a period of almost a month or slightly more (July–August) during which they remain flightless. The drab, henlike body plumage they acquire remains prevalent until late fall or even into winter.

This blue-winged teal drake preens at a loafing site— often a log—during the daytime.

Hens lead broods to water within 12 hours after hatching, often traveling distances of 100 yards, sometimes much more. Until their fifth week, ducklings usually swim in a tightly clustered block formation, sometimes appearing from a distance like a single swimming animal. Hens and broods frequently use old muskrat lodges as roosting or resting sites. They tend to remain more sedentary in rearing areas, wandering less than hens and broods of other duck species. Hens often renest if their first nests are destroyed, though incubating hens renest less frequently than those with earlier-stage nesting failures. Compensating for a relatively low nesting success rate (only 35 to 42 percent in many areas, owing mainly to predation), blue-wings display higher than usual rates of juvenile survival (7.5 birds per hatched brood), resulting in a net production of 1.3 juveniles per adult. Such figures account for the blue-wing's status as one of North America's most abundant ducks despite its high annual mortality.

Hens, fanning out widely, begin their eclipse molt soon after the broods disperse. On the Great Plains, many juveniles flock northward to Canada's prairie provinces. Adult drakes, wearing new flight feathers but still in drab body plumage, begin migrating by late summer, many moving directly eastward to the seacoast, then heading southward over the Atlantic. Other migration corridors angle obliquely to Florida and the Gulf coast. A frequent shorebird associate of blue-wings at migration stops is the greater yellowlegs.

Fall. After mid-September, most blue-wing flocks on the move consist of adult hens and young of the year. Flocks are usually small and, again, span huge nonstop distances over the Atlantic and Gulf of Mexico. Most blue-wings that migrate through the Northeast end up in eastern Venezuela and Guyana, but some travel below the equator to Brazil, Peru, and Argentina. Many also winter in Mexico and Central America. No other North American duck winters so far south in greater numbers. Since the hurricane of 1957 opened up Louisiana coastal marshes, many thousands of blue-wings continue to winter there and in Florida.

Winter. The drake's molt into breeding plumage occurs slowly, with much individual variation, often extending into January and February. As the white facial crescent gradually appears, the pace of courtship behaviors and pairing increases, reaching a peak as both sexes gain full nuptial plumage.

Blue-wings from Central and South America are already moving northward in February, joining coastal wintering flocks on the Gulf. By mid-March, most blue-wings have reached the continent and are beginning to move up their migration corridors.

Ecology. Open fields adjacent to marshes plus seasonal ponds and other semipermanent wetlands, including farm ponds, are favored breeding and brood-rearing habitats for blue-wings. A 50:50 ratio of open water to emergent vegetation is optimal. For nesting, the birds prefer grassy sites on dry ground. Extensive marshes provide molting cover in summer, and marsh and lagoon habitats are widely used on the winter range.

Nests, usually well concealed in tall grasses, hayfields, and sedge meadows, are usually placed within 100 feet or so of water. The hen scrapes a bare depression in the ground, then adds plant materials, often grasses, from the immediate vicinity. She also adds increasing amounts of down feathers throughout incubation. Surrounding vegetation is often arched over the nest, aiding concealment. Overgrown muskrat lodges or other slightly elevated sites are common nest locations.

Blue-wings consume more animal matter than most dabbling ducks—about one-quarter of the diet, mainly snails and insect larvae. Their main diet consists of aquatic plants, including filamentous algae, duckweeds, naiads, pondweeds, and widgeon-grass. They also favor seeds of sedges, bulrushes, nut-sedges, and smartweeds, among others. Ducklings feed exclusively on aquatic insects for their first week or so. On the South American winter range, blue-wings often invade cultivated rice fields; they also consume many water-lily seeds plus snails and water boatman insects (Corixidae).

Two other teals interact, perhaps competitively at times, with blue-wings. Cinnamon teals are known to hybridize with blue-wings where their ranges overlap and often associate with them on the winter range; green-winged teals often occupy the same feeding habitats as blue-wings in marshes and mudflats. Green-wings, however, are more exclusively vegetarian and feed to a greater extent on seeds than blue-wings, thus reducing food competition. Ring-necked pheasants occasionally lay eggs in teal nests; one researcher observed instances when the pheasant eggs hatched at the same time as the teal eggs: "One can imagine the situation that must have arisen when the duck took her brood to the marsh."

About 60 percent of nest losses are caused by predators including American crows, magpies, skunks, foxes, coyotes, minks, raccoons, and ground squirrels. Peregrine falcons sometimes capture flying adult teals. Mowing, fire, and flood destroy many nests, and ingestion of lead shot in marshland remains a toxic hazard.

Focus. The word *teal* is obscure in origin, its meaning uncertain. Biologically, as a bird name, it defines nothing more specific than "a small duck." Color technicians of paints and fabrics have adopted commercial descriptions of teal blue or teal green for certain hues, but how closely these may resemble actual teal plumages is questionable, since most plumage shades cannot be reproduced with any precision. Blue color in birds results from feather structure, not pigment, an interaction of light with microscopic facets and planes of the feather itself, which appears black or brown in unreflected light.

Apparently abundant in presettlement times, blue-wing populations underwent massive declines in the early 1900s, probably from combined habitat loss and unregulated hunting pressure. By 1940, they had again become common in much of the Northeast. Subsequent trends have shown both increase and decrease; this must be weighed against the fact that blue-wing populations normally fluctuate considerably, probably due in large part to annual water level changes in wetland habitats. Peaks and dips in local abundance seem to have occurred fairly regularly in each decade since 1950.

This bird, known as "the panfish of waterfowl hunting," has the highest annual mortality rate (65 percent) of any dabbling duck, probably due foremost to the hazards of its long overwater flights during migrations. Effects of wetland drainage have been somewhat offset by this bird's adaptability to field habitats for nesting. The blue-wing's fate, writes ornithologist James Granlund, "rests in our willingness and ability to preserve wetlands."

WATERFOWL FAMILY (Anatidae) - TYPICAL DUCKS - Dabbling Ducks

Northern Shoveler *(Anas clypeata)*

Its disproportionately large, spoon-shaped bill, longer than the head, immediately identifies this dabbling duck. Size, about 20 inches long, falls midway between blue-winged teals and mallards. Both sexes show large blue patches on the forewing, most visible in flight, and orange feet. The colorful drake has a dark green head that often appears black in poor light, bright yellow eyes, white chest, chestnut belly and sides, and a white flank patch at the rear. Except for the bill, the mottled brown hen much resembles the hen mallard, including the whitish tail. Drakes utter raspy, guttural "took took took" notes, especially during courtship; hens quack like mallards.

Close relatives. Three other shoveler species, all with large, spatulate bills, reside in South America, Africa, Australia, and New Zealand. Closest kin include all *Anas* species, especially the other blue-winged ducks: blue-winged and cinnamon teals and garganeys, among others.

Behaviors. Notwithstanding the shoveler's distinctive profile, novice birders and hunters often mistake it for a mallard. Plumage colors are somewhat similar (especially in hens), but in drakes, except for the green head, the shoveler *pattern* is much different. The drakes also show much more white than

Ducks often preen themselves, as this drake shoveler is doing, on the water; its large, spatulate bill is the shoveler's chief identity mark.

mallard drakes. Shovelers carry their heavy bills slanted downward at a 30- to 45-degree angle, appearing to ride down at the bow. Despite their name, they do not shovel with their prodigious mandibles but strain out zooplankton. Shovelers, more than any other ducks, are surface feeders, skimming the water with their heads half submerged, rarely tipping up to feed like other dabblers. The comblike *lamellae* (teeth) on the bill edges, which all surface-feeding ducks possess, reach their highest development in shovelers. Feeding shovelers often group in clusters *(pods)* of several to many birds, rotating in pinwheel-like formations called *cells.* These milling, circling shovelers are roiling the surface and often stirring the bottom mud with their feet. Such feeding usually peaks in early morning and evening.

In flight, shovelers sometimes exhibit erratic, teal-like twists and turns. Their wings seem placed far back, owing to the added length of the bill, and they appear chunky, somewhat humpbacked. Flocks are usually small; 5 to 10 birds is typical. Flocks have a tendency to drop suddenly to the water rather than coast down. On taking off, their wings make a characteristic rattling sound.

Labeled one of the most cosmopolitan of ducks, northern shovelers breed across most of the Northern Hemisphere. In North America, they center in Canada's prairie provinces and the Great Plains. Their breeding range also extends across Eurasia south to the Mediterranean, Mongolia, and Japan.

Spring. Shovelers, like their blue-winged teal kin, are late arrivals in spring, flying both day and night in small flocks of 10 to 25 birds. They often travel leisurely over an extended period from late March through late May. Usually there is a surplus of drakes (about 60 percent of the spring population), and unpaired drakes often home to their natal areas. Hens, most having paired on the winter range, commonly home to their natal or previous breeding areas, accompanied by their mates. Most yearling birds breed. Upon arrival, flocks break up as pairs disperse. Each pair settles on a home range of 20 to 100 or more acres, its boundaries often overlapping the home ranges of other pairs. Each home range contains a core waiting area, where the pair loafs and feeds; peripheral ponds often shared with other pairs; and a nest site selected by the pair over a period of a week or so. Considered the most territorial of all North American dabblers, drake shovelers aggressively defend their core areas and a space of 3 to 6 feet around mobile hens. Drakes abandon their mates during incubation, some very early, others late in the period.

EGGS AND YOUNG: typically 9 to 11; eggs pale olive or greenish gray. INCUBATION: about 23 days. FLEDGING: 38 to 66 days, apparently depending on longitude and consequent day length for feeding.

Summer. Most hatching occurs in June. Hens lead their broods to ponds formerly used as waiting areas but usually move them on to other ponds within days. Though nesting success is relatively high (about 60 percent), broods typically suffer a 22 percent decrease in size by fledging time due to accident and predation. Hens often renest if the first nest fails. Drake shovelers, in the meantime, begin moving to large lakes, at first flocking in groups of 10 to 40 birds. Then, hidden and secretive in marsh or shoreline vegetation, they remain flightless for about 35 days during their annual molt into eclipse plumage. They apparently feed little during this period. Following fledging of the juveniles, the hens likewise undergo their annual molt, tending to remain in the local area.

Fall. Late September to mid-October is the peak time of shoveler southward migration. By this time, the ratio of immature to adult birds is, in most years, about 2:1. Drakes begin migrating before hens and young. Less than 3 percent of the total population travels east of the Mississippi River. The largest numbers move through the eastern Great Plains to coastal Louisiana and down through California to Mexico; relatively small numbers diverge eastward from Manitoba and Tennessee to the Atlantic coast.

Winter. Most North American shovelers winter in California's San Joaquin and Sacramento valleys and in Louisiana coastal marshes. Large numbers also reside in western Mexico and, in lesser abundance, south to Panama and eastward to South Carolina, Cuba, and the Dominican Republic. Small numbers occasionally winter as far north as Long Island and the southern Great Lakes.

As the drakes slowly develop their colorful nuptial plumage, usually beginning in November, courtship and pair bonding proceed on the winter range. Compared with that of some other duck species, shoveler courtship "does not amount to very much as a spectacular performance," wrote ornithologist Arthur C. Bent. Drakes nod, bow, often group around a single hen or chase her in flight. Most shovelers probably are paired by the time they begin moving northward in spring.

Ecology. Shovelers favor shallow, open ponds and marshes, but they also surface-feed in deep-water lakes and slow, muddy creeks. They increasingly utilize sewage lagoons. For nesting, the birds require areas of dense grass, sometimes choosing hayfields and meadows. Coastal marshes and lagoons are the usual winter habitats.

Shovelers usually locate their nests in grass less than a foot tall within 200 feet of water, often near their pond-site waiting and loafing areas. The nest itself consists of grasses from the immediate site lining a scrape in the ground, with added down feathers.

The large, lamellate bill is well adapted for filter feeding, straining out zooplankton from surface waters. This animal life, plus snails, fingernail clams, cladocerans (water fleas), amphipods, aquatic beetles, and insect larvae probably constitutes more than half of the total diet, especially in summer. In mudflats and shallow waters, shovelers often bill-sweep the bottom muds, obtaining much animal food this way. Seeds of bulrushes, nut-sedges, pondweeds, smartweeds, swamp loosestrife, and buttonbush form most of the vegetative diet, along with duckweeds and pondweed leaves and stems. Shovelers are not repelled by thick algal bloom on overfertilized ponds or lakes—"the thicker the soup, the more they seem to relish the straining," an observer noted. Another "spin feeder," the Wilson's phalarope, a shorebird, often forages in the wake of swimming shovelers.

Competition for food and nest sites appears negligible. Shovelers' feeding patterns probably allow them to exploit food resources largely bypassed by other surface-feeding waterfowl. Shovelers may be seen feeding with gadwalls, American wigeons, blue-winged teals, and other ducks. Skunks are the foremost shoveler nest predators. American crows, magpies, gulls, ground squirrels, and red foxes also raid shoveler nests.

Focus. Shovelers reportedly are among the easiest ducks to lure with decoys because of their curiosity and gregariousness. Hunters often call them "spoonbills," "spoonies," or "grinning mallards" and nickname their cell feeding techniques "sewing circles." Shovelers rank low as preferred game ducks, however, probably because of the high proportion of animal matter in their diet and consequent gamy taste. Another hunter's term, "neighbor's mallards," refers to the story that, according to biologist Frank C. Bellrose, "hunters pass them off to their neighbors as mallards—a good way to lose a neighbor!" Shovelers account for about 2 percent of the total duck kill by hunters each year.

Spatulate bills are uncommon in the bird world; an extreme example is the roseate spoonbill *(Ajaia ajaja),* a long-legged wading bird of the Gulf coast and southward. The spoon-bill sandpiper *(Eurynorhyncus pygmeus),* another example, is an Asian resident. All of these birds may be said to belong to the *guild* of filter feeders.

Shovelers have shown a slow trend of increase over the past few decades, perhaps because of artificial habitats created by overfertilized ponds, water impoundments, and sewage lagoons. One wild shoveler on record survived 16 years, but even 5 years is probably extreme longevity for this species.

WATERFOWL FAMILY (Anatidae) - TYPICAL DUCKS - Dabbling Ducks

Northern Pintail *(Anas acuta)*

Its long, needle-pointed tail, one-quarter of the bird's total length (about 26 inches), is the drake pintail's most distinctive feature. Easily seen too are the chocolate brown head marked by a finger of white extending up the neck on either side from the white foreneck, chest, and belly; grayish back and sides; and white flank patch at the rear. Hens, mottled brown, have a less lengthy pointed tail and a rather streaked appearance of various shades of brown. In flight, the pintail's long, narrow wings appear almost gull-like; drakes show an iridescent green-brown *speculum* (wing patch), hens a brown one. Drakes utter a distinctive, double-toned "whee"—"like a wheezy train whistle," according to one observer; hens voice low quacks.

Close relatives. Only 3 pintails exist. The white-cheeked pintail *(A. bahamensis)* inhabits the West Indies and South America; another South American species is the yellow-billed pintail *(A. georgica)*. All other dabbling ducks *(Anas)* are related.

Behaviors. Pintails are slender ducks that measure longer than mallards but weigh less. They have longer necks than most ducks. Its trim, elegant appearance and swift flight (up to 65 miles per hour) have given this duck the label "greyhound of the air." A characteristic flight pattern is a sudden zigzag descent from the heights, leveling off at water level just before landing. On the water, it is shy, difficult to approach. Pintails characteristically ride high in the water, tipping up to feed, legs paddling for

The drake pintail's two long, central tail feathers, present for about half the year, give this duck a distinctive profile.

balance. "Frontal views of the white-necked drakes," wrote one observer, "bring to mind flotillas of toy sailing ships." Often they feed in mixed flocks with other dabblers. They frequently accompany green-winged teals in flight.

Northern pintails range farther over the globe than any other waterfowl species. Their circumpolar breeding range extends to southern Europe and Siberia, the winter range to India, central Africa, and Pacific islands. In North America, only scaups outnumber them as breeding ducks in the Arctic. The American breeding range extends northward from the Great Lakes and Great Plains states. Foremost breeding areas are the prairie provinces and tundra regions of Canada.

Spring. Most bird migrants that arrive early depart late, whereas late-spring migrants usually leave by early fall or before. Describing the pintail as "the most paradoxical of ducks in its seasonal migration," waterfowl biologist Frank C. Bellrose noted this bird as one of the earliest migrants in both seasons. Large flocks of pintails begin arriving on their northern breeding range in early spring, sometimes by late March. Courtship behaviors, begun on the winter range, continue during migration and after the birds arrive; many pintails, however, are already paired by this time. Most begin breeding as yearling birds. Pintails show an elastic, adaptive tendency to wander and pioneer new breeding areas—more so than most other waterfowl—when drought reduces the northern prairie potholes, often move farther northward at such times. Where habitats are stable, the hens home to their natal or previous breeding sites. They are accompanied both by their mates and by unmated drakes (spring populations consist of about 3 drakes for every 2 hens). Arriving flocks settle in the shallows where ice has melted, soon dispersing as pairs establish home ranges and begin to nest, usually by early April (later in the far northern range).

The only territory defended by drakes is the hen's immediate proximity, though home ranges may extend more than 1,000 acres. Late snowstorms sometimes cover the backs of incubating hens, causing some to abandon nests. Paired drakes often become promiscuous, chasing other mated hens during this period, engaging them in forced copulations. This behavior, according to researcher Robert

I. Smith, "tends to disperse the flock functions more effectively than territorial behavior in the traditional sense," resulting in a wider spacing of nests than might otherwise occur. A 1987 study by David C. Duncan refutes this hypothesis, however, indicating that drake pursuit has little effect on nest dispersion.

Nest predation is extensive in this species owing to its early-season nesting and open nesting sites (see Ecology); renesting in the event of first-nest destruction may or may not occur. Most broods hatch by early to middle June. Hens lead broods overland, sometimes for hundreds of yards, to the nearest water. Once there, the flock often continues to journey from pond to pond through the brood-rearing period. Drakes usually desert their mates soon after incubation begins— "poor husbands at best, and, as is true of most ducks, fathers in name only," noted one observer.

EGGS AND YOUNG: typically 6 to 8; eggs olive green to grayish. INCUBATION: by hen; about 24 days. FLEDGING: 7 to 8 weeks.

Summer. As brood rearing proceeds, drakes congregate, then travel on *molt migrations.* They usually fly southward, sometimes for extensive distances, often to the same marsh sites from year to year. Here, mainly in July and August, they replace their trim breeding plumage with a drab, henlike eclipse plumage. They remain flightless for about a month as they grow new wing and tail feathers. Hens begin their annual molt, probably near the breeding area, soon after their broods begin to fly. By late summer, the uniformly drab pintails are beginning to *stage* (gather) in large flocks and move southward from their far-northern range.

Fall. Flying in long, irregular lines at night, the migrant pintail population peaks in September and October. More than half of the pintails in North America move from Canada's prairie provinces to California's Central Valley and southward. Most of the rest drop through the Central and Mississippi flyways to the Gulf coast and Mexico. Eastern and Atlantic coastal movements are relatively sparse. Drakes and hens tend to flock and travel separately, the drakes preceding the hens and young. Most drakes have gained their new breeding plumage by late November or December. Fall age ratios show about 1 immature pintail per adult bird.

Winter. Coastal marshes in California and Louisiana host the greatest abundance of wintering pintails. Smaller numbers winter on both Mexican coasts and through Central America to Colombia. In the East, pintails winter from South Carolina to the West Indies; a few typically remain as far north as the Great Lakes and New England. Pintails show strong fidelity to their wintering sites.

The flocks commonly feed morning and evening in dry fields at this season, at night in flooded fields and wetlands. Like all ducks, pintails form new pair bonds each winter. Courtship behaviors, including pursuit chases and drake grouping and posturing around hens, begin in December and January. The "burp display," unique to pintails, is a kind of head and neck hiccup movement, and much mutual head pumping occurs. Drakes often "stand" on the water, displaying their white underparts and erect tails.

Many pintails are moving northward in February, with migration building to peak numbers in March and April.

Ecology. This is predominantly a duck of the short-grass prairie. Pintails strongly favor areas of sparse vegetation and temporary water, as in flooded fields. Like all prairie ducks, they require open, marshy wetlands for feeding, brood raising, and molting. They often choose drier uplands near water or fields in farmland habitats for nesting.

The nest, a scrape in the ground, is lined gradually during incubation with whatever vegetation is at hand plus down feathers. Pintails nest on dry, often open ground where vegetation is low or sparse, averaging about 40 yards, but often up to a mile or more, from water. Grassland areas and grain stubble fields are frequent nest-site choices. Little effort at concealment is apparent.

Pintail diet is about 90 percent vegetarian, mainly seeds. Bulrush, smartweed, pondweed, wild rice, and various grass seeds rank high, but pondweed leaves and stems are also relished. On the winter range, in addition to the plants mentioned, seeds of ditchgrass, stoneworts, and glasswort are favored. Pintails also feed in grain stubble fields, consuming much wheat, barley, oats, and rice where available. In the prairie provinces, crop damage by pintails and other waterfowl poses a serious problem for wildlife managers, wrote Bellrose, "because it results in a greater incentive to drain wetlands." Most crop damage occurs in grain-swathed fields before harvest combining begins. Hens and ducklings, especially, consume aquatic invertebrates, minnows, and tadpoles in spring.

Potential competitors include other surface-feeding waterfowl and granivorous birds, but actual competitive interactions seem rare in this species.

Predators frequently destroy entire nests or broods; high rates of nest loss probably result from the pintail's early nesting and exposed nest sites. American crows, magpies, gulls, skunks, raccoons, red foxes, and ground squirrels are the foremost nest predators. When pintails nest in stubble fields, spring plowing and other farming operations disrupt many nests. In marshes, lead shot ingestion is a frequent killer.

Focus. The 2 long, central tail feathers *(rectrices)* seen in the drake are also characteristic of the unrelated drake oldsquaw *(Clangula hyemalis)*. Many drake pintails lack their long tails for almost half the year (summer to late fall), owing to slow replacement after the eclipse molt; their frequently nondescript body plumage at this time often gives only subtle cues to their identity. The pintail is a duck hunter's favorite, noted for its excellent table qualities. "Sprig" and "spike" are common hunters' names for this species.

Pintails declined by about 50 percent from the 1970s to 1990s. Apparently, populations are normally subject to radical swings in abundance, probably owing in large part to prairie droughts and the hazards and vagaries of early nesting. Once past their first year, during which mortality may approach 90 percent, the birds show much higher survival rates. Maximum recorded longevity for pintails in the wild is 21 years.

Diving Ducks

Also called divers, bay ducks, or pochards, all members of this tribe (12 species worldwide) belong to the genus *Aythya*. In addition to the 3 species presented in the following accounts, other North

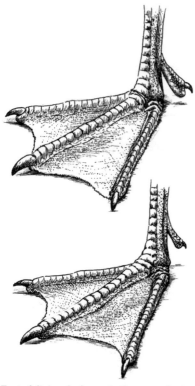

American divers include redheads *(A. americana)* and ring-necked ducks *(A. collaris).* The common pochard *(A. ferina),* ferruginous pochard *(A. nyroca),* and tufted duck *(A. fuligula)* are Eurasian residents. Sea ducks also dive but, being of different genera, are not labeled divers.

Seldom as brightly colored as dabblers, most divers exhibit various patterns of black and white or other subdued coloration. Also in contrast to dabbling ducks, divers are more or less restricted to large, open bodies of water, mainly because of their anatomy. Their wings are smaller relative to body size and weight, necessitating a running start across the water, often for a considerable distance, when taking flight. Their short legs and large feet, set farther to the rear than in dabblers, make these ducks exceedingly awkward on land, and thus they seldom feed in

Feet of diving ducks, as in the scaup foot (top), have a lobed hallux (hind toe), in contrast to the smaller hallux of dabbling ducks (mallard at bottom).

crop fields. The hind toe *(hallux)* is lobed, with a paddlelike flap.

Divers feed primarily beneath the water surface, also occasionally dabbling at the surface, and their diet is mainly animal rather than plant. These ducks dive by arching up, then nosing downward, exhaling before they dive. Underwater, they swim by foot propulsion, holding their wings tightly against their *feather pockets,* flank feathers that form a slight hollow on each side of the body and keep the wings dry and ready for flight.

Although dabbling ducks sometimes frequent the same open-water habitats as divers, both kinds of ducks partition the resources of such habitats, dividing them "in a manner analogous to the way in which some warbler species divide trees in which they forage," wrote one research team.

Aythya courtship displays, seen mainly in winter and spring, are fascinating exhibitions of ritualistic contortion and attention-grabbing moves. Head-throw displays are maneuvers in which drakes rest their heads far back, their throats aimed skyward, then abruptly jerk their heads forward. Other common displays include the sneak posture, wherein drakes stretch out, flattening themselves on the water when swimming around hens; neck stretches; rearing up; and head bobbing.

Diving ducks pair in late winter and spring, in contrast to fall-pairing dabbling ducks. *Aythya* sex ratios are heavily unbalanced, with some species numbering 3 or more drakes for every hen. Such skewed numbers mean that population censuses of these species do not accurately reflect potential breeding populations, which are considerably lower, since most pairs are monogamous. Hunters often lump divers under the collective term "raft ducks" for their tendency to float in large flocks like unmoving rafts.

WATERFOWL FAMILY (Anatidae) - TYPICAL DUCKS - Diving Ducks

Canvasback *(Aythya valisineria)*

Recognize the canvasback by its chunky mallard size (about 20 inches long); its large, blackish bill; and its long, sloping head profile. Drakes have a chestnut red head and neck, black chest, and white back and sides. Hens show a brownish head and neck merging into darker brown chest and foreback and grayish body plumage. Like most divers, cans are silent most of the time. Drakes utter low croaks, coos, and growls; hens quack and voice low purring notes.

Close relatives. All other diving duck *(Aythya)* species are related. The redhead *(A. americana),* though similar in drake plumage pattern, is smaller with a grayer back and sides, and a smaller, bluish bill.

Behaviors. Its unique wedge-shaped head profile immediately identifies the canvasback, largest of the divers. In prolonged flight, flocks of 5 to 30 cans form lines and evenly shaped Vs; flying in

Although canvasback (top) and redhead (bottom) coloration is similar and both birds are divers, their head profiles are much different.

feeding areas, the flocks are usually compact and irregular in shape. Cans are said to be the fastest flying of the large ducks (up to 70 miles per hour), but they probably do not outspeed teals, scaups, and ring-necked ducks. Highly gregarious except when nesting, canvasbacks typically gather in huge offshore rafts, sometimes numbering thousands of ducks,when feeding or staging for migration.

Canvasbacks breed primarily in Canada's prairie provinces and the Dakotas, also nesting in Alaska and the high Arctic. In the Northeast, we see them mainly during spring and fall migrations.

Spring. Canvasbacks are moving rapidly northward from their winter range by early spring, numbers and arrivals on their breeding areas peaking in April. Hens are highly *philopatric,* usually returning to their natal areas, but drakes rarely do so. Much pairing occurs during northward migration, but usually less than half of the arrivals are already paired, and courtship displays resume or begin upon arrival. Yearling hens nest when habitat conditions are optimal but often do not if conditions are adverse. Canvasbacks are slow-maturing ducks; many do not breed before age two or three. Three to 5 drakes commonly cluster about a hen, pursuing her for brief chases in the air and on and below the water surface. "Although the hen appears to play a submissive role," observed waterfowl biologist H. Albert Hochbaum, "she is, nevertheless, the dominant character in any courting party . . . should the displays and attentions of her suitors seem to lag, then she may become the aggressor, assuming the neck-stretch [display] as if to encourage further display." Unpaired hens diminish in number as courtship proceeds, and flocks of courting drakes pursuing single hens may grow to a dozen or more birds.

Home range of a pair, sometimes more than 1,000 acres, usually includes several pothole ponds, some of which are used as nesting, feeding, and loafing areas. These sites are usually not defended from other pairs. A drake may defend an area of several feet around his mate at times, and at other times ignore nearby drakes. By late April and early May, nesting has begun. "The presence of a lone drake in the morning, and a pair together in the afternoon on the same water day after day," wrote Hochbaum, "is a reliable indication of a nest nearby." Drakes desert the hens usually within the first week or so after incubation begins; they gather in small bands on open bays, their numbers increasing as the breeding season advances.

Canvasback hens exhibit a relatively high rate of nest desertion, in most cases owing to brood parasitism (the principal cause; see Ecology), predation, or flooding. Deserting hens may or may not renest, depending on various factors.

EGGS AND YOUNG: 7 to 9; eggs greenish olive. INCUBATION: by hen; about 25 days. FLEDGING: about 2 months.

Summer. Most hatching occurs in June. The most mobile of duck broods, except for pintails, canvasback ducklings are guided by hens through a succession of marshes and pothole ponds. Hens often abandon their young a week or more before they can fly. A few other duck species also do this; as Paul R. Ehrlich et al., the authors of *The Birder's Handbook,* point out, a conflict often exists "between the evolutionary interests of parents and young, it being best for the parents to cease care before it is best for the young to be on their own."

Unlike the drakes, most hens remain solitarily in the breeding marshes during their molting and flightless period (3 to 4 weeks, usually in August). They replace their grayish body feathers with an almost solid brown eclipse plumage. Drakes, in the meantime, have fled to the open waters of large lakes or bays, assembling in large rafts. Here, also in August, they cast their flight feathers, remaining flightless in the open for 3 to 4 weeks. The eclipse plumage is drab and dusky gray, with cinnamon brown head and chest. By early September, many drab-plumaged cans are beginning to move southward.

Fall. Drakes probably move southward directly from their molting lakes, joining hens and juveniles on the winter range. Late October and early November are peak migration periods for canvasbacks. Most drakes have gained their bright breeding plumage by late October, coinciding with their southward passage. The main migration corridors diverge east and west from prairie breeding areas to the Atlantic and Pacific coasts; the major eastern corridor culminates in Chesapeake Bay, the western in San Francisco Bay. Substantial numbers also fly the more conventional flyway routes to the Gulf coast and central and eastern Mexico. Banding data show that many brood mates of the year migrate in separate flocks.

Winter. As birds of "big water," canvasbacks spend most of their time feeding and resting in large offshore rafts. Most cans frequent Chesapeake Bay and other coastal bays and estuaries of the Atlantic and Pacific oceans and Gulf of Mexico. One of the highest winter concentrations gathers at Bitter Lake National Wildlife Refuge in New Mexico. Large flocks also winter inland as far north as the southern Great Lakes. By early February, flocks are becoming restless, and many canvasbacks begin departing their winter areas as inland waters on their migration routes open up. Some evidence exists that portions of the population change migration corridors from year to year.

Ecology. Canvasbacks favor open water areas containing substantial growth of submersed aquatic plants on both summer and winter ranges. For breeding habitat, they require large marshes and prairie ponds of diverse size. In winter, they favor the more brackish estuaries and bays over saline water areas.

Cans usually nest in the cover of emergent aquatic plants, within 60 feet or less of open water. Other common nesting cover includes sedges, reeds *(Phragmites),* and shrub willows. Most nesting cover rims prairie ponds of less than an acre in size. Egg laying often begins on only a shallow platform of cattails or other surrounding vegetation, the hen gradually building up the nest and lining it with down feathers as incubation proceeds. "Nests well hidden in tules [bulrushes] may later be stripped of cover within reach of the incubating bird," observed one researcher. Heavy rains or rising waters test the hen's adaptability; she "is deft at building beneath the eggs so that as the nest is raised, so are its treasures." Receding waters may strand the nest over dry land. One or more ramps of plant material usually lead from the nest rim to the water, and the hen keeps clear of debris a narrow lane running through emergent plant cover from the nest to open water.

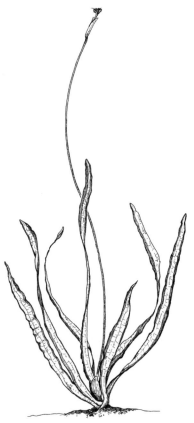

Along with the closely related redheads, canvasbacks are the foremost plant feeders among diving ducks, vegetation forming about 80 percent of the total diet. Highly favored foods are the tubers and seeds of wild celery *(Vallisneria americana),* the submersed aquatic plant from which the bird derives its specific Latin name *valisineria.* Ranking even higher as food plants, however, are sago pondweed tubers, leaves, stems, and nutlets. This pondweed *(Potamogeton pectinatus)* has been called the single most important food not only for cans but for many other waterfowl as well. Other favored plant foods

A favored food of canvasbacks and many other duck species is wild celery (Vallisneria); *the can takes its Latin species name* (valisineria) *from this aquatic plant.*

include arrowhead tubers, wild rice grains, bulrush seeds, and ditch-grass. But canvasbacks are also opportunistic feeders. When plant resources fail, they turn to small mollusks, insect larvae (mostly caddisflies and midges), worms, crabs, and small fish; much of the summer diet normally consists of these animal foods. Cans typically dive from 3 to 12 feet for food, sometimes down to 30 feet.

Some diving ducks, including cans, benefit surface-feeding waterfowl by uprooting aquatic plants, causing them to float up, and by bringing aquatic tubers to the surface. American wigeons often accompany feeding canvasbacks, as do American coots; both often attack surfacing cans, pirating what they can. In coastal wintering areas, great black-backed gulls commonly harass cans, stealing invertebrate food the ducks bring to the surface. The canvasback's strongest competitor on much of its breeding range, however, is the redhead duck. The latter has similar habitat requirements, and its frequent laying of eggs in canvasback nests *(brood parasitism)*, often resulting in canvasback desertion, gives it a competitive edge. In many areas, redheads parasitize more than 50 percent of can nests, usually laying 3 or more eggs in a nest. One study found that in cases where the hen canvasback did not desert, only about 30 percent of the redhead eggs hatched; another study indicated that in Manitoba habitats, about half of all redheads had been reared in can broods. This redhead proclivity, suggested researcher Michael D. Sorenson, may represent a "low-cost alternative" to typical nesting. It is, at any rate, a common aspect of redhead-canvasback nesting. Redheads are not as adaptive in their diets as cans; they are more exclusively plant feeders and tend to feed in shallower waters. On the winter range, they frequent more saline waters than cans.

Canvasbacks also brood-parasitize the nests of other cans, probably at a much higher frequency than generally recognized. A 1993 study area showed 36 percent of can nests parasitized by other cans; the parasitizing hen, in such cases, may be one that has abandoned her own nest because of brood parasitism by redheads or other cans.

Since about 1950, raccoons have become the foremost canvasback nest predators in southern portions of the breeding range, destroying thousands of nests. American crows, magpies, northern ravens, and skunks also raid many nests. Because of their bottom-feeding habits, canvasbacks are among the commonest victims of lead-shot toxicity *(plumbism)*. Floating oil slicks have also killed many.

Focus. Labeled the "king of ducks" by hunter-epicures, the canvasback is among the wariest and wildest of waterfowl. "Those who have forgotten the skills of hunting, or who have never learned them," wrote Hochbaum, "are not worthy of the Canvasback." Today Hochbaum's criteria have become largely academic, for, 50 years after he wrote those words, canvasbacks have become the least abundant of North American duck species. After decades of closed seasons on this species, a limited, one-duck-per-day season nationwide was commenced in 1996. Their long-term trend of decline since the 1950s is hardly surprising; the competitive and predatory pressures, the exceedingly top-heavy ratio of drakes to hens (about 7:3), and the loss of wetland habitats and prime aquatic plant food sources have combined to depose the "king of ducks." Annual survivorship of drakes is about 75 percent; of hens, about 56 percent. The hen's higher mortality rate accounts for the sex-ratio differential; a variety of environmental stresses combined with the timing of the hen molt seems to operate against the female. Thus about three-quarters of the drake population cannot pair in any given year.

As an important index species of the environment, the canvasback reveals, more than any other North American duck, the insidious contamination of many of our waters and wetlands. Owing to pollution and turbidity, beds of wild celery, to cite just one example, have virtually disappeared over much of its former range, depriving waterfowl of a once-important food source. In view of the environmental degradations we allow our leaders to permit, it appears that few of us today can claim ourselves very "worthy of the Canvasback."

The name canvasback, in common usage since 1800, refers to the drake's back plumage with its grayish vermiculations, thought to resemble canvas fabric. The canvasback was once believed identical to the closely related pochard, a duck familiar to colonists from Europe. Wild cans have survived to 15 years, but relatively few probably live beyond 2 or 3 breeding seasons.

WATERFOWL FAMILY (Anatidae) - TYPICAL DUCKS - Diving Ducks

Greater and Lesser Scaups
(Aythya marila, A. affinis)

Both scaups appear black at both ends and white in the middle. The lesser scaup, averaging about 17 inches long, is almost 2 inches shorter than the greater. Drakes of both species show bluish bills, dark heads and chests—green in the greater, purple in the lesser—and black tails, with white to light gray back and sides. Size and color distinctions are not readily visible except at very close range, however. Hens are uniformly dark brown with a white facial patch surrounding the bill. In flight, both species exhibit a broad white stripe on the trailing edge of the wings. Drakes voice soft "whew" whistles and purring notes; hens utter low rattling notes. Both sexes occasionally emit harsh "scaup" quacks.

Close relatives. All other *Aythya* species bear certain visible similarities to scaups, especially in plumage patterns, as well as distinctive differences.

Behaviors. "Bluebills," as hunters label both scaup species, are some of the most common winter divers in eastern North America. Viewed at a distance on the water, they appear simply black and white; identifying which species you see, when possible at all, requires meticulous observation (even Audubon failed to distinguish them). The most consistently reliable differences, though subtle, lie in the amount of white on the wings in flight and shape of the head profile. Greater scaups have a white stripe extending almost the full length of the wing, whereas the stripe on lesser scaups is limited to only half the wing length closest to the body. Greater scaup heads are round in profile; lesser scaup heads show a somewhat peaked shape owing to their thicker crown feathering. Although head shapes "are very subjective field marks," wrote ornithologist

James Granlund, "with practice observers can separate many individuals using them." Winter distribution differences also exist. Even though much overlap occurs, greaters frequent the seacoasts and Great Lakes, whereas lessers more often occur on inland lakes and smaller bodies of water.

On the water, scaups usually gather in flocks of varying size, often associating with ring-necked ducks, buffleheads, American goldeneyes, and American coots.

Behaviorally, both species are much alike, feeding by diving and grubbing food from mud bottoms. Drift feeding is common; rafts of scaups float past feeding areas, the birds constantly diving, then the flock flies back to the beginning of the drift current. Greaters typically dive to greater depths—at least 20 feet—and can remain submerged for about a minute. Lessers tend to dive shallower—5 or 6 feet—but can also go much deeper. In a typical feeding raft, some ducks will be up, others down at any given time—but unlike many waterfowl feeding flocks, no sentinel birds warn of impending danger.

In flight, both species move in compact flocks of 30 to 50 birds. Wings of greater scaups often produce a loud, rustling sound as the birds fly over. Lesser scaups seem more nervous and erratic, twisting and turning in flight.

Lesser scaups are one of the most common winter ducks in the Northeast; these drakes show the somewhat peaked head shape typical of this species.

Greater scaups are circumpolar, breeding in arctic and subarctic regions worldwide, except for Greenland and northeastern Canada; the foremost breeding area in North America is the Yukon delta. Lesser scaups breed exclusively in North America, mainly in Alaska and western Canada.

Spring. Spring migration for scaups is a long, drawn-out affair, the most protracted movement of all North American ducks. Some begin following the progression of ice retreat from lakes in earliest spring; others are still moving northward in May. Hens are *philopatric,* homing to their natal or previous breeding areas; drakes rarely are, following the hens. Most hens are paired by the time they arrive, and pairs disperse from the arriving flocks to establish ill-defined home ranges, usually some portion of a lake and lake edge. Home ranges often overlap with those of other pairs. Several pairs may associate in feeding and loafing sites, especially during afternoon hours, and territory is restricted to the mobile proximity of each hen.

Nesting appears semicolonial for both species in some areas, where nests are spaced less than 10 feet apart and number more than 20 per acre, though greater spacing is more typical. Most scaups do not begin breeding until their second year (though exceptions occur), and most nesting begins from early to mid-June. Hens gain new body feathers in March and April, and many drakes continue to undergo their winter body molt at this time.

EGGS AND YOUNG: 8 or 9 (greaters), 9 to 12 (lessers). INCUBATION: by hens; about 25 days. FLEDGING: about 40 days (greaters), about 50 days (lessers).

Summer. Hatching season for most scaup broods peaks in July and early August. Drakes desert their hens during the first week or so of incubation, joining with thousands of other drakes on *molt migrations* to interior lakes, where they remain settled in flightless rafts on open water for about 3 weeks in July and August. Here, in brown and mottled eclipse plumage, they gain new flight feathers.

Hens, in the meantime, often desert their broods when they are still in the downy stage (up to 3 weeks old), but duckling mortality is low. Deserted ducklings often join other, parented broods, sometimes resulting in multiple broods *(creches)* escorted by a single hen. Two or three broods with hens may also combine. By early September, many northernmost scaups are beginning to move southward.

Fall. Scaup migration through the United States peaks in mid-October to mid-November. The two species use different migration corridors and primary wintering areas. Greater scaup movement is mainly east-southeastward from Alaska and northwestern Canada to the Atlantic coast, often in huge mass movements. Smaller numbers head southward along the Pacific coast and to the Gulf coast. Few, if any, leave the North American continent. Most lesser scaups move more directly southeastward to the Gulf coast and Mexico, flying in flocks of 20 to 50. Some also head for the Atlantic and Pacific coasts, Central America, and the West Indies. Scaups travel mainly at night.

Winter. About 60 percent of the greater scaup population winters on the Atlantic coast, most along New England and Long Island shores. Smaller percentages winter on the Great Lakes and from coastal Alaska to San Francisco Bay. Most lesser scaups winter in Louisiana and Florida, but many also winter on the seacoasts from Puget Sound and Long Island southward. Relatively few winter on inland lakes. Thus the two species, though they intermingle in some areas, remain largely apart on the winter range.

Winter is the primary courtship and pair-bonding season for most divers, including scaups. Most drakes gain their full black and white breeding plumage in December; hens continue their molt into late winter and early spring. Common drake displays are head throws and turning the back of his glossy head toward an inciting hen.

Gradual departure from some wintering areas begins as early as February.

Ecology. Like all diving ducks, scaups require large open-water areas for feeding, resting, and molting. Breeding habitats of the two species differ, however, tending to separate them even though they occupy much overlapping range. Greaters favor lowland tundra sites for nesting; lessers tend to select upland sites adjacent to lakes, pothole ponds, and wetlands. In winter, greater scaups frequent marine habitats more than lessers, which favor inland freshwater areas.

Greater scaup hens scrape nest hollows usually within 20 feet of water, often on slight rises near tundra ponds. They mat the scrape with grass and, as incubation proceeds, with down. Lesser scaups seem more opportunistic in nest-site locale, generally favoring more cover than greaters. Many nest on islands, in grass, sedge, and rush growth, and in mixed prairie vegetation at varying distances from water. But not all choose upland sites; many also nest on floating mats of vegetation. Pothole pond vicinities are strongly favored, especially ponds from 2 to 5 acres in size—"larger, deeper, and more stable than those preferred by dabbling ducks," according to waterfowl biologist Frank C. Bellrose.

Both scaup species feed on plant and animal matter, the latter predominating in most areas and seasons. Greater scaups feed heavily, at times almost exclusively, upon mollusks, mainly small clams of several species; they also consume larval insects, barnacles, and crabs. Plant foods include pondweed seeds and leaves, wild-celery, naiads, and stoneworts. Lesser scaups favor snails, small clams, leeches, and aquatic insect larvae. Amphipod crustaceans rank high as important summer foods. Seeds and leaves of pondweeds, wild-celery, naiads, and arrow-heads are important plant foods, as are wild rice, bulrush, and water lily seeds and (on the winter range) ditch-grass.

Evidence exists of occasional conflict between the two scaup species over nesting sites, and food competition is also possible. Greater scaup nests are often parasitized by invading greater scaup hens, resulting in egg clutches of 16 or more; density of nests and overlapping home ranges may account for this. Redheads also parasitize scaup nests, and both scaups occasionally parasitize the nests of other duck species. The two scaup species, however, rarely parasitize each other's nests. Hybrids remain unknown, though, should they exist, "their recognition would prove to be extremely difficult," as biologist Paul A. Johnsgard comments.

Skunks, ground squirrels, and weasels are the foremost nest predators. Magpies and American crows also raid nests.

Focus. The name *scaup* supposedly derives from the British term *scalp,* referring to the shellfish diet of pochards—though it may also stem from one of the drake's call notes.

Scaups may have the largest surplus of drakes to hens of any North American duck (except, perhaps, the canvasback)—in some populations almost 3:1. One study estimated an average annual mortality rate of 42 percent for adult lesser scaups. The figure is probably comparable for greaters. Greater scaup populations, however, may be decreasing in North America. "An apparent long-term decline has us concerned," says waterfowl biologist Joe Johnson— "from 6 to 7 million in the 1970s to less than 5 million in the 90s." Banded scaups have been retrieved at ages 10 to 13, but most scaups probably survive less than half that long.

Sea Ducks

Though these ducks, most of which frequent the oceans during winter, are known as sea ducks, many breed and also winter in freshwater wetlands. In eastern North America, we see them mainly during their migrational passages. Like the divers, sea ducks also feed by diving, but they differ from the other duck tribes in their breeding schedule, beginning nesting in their second rather than first year. Their elaborate courtship displays also are uniquely different from those of other ducks. Nineteen species reside worldwide, most of which are also North American.

Most sea ducks show striking patterns of black and white or iridescent colors. Besides the two species accounts that follow, plus listed relatives, other North American sea ducks include the eiders *(Somateria, Polysticta),* scoters *(Malanitta),* harlequin duck *(Histrionicus histrionicus),* and oldsquaw, or long-tailed duck *(Clangula hyemalis).* The Labrador duck *(Camptorhyncus labradorius),* extinct since 1875, was also a sea duck.

Similar to other maritime bird species, sea ducks often develop salt glands, enlarged, paired nasal glands that eliminate excess salt acquired in the seawater environment, from the bloodstream.

Common Goldeneye *(Bucephala clangula)*

Measuring about 19 inches long, this common winter duck is easily identified. The drake has a puffy, iridescent, dark green head that appears black at a distance, marked by a large white spot between eye and bill; neck and body are all white, back and tail black. The hen has a dark brown head, white neck collar, and gray body. Both sexes show bright yellow eyes and, in flight, large white wing patches. Also distinctive are their whistling wings, enabling an observer to detect a flying flock from half a mile away. Hens utter low-pitched quacks, but these ducks are usually silent except during courtship displays (see Winter).

Close relatives. Only three *Bucephala* species exist. Barrow's goldeneye *(B. islandica)* is primarily a western continental resident; the bufflehead *(B. albeola)* breeds across the continent.

Behaviors. Also known as whistlers because of their singing wings, common goldeneyes fly in fast (about 50 miles per hour),

compact flocks of 6 to 12 ducks. Extremely wary of intruders and disturbance, they can take flight with a shorter running start than other diving and sea ducks, often rising in rapid spirals. Their short necks and chunky bodies also help identify them in flight. On the water, the goldeneye typically floats with its head tucked in so that the dark head and back seem to merge in a continuous black band.

The white-spotted head profile of the common goldeneye drake is distinctive; its yellow eye is only visible close-up.

Accomplished divers, goldeneyes commonly feed in water less than 10 feet deep but can dive to at least 20 feet. Usually they remain submerged less than half a minute, propelling themselves with their feet. On the bottom, they often overturn loose stones in seeking food. Goldeneyes preening on the water commonly roll half over, feet aloft, for a minute or so, then roll over on the other side, as they fuss with their feathers.

Common goldeneye breeding range spans the forested areas of the continent, mainly north of the United States. The species is circumpolar, breeding also in Eurasia. Drakes outnumber hens by about 60 percent in North America.

Spring. Among the earliest spring migrants, goldeneyes begin to arrive on their breeding areas as soon as open water appears. Most hens are paired by this time, though courtship activity of unpaired birds continues (see Winter). Hens show strong homing instincts *(philopatry),* returning to the same areas—often the same nest cavity—but with a different mate each year. (Like some other sea ducks, but unlike most ducks generally, common goldeneye pairs may occasionally reunite for more than a single breeding season.) Nesting begins in mid-April to mid-May, and most broods hatch before summer. If nests are destroyed by predators, goldeneyes rarely renest.

Goldeneye drakes defend fixed breeding territories, which vary in size, from other goldeneyes and from the closely related buffleheads. The home range consists of the nest site plus adjacent water areas where the pair feeds and preens. Drakes desert their hens soon after incubation begins, dispersing to lakes on molt migrations. Ducklings emerge from their tree cavity nests a day or so after hatching, tumbling to earth in much the same manner as wood ducklings, and follow the hen to the nearest water. Hens often move broods from the nest-site lake to rearing lakes that offer more abundant food.

EGGS AND YOUNG: 7 to 10; eggs pale greenish. INCUBATION: by hen; about 4 weeks. FLEDGING: about 60 days.

Summer. Many hens apparently abandon their young at 5 or 6 weeks, before they can fly. Motherless broods often combine in groups of 20 or more *(creches).* In early summer, however, when some hens are still incubating or shortly after hatching, many yearling hens and hens with failed nests go prospecting for future nest cavity sites. Often traveling in small groups, they utter characteristic "cuk cuk cuk" notes as they fly around and enter potential cavity sites. This behavior is believed to be advance preparation for selecting nest sites the following spring. After leaving their broods, many, if not most, hens depart their nest-site lakes and begin molting their flight feathers and body plumage. Drakes, flightless on their molting lakes for 3 to 4 weeks in July and August, exchange their breeding plumage for eclipse coloration similar to hen plumage—brown head with an obscure white spot between head and bill. Both adult and young goldeneyes tend to move not south but northward after gaining their flight feathers, sometimes massing by thousands on lakes to which they return each year at this time.

Fall. Noted as one of the latest fall migrants and a harbinger of winter, the goldeneye typically moves southward on broad fronts just ahead of freeze-up on the northern lakes. Travel is in full swing by mid-October, peaking a month later. Migration corridors have been difficult to establish for this species because of the birds' tendency to remain as far north in winter as open water permits. Goldeneyes always favor cold waters, and few fly as far as the Gulf coast and Mexico. Most of the population heads for Atlantic and Pacific coastal bays, but many also move more directly southward to the Great Lakes and along the Mississippi River. Juveniles tend to fly farthest south, drakes winter farthest north, with hens in between— but obviously much overlap occurs, or winter courtship couldn't proceed. The birds concentrate in dense, offshore rafts at night during fall and winter. Most adult drakes begin to molt into new black and white breeding plumage in the fall before or during migration, a molt usually completed by late October. Immature birds of both sexes retain their henlike plumage for a year, with gradual changes, until their second winter.

Winter. Largest winter concentrations of common goldeneyes range along the Pacific coast from southeastern Alaska to British

Columbia, and along the Atlantic coast from Long Island Sound to North Carolina. Lesser numbers string out southward along both coasts, in the Mississippi basin, and throughout the Great Lakes region. On many interior lakes and rivers of the Northeast, common goldeneyes, along with mallards, rank as the most commonly seen winter ducks.

Courtship behaviors begin in earnest by December, lasting through winter, as small groups of drakes posture and display before one or two hens. Goldeneye courtship displays are spectacular; the restless drakes perform snapping head-throw movements with much complex nodding, ducking, and utterance of double squawking notes similar to those of common nighthawks. The hen's inciting display is a prone, floating, stretched-out position in the water, lasting up to 15 minutes.

Goldeneyes develop yellow tips on their bills, which fade after the breeding season. Most yearling goldeneyes gain their first adult plumage during winter. Hens complete their body molts by early December.

By late winter, most goldeneyes are trending northward, probing interior lakes and bays for open-water areas, "rushing the season" in accord with their early-timed patterns.

Ecology. Common goldeneyes require inland lakes and streams bordered by nest-cavity trees—either coniferous or deciduous—for breeding habitat. For feeding and loafing, they favor clear lakes without much emergent or submersed vegetation, often selecting fishless lakes over more productive ones. This is the only North American duck known to benefit from lake acidification caused by acid rain. Lakes selected, however, especially for brood rearing, must contain ample food supplies of acid-tolerant invertebrates. Thin bulrush stands and shoreline logs for brooding and loafing sites are also typical of goldeneye habitat. Winter habitats are mainly coastal bays and estuaries and large, icefree, freshwater lakes and rivers. Goldeneyes increasingly frequent shoreline discharge areas near industrial or power stations, probably because of the increased food supply generated by the warmer waters of such outlets.

For nesting, the common goldeneye favors large, mature trees containing cavities, usually 20 to 30 feet high, with an entrance hole diameter of about 5 to 9 inches. These ducks also frequently use roofless bucket or chimney type cavities—broken-off hollow tops of trunks. Old cavities created by pileated woodpeckers provide some nesting sites, as do nest boxes placed about 20 feet high in trees along fairly open lakeshores. The ducks favor boxes with rectangular openings of about 4 by 5 inches and a depth of about 2 feet. Occupied cavities often show bits of down clinging to the outside entrance. Hens bring in no materials for the nest, using only wood debris of the cavity itself plus their own additions of down feathers, forming a thick mat as incubation proceeds.

At least three-fourths of the common goldeneye diet is animal food, mainly crustaceans (crabs, crayfishes, amphipods), insect larvae, and mussels. Ducklings feed mainly on dragonfly and damselfly nymphs and caddisfly larvae. Foremost plant foods consist of pondweed seeds, leaves, and tubers; wild celery; and seeds of bulrushes and water lilies.

Most goldeneye competitors are other cavity nesters seeking space for their own nests. Tree cavities of suitable size are often scarce in otherwise optimal habitats; their availability is usually the chief limiting factor for goldeneye breeding abundance. Other North American tree-nesting ducks—wood ducks, buffleheads, and common and hooded mergansers—may compete where breeding areas overlap, but range and habitat differentials usually preclude intense competition from these species. In areas where wood ducks are present, goldeneyes tend to seek cavities in more open stands and along field or marsh edges; the wood ducks prefer denser woods. Goldeneyes may, at times, invade occupied wood duck nests, taking them over as their own. But tree swallows, European starlings, squirrels, and raccoons probably offer greater competition than other ducks for nest cavities. In nesting areas that offer few tree cavities, dump nesting often occurs as one or more goldeneye hens deposit eggs in another goldeneye nest. The original nesting hen often accommodates the addition of several eggs, reducing her own clutch by a like number, but she usually deserts the nest if more than 7 eggs are added, and the eggs never hatch. (Some biologists argue that moderate brood parasitism in ducks, which is fairly common, is favored by kin selection; the brood parasites probably share the parasitized hen's gene pool owing to hen *philopatry,* or homing.) Food competition seems negligible in most areas, probably an aspect of the goldeneye's unique tolerance of acidic lake habitats, where fish are not present to compete for animal food. In lakes where fish do occur, a study revealed that yellow perch compete strongly with goldeneyes for invertebrate foods.

Nest predators include northern flickers, European starlings, raccoons, red squirrels, minks, and black bears. Northern pike, hawks, owls, and eagles raid broods, and occasionally a threatened or intruding goldeneye hen or common loon attacks a duckling. Studies indicate that common goldeneye broods suffer unusually high rates of loss, up to a quarter or more of original brood sizes.

Focus. The goldeneye is not a popular hunter's duck, ranking low as table fare. Its characteristic wing-whistling sounds, however, probably draw more attention from overeager gunners than a silent flier might, resulting in added gunshot mortality.

It is interesting to speculate on what effects the zebra mussel *(Dreissena polymorpha),* a recent pernicious invader of many northeastern lakes, may have on goldeneye habitats. The plankton-feeding habit of these small mollusks often results in clear-water lakes that closely resemble the acid-environment lakes favored by goldeneyes. Another aspect of this potential interaction is the fact that goldeneyes do feed heavily upon mussels in some areas. Could the ducks provide a significant biological control on the proliferation of zebra mussels? Such questions still await the focus of researchers.

Maximum longevity for goldeneyes is probably 11 or 12 years, though not many survive that long.

WATERFOWL FAMILY (Anatidae) - TYPICAL DUCKS - Sea Ducks

Common Merganser *(Mergus merganser)*

Recognize this large, 2-foot-long or more duck by its sleek, elongated profile and red, spike-shaped bill with sawlike "teeth." Feet are also red. In flight, the birds show large, white wing linings. The drake, boldly patterned, has a glossy green head, white chest and sides (tinged with pinkish), and black back. The hen, with reddish brown head and white throat patch, has a ragged, swept-back head crest, white chest, and silver-gray body plumage. The birds are mostly silent except during courtship displays (see Spring).

Close relatives. Four of the 7 merganser species occur in North America: the common merganser; the red-breasted merganser *(M. serrator);* the smew *(Mergellus albellus),* a Eurasian species that appears in the Aleutians; and the hooded merganser *(Lophodytes cucullatus).* Common mergansers are known as goosanders in Europe.

Behaviors. All waterfowl have serrations on the edges of their bills, but the larger, sawlike teeth slanting backward and the bill shape itself—round instead of flattened, and slightly hooked at the end—are distinctive in mergansers, accounting for the vernacular name "sawbills." These are adaptations for catching and holding fish, the main diet of mergansers. Mergs also have a distinctive flight style, usually swift, single-file, trailing lines low over the water. From bill to tail is a straight horizontal axis, enabling instant identification of a merganser in flight.

Common mergansers, the most abundant of all North American mergs, are often seen during winter in large, open-water areas. The whiteness of drake breeding plumage makes them visible from far off. Fast swimmers both on and beneath the water surface, they can (like grebes) sink slowly out of sight as well as dive in a flashing arc.

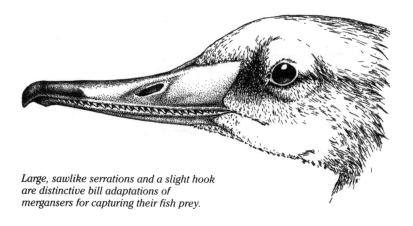

Large, sawlike serrations and a slight hook are distinctive bill adaptations of mergansers for capturing their fish prey.

Often they cruise with only their heads submerged up to the eyes before diving for food. ("Audubon thought mergansers swimming with their heads submerged were checking on the density of local fish populations by tasting the water," wrote naturalist Alan Pistorius.) They prefer to feed in waters less than 6 feet deep, though they can dive to 30 feet or more. Most dives last less than 20 seconds. This merganser has small wings relative to body weight and must patter across the water for several yards to launch into flight, usually heading upwind or downstream. As fish eaters, merg groups, usually 5 to 20 birds, exhibit cooperative feeding behaviors; sometimes they wing-splash in a line as they drive schools of fish into pools or shallows for easier feeding.

Common mergansers breed in the Northern Hemisphere around the world. In North America, their breeding range spans the continent from New York to the upper Great Lakes, the Rockies, and California, extending north to the timberline in Canada and Alaska.

Spring. Early migrants, common mergansers move northward both day and night, flying high in small flocks, close on the heels of icemelt in late winter and early spring. Most travel occurs in March and April, the hens homing to their natal areas with unerring site fidelity *(philopatry).* Courtship activity is continuous en route and after arrival, as groups of 5 or 6 drakes swim in compact masses or strung-out lines around a hen, abruptly turning, tilting up, bobbing, splashing in kick displays, and striking at each other. Hens are highly aggressive toward courting drakes, often jabbing at them while voicing harsh "karr karr" notes. Drakes utter low, twanging croaks. Hens incite mating by flattening themselves, remaining motionless and half submerged, floating like dead ducks. Because of the unbalanced sex ratio (about 65 percent drakes), as is typical in ducks, many drakes go unpaired. These, along with the yearling ducks, which do not breed, remain in segregated flocks throughout the season. Paired mergs disperse from the courting flocks, spacing themselves apart; home range size remains unknown. Hens often select the same nest site they have used previously.

Most nesting begins from mid-April to mid-May, later in some locales. Drakes abandon their mates soon after incubation begins, congregating on large lakes and coastal estuaries. The first broods, spilling from the tree-cavity nests like wood ducklings, appear in early June as hens lead them to the nearest water, sometimes as far as 200 yards.

EGGS AND YOUNG: typically 9 to 12; eggs pale buff or ivory-yellow. INCUBATION: by hen; about 1 month. FLEDGING: about 65 days, often longer.

Summer. Many hens abandon their broods several days or weeks before they are able to fly, resulting in mixed broods of ducklings *(creches)* numbering 20 or more, often, but not always, guided by a remaining hen of a brood. Merg ducklings are hardy, however, and studies indicate unusually high rates of nest success and duckling survival. By mid-June, most drakes and yearlings have flocked to the seacoasts or large inland lakes. There they begin their wing molt, remaining flightless for about a month. Adult drakes are in eclipse plumage by late summer, closely resembling the hens and juveniles. Adult hens, on a somewhat later molt schedule, as is typical of most waterfowl, begin their flightless period about mid-August.

Fall. Hens gain their new flight feathers by late September or early October, at which time the adult and yearling drakes are beginning their prenuptial body molt. By late November, they wear brilliant new breeding plumage.

Common mergansers are extremely late migrants, remaining on their northern range until ice rims the lakes, seldom moving in force until mid-November. During migration, many flocks tend to home to the same water areas en route year after year for resting and feeding, and to the same wintering lakes as well, though annual shifts may occur as ice formation and food supplies vary. Many mergs fly south only as far as they must to find large bodies of open water. More than half the total population travels to interior lakes, reservoirs, and dam discharge areas of the Central, Pacific, and Mississippi flyways, the rest to bays, river mouths, and estuaries along the seacoasts. Relatively few reach the Gulf and northern Mexico or, in the eastern United States, south of Tennessee.

Winter. Migration continues to late December. Courtship activities occur sporadically on the winter range. On their southernmost range, mergs begin departing northward by mid-February, but most movement occurs in March.

Ecology. Common mergansers require lakes and streams bordered by forest on their breeding range. Although they favor clear water for feeding, lake or stream turbidity does not seem to exclude them; on winter rivers, they often gather to dive and feed at fast, unfrozen rapids. The major food habitat requirement is the abundant presence of fish.

These ducks commonly nest in tree cavities ranging from 15 to 50 feet high. The site typically is in a living maple, ash, or other deciduous tree. Nest-cavity availability is probably the major factor in common merg distribution, influencing the density of nesting pairs. Where tree cavities are lacking, common mergs prove their adaptability by nesting in a variety of well-hidden sites: streambank hollows, logs, root crevices, rockpiles, dense shrub thickets, occasionally in nest boxes. Ground nests are usually bulky masses of dead weeds, fibrous roots, lichens, and mosses.

Fish is the staple diet of common mergansers year-round. The ducks are highly opportunistic fish feeders, taking whatever kind happens to be in abundance. Adult birds require about a pound per day. Most prey is small fry, but captures more than a foot long have also been recorded. In clear waters, mergs can see fish up to 10 feet away. The ducks also consume frogs, salamanders, crayfish, snails, worms, and insect larvae. Ducklings feed heavily upon mayfly larvae and adults. Plant food, consisting of roots and stems of aquatics, is negligible.

Nesting cavities are always in high demand and often relatively scarce. "There are few stranger springtime sights," wrote Pistorius, "than a coterie of two or three big, ungainly common merg hens crashing about the treetops prospecting for nest sites." The degrees of scarcity and resulting competition for such sites are generally indicated by the amount of egg dumping, or brood parasitism, that occurs in many duck species but especially those that use tree cavities: wood ducks, common goldeneyes, buffleheads, common and hooded mergansers. Usually no more than 2 hens lay simultaneously in the same nest, resulting in a multiple clutch of 13 or more eggs. More competition for cavities probably comes from squirrels and raccoons than from other tree-nesting ducks. Potential food competitors include other fish-eating ducks plus common loons, ospreys, belted kingfishers, and a few other birds, but little evidence exists of actual pressure from these species. The closely related red-breasted merganser shares similar foraging habits and food, but this is mainly a saltwater duck for much of the year, and not much actual competition occurs. Herring and ring-billed gulls are major food competitors, often attracted to merganser flocks and pirating fish brought to the surface. Bald eagles also occasionally pirate from common mergs. In certain fisheries, the human angler must also be ranked as a foremost competitor (see Focus).

Nest predators are relatively few. Raccoons (where present), American crows, and common ravens probably raid nests occasionally.

Focus. Owing to their diet, mergs are not favored table ducks, thus are not eagerly sought by most hunters. Fishermen, however, have historically considered and treated the "fish duck" as an enemy, believing it a rapacious predator on game fishes such as trout, bass, and salmon fry. Numerous studies on merg food habits, however, have revealed that such prey ranks low in percentage and frequency. In lakes and hatcheries managed for trout and salmon culture, mergs can and do consume these fishes on occasion. But most of their fish diet consists of slower-swimming, rough and forage fishes such as suckers, chubs, shiners, carp, gizzard shad, and eels. Fishery biologists have long recognized that mergs and other fish-eating birds often benefit lakes overpopulated with half-grown fish; thinning the fish populations below full carrying capacity promotes the rapid growth of survivors, often resulting in excellent fishing, as in wilderness lakes. So the fisherman's enmity is, more often than not, a bum rap.

The name *merganser* originates from the Latin words *merger* ("to dive") and *anser* ("goose"). Longevity of this species remains unknown.

2

Belted Kingfisher *(Megaceryle alcyon)*

Kingfisher family (Cerylidae), order Coraciiformes. Its big, raggedly crested head, spear-shaped bill, and blue-gray plumage identify this 13-inch-long fish predator. A white collar circles the throat, dividing the head from the dark chest band and white belly. Females additionally show a rusty red chest band beneath the upper one. A white spot in front of each eye is conspicuously displayed when the bird is alarmed. Listen for the kingfisher's loud, distinctive rattle of notes as it flies over its territory, sometimes described as sounding like a heavy fishing reel.

Close relatives. Other *Megaceryle* kingfishers include the giant kingfisher *(M. maxima)* of Africa and the crested kingfisher *(M. lugubris)* of Asia. Only 3 of 9 worldwide cerylid kingfisher species reside in North America: the belted, ringed *(M. torquata),* and green *(Chloroceryle americana)* kingfishers; the ringed and green are southwestern and tropical species. Two other kingfisher families contain many more species. The most widely distributed kingfisher (in the family Alcedinidae) is the common kingfisher *(Alcedo atthis)* of Eurasia. Related birds in the same order include the hoopoes, trogons, motmots, and bee-eaters.

Behaviors. Often heard before it is seen, the belted kingfisher courses swiftly along streams and shorelines, voicing its rattle call. When it spots a fish, it often hovers on beating wings 20 or more feet above the water, then plunges headlong. It flies with its captured prey to a perch, often a habitually used dead limb projecting over the water, beats the fish repeatedly against the limb, tosses it up, and swallows it headfirst. The bird periodically ejects small pellets of undigested fish bones and scales; if the perch is over ground,

Conspicuous by sound and sight, the belted kingfisher travels its feeding territory, capturing about 10 fish per day; two chest bands identify this bird as a female.

the litter of pellets and whitewash (droppings) is always a good sign of kingfisher presence. Because of their body shape, kingfishers look somewhat squat and top-heavy when perched. Diving obliquely from the perch into the water for a meal is a more energy-efficient method than hovering, which researcher William James Davis called "a default mode of foraging" where lookout tree perches are unavailable.

Kingfishers catch most fish in shallow water. "With their eyes closed," wrote Davis, "they grab their prey with a pincerlike action of the bill; to catch a meal their aim must be perfect." That perfect aim, some biologists believe, is facilitated by the two white "false eyes" in front of the bill. These may function as sighting devices along the line of the bill, enabling the eyes to fix binocular vision on the prey, also correcting for refraction of the water surface. (Another suggested use of the light-gathering eye spots is in enabling the young within the dark nest burrows to see and peck at them and thus be fed.) The bird's success rate at prime feeding spots may exceed 40 percent, Davis estimated.

At night, kingfishers, if not on the nest, often roost in trees or sometimes dig roosting burrows near the nest burrow. All birds of this order have short legs and *syndactyl* feet—that is, the third and fourth toes are fused for part of their length, probably an adaptation for nest excavation.

Belted kingfishers range throughout most of North America north of Mexico. Most individuals are migratory, though many males tend to remain year-round on their breeding territories if ice-free.

Spring. Kingfishers begin arriving on their breeding territories in late winter and early spring. Males, unless they remained through winter, usually arrive first. Kingfishers are seasonally monogamous; the same pair may sometimes remate in succeeding years, especially where males remain on the breeding territory over winter. Sometimes a pair even reuses its previous nesting burrow. Generally, however, site fidelity *(philopatry)* is weak in this species, perhaps owing to the ephemeral nature of sandbank habitat, which is widely subject to flooding and erosion along streams.

Once arrived, both sexes become strongly territorial, especially the females. The pair defends linear stretches of stream or shoreline that average about 1,000 yards long. One study estimated a breeding density of 1 pair per 1.8 square miles. Opinions differ on whether territory size depends upon food resources. Some data indicate that the richer the food supply in a given area, the smaller the territory; other studies seem to show no strong connection. Often the birds expand their territories when they begin feeding nestlings. Where nesting banks are scarce along streams, however, feeding and nesting territories may be separated, up to a mile or more apart. Each territory is aggressively defended from other kingfishers. Courtship feeding occurs as males catch fish, presenting them to their mates. Also at this time, kingfishers utter prolonged series of mewing calls quite unlike the typical rattle call. Another behavior, so far unexplained by observers, occurs when several birds fly up together, perhaps to several hundred feet, then circle, chase, and loudly rattle.

Kingfishers display a degree of sex-role reversal, as seen not only in the female's greater territorial aggressiveness but also in nest building, incubation, and parental care; the male gives more time and energy to these activities than the female. Nesting occurs from late April through early June, sometimes later. Nestling mortality is usually low, but if nest failure occurs before mid-June, the birds may renest. Disturbance at the nest site often results in nest desertion. A disturbed kingfisher often screams, spreads its wings, and lifts its white eyespots.

EGGS AND YOUNG: typically 6 or 7; eggs glossy white. INCUBATION: by both sexes, females mainly at night; about 23 days; nestlings altricial. FEEDING OF YOUNG: by both sexes, especially by male; regurgitated fish, crayfish, and insects; whole fish after 5 days. FLEDGING: about 27 days.

Summer. Parent birds—again, males foremost—continue to feed the fledglings for a week to 10 days. Some observers maintain that parents teach their young to fish by dropping dead prey into the water for retrieval; studies have demonstrated, however, that the juveniles learn quite adequately on their own. Families split up about 3 weeks after fledging, both females and juveniles dispersing and remaining solitary until the next spring. Adult males tend to remain on the territory even through winter if feeding areas remain icefree. Solitary juveniles can be recognized by their short bills and brownish breast bands. The annual plumage molt begins about July, sometimes extending to October.

Fall. Migration begins about mid-September in the North, lasting through October. This species exhibits differential migration in both spring and fall; females usually travel farther south than males, which tend to move no farther than they must to find unfrozen streams and shorelines. The winter range extends to the Caribbean islands and northern South America. Migration, nocturnal, at least at times, is solitary and generally follows shorelines of major rivers and lakes. The birds sometimes establish temporary feeding territories at stops during their passage.

Winter. The degree to which kingfishers home to previous winter areas remains unknown, but both sexes invariably establish winter feeding territories and aggressively defend them. Female winter territories are usually larger than those of males.

Ecology. The fact that the kingfisher is one of the most widely distributed land birds in North America seems a bit surprising in view of its quite precise habitat requirements. For nesting, it needs bare, near-vertical sandbanks, usually but not necessarily near water. For feeding, the birds, dependent on vision, require clear water; kingfishers rarely feed in turbid or muddy waters. Stream riffles, where small fish gather, are especially favored. "For a kingfisher," wrote one researcher, "a section of stream with well-stocked riffles is prime real estate." Although open, fast-running streams are preferred, kingfishers also feed and reside along sheltered coves and shallow bays of lakes. Very important are perching posts—usually dead limbs—overlooking the water and nest burrow. On the southern winter range, kingfishers inhabit coastal lagoons and bayous, mangrove swamps, and offshore islands.

Sandbanks selected for nesting must be compact enough to hold without caving yet soft enough for the birds to excavate. One study estimated that a sand-clay ratio of about 75:7 percent is optimal. Both sexes of a pair work alternately at excavating the burrow, the male usually digging about twice as long as his mate. Each bird's digging session lasts up to 4 minutes at a time, usually performed in early morning; the entire project may take several days to complete. A kingfisher digs with its bill, typically ejecting showers and plumes of sand from the hole with its feet as it digs (a sand-spouting burrow can be a startling thing to see if one happens upon a kingfisher nest in progress). Burrows are started in the upper level of a bank, usually 1 or 2 feet from the top, and channel inward 3 to 6 feet, sometimes more. The entrance hole is 3 or 4 inches in diameter, and the tunnel often slopes slightly upward. At the end, the birds hollow a circular, dome-shaped chamber about 10 inches in diameter and 7 inches high. They bring in no materials, but regurgitated fish bones and scales accumulate over time, especially in reused burrows, providing a nest lining of sorts. The chamber gradually enlarges due to nestling behavior: Unlike many nestlings, kingfisher young excrete not in fecal sacs but in liquid streams vented against the sand walls; they peck at the walls, caving the sand and thus burying their excreta while expanding the chamber as they grow. Kingfisher pairs often dig multiple burrows in a bank before nesting in one. A good way to identify an occupied burrow is by the 2 slight grooves or furrows that appear at the entrance;

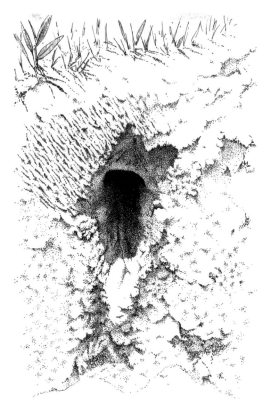

A kingfisher burrow in a near-vertical sandbank often shows double grooves made by the birds' feet as they enter and exit.

these are created by the birds' feet as they enter and exit. Steep-banked gravel pits and road cuts created by human industry have benefited kingfishers, providing many additional bank nesting sites.

Each adult kingfisher consumes about 10 fish per day in optimal feeding habitats. Most prey is fingerling size (3 to 4 inches long), the major source being stream riffles and shallows. When the parents are feeding young, the number of fish required dramatically increases. The birds are opportunistic feeders as concerns fish species, taking whatever is in greatest abundance, including minnows and occasionally trout. A larger-than-usual fish may remain crammed in the bird's gullet, slowly inching down the throat over minutes as rapid digestion works away at the swallowed end. Like most fish-eating birds, kingfishers have a distensible gizzard rather than a crop. Other foods include mussels, large tadpoles, frogs, lizards, crayfish, small snakes and turtles, and insects. A possible commensal relationship (wherein one species benefits, neither is harmed) between feeding egrets and wintering kingfishers has been observed in Florida, where the latter hover over the heads of the egrets, ready to plunge after an escaping morsel. Kingfishers also occasionally feed on berries, probably their only plant food.

Competition with other species seems rare. Kingfishers often share bank nesting habitats with bank swallow colonies, especially in gravel pits, but contact between the two is negligible. Northern rough-winged swallows, which require ready-made burrows, sometimes try to co-opt kingfisher burrows for their own nesting, but the kingfishers readily displace them. Occasionally a territorial contest between kingfisher females results in brood parasitism and egg dumping; the winner destroys any eggs of the other and starts relaying. Kingfishers often rankle anglers and hatchery managers, many of whom regard these birds as definite competitors for game fish species. Little evidence exists, however, that kingfishers habitually deplete fishery resources. Indeed, they probably benefit them more often than not by thinning surplus populations, thus fostering the optimal growth of survivors.

The foremost nest predators are snakes, skunks (which dig into nest burrows from the ground above), minks, and raccoons. Juvenile kingfishers, which fly weakly, are especially vulnerable to capture by hawks, mainly northern harriers and Cooper's hawks.

Focus. An extensive mythical lore surrounds this "chief of the fishers," the original meaning of this bird's name; most tales refer to the Eurasian kingfisher, *Alcedo atthis.* A French legend relates that Noah, after releasing a dove from the ark to search for dry land, next released a kingfisher. Bad choice. Struck by lightning, then scorched by the sun (thus accounting for its colors), this incompetent bird never made it back to the ark; to this day, it roams the river valleys still searching for the boatman who did him such favor. Another old word for kingfisher was *halcyon,* derived from Halcyone, a minor Greek goddess. She, a grief-stricken suicide after her husband Ceyx drowned, was transformed by the mercy of higher gods into a kingfisher along with Ceyx. This tale led to the mariners' belief that kingfishers were seabirds that created nests of fish bones on the ocean surface in December. To facilitate their incubation, Zeus declared that he would henceforth calm the sea during the solstice period (hence "halcyon days"). Cherokee natives also told a tale about how the belted kingfisher got its stout, spearlike bill: Originally the bird was ill equipped for anything, but a council of animals took pity and fashioned a spear, attaching it to the bird's mouth. It's interesting that tales from both the Old World and the New seem to establish this bird, at least initially, as a real loser.

Some researchers believe that kingfishers occupy a midpoint on the evolutionary continuum of sex-role strategies, in which males assume a more equal function with females in nest building, incubation, and care for offspring. The continuum extends, especially in some shorebird species, to almost complete role reversal, with males assuming nearly all parental activities. Female energy potential and losses during egg laying may account for this trend in some bird species that breed and lay large clutches within a short time span.

Recent surveys indicate that continental kingfisher populations are declining at about 1 percent per year. The bird's average longevity remains unknown.

3

Sandhill Crane *(Grus canadensis)*

Crane family (Gruidae), order Gruiformes. Standing 3 1/2 feet tall, the gray-bodied sandhill crane displays drooping rump feathers and a bald, red forehead patch. Body plumage often becomes stained rusty brown. In flight, the long neck is stretched straight out (unlike herons in flight), and the wingspan is 6 to 7 feet. The bugling, gargling call, often the first sign of migrating cranes passing high, is loudly distinctive. Males are slightly larger than females. Six subspecies exist; north-central populations mainly consist of the greater sandhill crane subspecies *(G. c. tabida).*

Close relatives. Thirteen *Grus* species exist worldwide. Nearest North American kin is the whooping crane *(G. americana),* an endangered species. Sandhills appear most closely related, however, to the Australasian cranes, including the sarus, brolga, and white-naped cranes. The common crane of Eurasia *(G. grus)* closely resembles the sandhill.

Behaviors. Novice observers often confuse these birds with herons or storks; despite superficial similarities, however, all are unrelated. Sandhills are graceful in flight, with snapping upstrokes of wings and slower downstrokes. Landing can be somewhat bumpy and awkward; as the birds sail down, they drop their legs like landing gear, tilting and veering as if about to lose balance. This crane's habit of foraging in the mud, then preening its feathers, often results in plumage discoloration, especially with reddish iron mineral (ferric oxide), producing a more brownish than gray appearance. Sandhill cranes can also swim, though infrequently do so. Highly gregarious except during nesting, most sandhills begin

Sandhill crane pairs, both sexes with similar plumage, are among the most monogamous of bird species, remaining together throughout the year.

breeding at age three or four, usually pairing for life. Family groups remain together throughout 10 months of the year.

A spectacular behavior, performed by one or many cranes regardless of age, sex, or season (though it occurs most frequently in spring), is the sandhill dance. The birds bow low, then leap straight up 6 to 8 feet, often tossing bits of grass and debris as they do so. Sometimes a bird continues the performance for minutes at a time. In any large flock, one can usually see at least several (sometimes many more) sandhills "bouncing like rubber balls," as ornithologist John K. Terres described it, simultaneously voicing their deep, vibrant "garooo-a-a-a" calls. The dance is basically a courtship behavior serving to establish and maintain the pair bond; it is believed "to synchronize mates for successful copulation," one research team reported. As crane observer Ann Swengel wrote, "unison behavior of all sorts is a sign of a good crane marriage." Members of a pair often mimic each other: "Couples tend to move either in exact likeness or mirror image."

Sandhill crane breeding range extends throughout much of Canada from Ontario and Hudson Bay west to Alaska and to eastern Siberia; and in the United States mainly from the Great Lakes westward through the northern prairie states. Outlying populations also exist in Pennsylvania, Ohio, Oregon, and California. The greater sandhill subspecies resides mainly in the Great Lakes states and Ontario, and it migrates; three southern subspecies do not migrate.

Spring. Most northeastern sandhills are already on their breeding marshes by early March, established pairs having returned to their previous territories. The one or two young offspring of the previous year that have accompanied the parent birds northward are driven off; until they pair (at age three or more), these nonbreeding birds usually form stable flocks that remain separate. Unpaired males sometimes establish a breeding territory, which unpaired females seek out. Strongly territorial, the pairs engage in mutual dancing and unison duet calls, often at dawn and dusk. Territories range in size between 100 and 200 acres. Both sexes construct the nest, usually from early April to May. The 2 eggs are laid about 2 days apart, incubation beginning with the first.

EGGS AND YOUNG: 2 (more than 2 eggs usually indicates nest dumping by an invading female crane); eggs buff-olive with brown spotting. INCUBATION: by both sexes, females predominating; about 1 month; hatching asynchronous; chicks precocial. FEEDING OF YOUNG: by both sexes; mainly insects, aquatic invertebrates. FLEDGING: 65 to 90 days.

Summer. Asynchronous hatching leads to fierce sibling rivalry in competing for food. In many instances, the younger sibling becomes the victim, through starvation or attack, of the older. In such situations of *obligate siblicide,* the second egg provides, in the words of one researcher, "insurance against loss of the first egg from infertility, predation, or damage, rather than . . . a means of rearing two chicks." Thus many sandhill pairs seldom raise more than a single chick to fledging. Those that do have been observed "to keep the hellions apart," as naturalist Ann Zwinger writes, with each parent guiding and feeding a separate chick during family forays. A chick leaves the nest with parents about 8 hours after hatching but is brooded for 2 or 3 weeks; it must also be fed for several weeks as it gradually learns to feed itself.

The molt of body feathers in parent sandhills usually begins soon after the eggs hatch, continuing for several weeks. Nonbreeding sandhills often begin and end their plumage molts earlier. Replacement of the large flight feathers is a much lengthier, more gradual, and irregular process, requiring 3 or 4 years to complete. The birds may have a brief flightless period before the chicks fledge, but this remains uncertain. Parents and chicks stay on their territories for most of the summer until the latter can fly.

Flocks of nonbreeding or bachelor cranes often forage together in fields during the day, flying to communal roosting areas in marshes as nightfall approaches. In late summer, family groups also become more social, deserting their territories and flocking together in restless, premigrational assemblages. Many cranes are moving southward by early September.

Fall. Eastern sandhills travel overland through Indiana, Illinois, Ohio, Tennessee, and Kentucky on their migration routes. Sandhill cranes are well known for their interim stopovers during migration at *staging areas.* These are usually large marshes used by generations of sandhills for resting and as home bases for feeding flights to nearby fields. High, incoming flights join thousands of previous arrivals during September and October. Family groups remain cohesive even within the larger flock context, similar to Canada geese. Despite one's first impressions, a large flock is hardly a disorderly mass, as Swengel points out. In any fall or winter flock on the ground, one can usually recognize individual families of 3 or 4 cranes, as well as other social units—bachelors and chickless pairs—by their relative behavioral unity. East of the Mississippi, the main staging area is Jasper-Pulaski State Wildlife Area ("an oasis in a desert of farmland," one nature writer termed it) in northern Indiana. Here the majority of the midwestern population—about 30,000 greater sandhill cranes—stops en route to Florida and southern Georgia, their chief wintering destinations. Many cranes remain for several weeks. Most have departed southward by early December, though during recent winters, a few have remained in Jasper-Pulaski. Major staging areas for western sandhills include the Platte River in Nebraska (spring migration), Monte Vista National Wildlife Refuge in Colorado, and Malheur National Wildlife Refuge in Oregon.

During migrations, sandhill flocks fly in V-shaped formations at average heights of 1 to 6 miles (up to 30 miles high), at speeds to 50 miles per hour or more. They also soar on thermals at times, spiraling like turkey vultures.

Winter. Eastern sandhills concentrate on traditional wintering sites, large marshes and lowland sites in Florida and Georgia. They roost in shallow water at night and fly at dawn to feeding areas up to 10 miles away. Juvenile cranes now acquire their red forehead patches but continue to be fed on occasion by their parents. By mid-February, the birds are launching northward. Many stop at their fall staging areas en route, but most eastern sandhills bypass them. Migration peaks in early March, continuing throughout the month. Sandhill cranes rank among the earliest migrants of the year.

Ecology. For nesting, sandhill cranes favor large, deep marshes isolated from human activity. Yet the birds also show adaptability to more fragmented wetland sites, including smaller marshes, sedge meadows, swamp openings, and bogs. Primary feeding areas include upland fields, open grasslands, and drier marshland sites.

The nest, built by both sexes, consists of a bulky mound of wetland plants acquired from the immediate vicinity—cattails, bulrushes, leatherleaf, or sphagnum mosses, depending on the locale—piled some 6 to 8 inches above the water. Cranes usually locate their nests, which may measure 3 to 5 feet in outside diameter, in knee- to shoulder-high vegetation if in a marsh. Sometimes the birds use old muskrat lodges as nest bases.

The sandhill's diet is omnivorous, though mainly vegetarian. It contains a large variety of seeds, berries, roots, tubers, and plant foliage. The birds have incurred some enmity from farmers in winter and spring because of their liking for corn, wheat, and rice sprouts; in summer and fall, they glean large amounts of waste grain in harvested fields. Probing for seeds, insects, and earthworms with their long, straight bills, they probably benefit more than harm agriculture by their aeration of soil and removal of pest insects. When feeding in marshes and during the nesting season, the diet is mainly animal matter, including grasshoppers, beetles, aquatic insects, earthworms, caterpillars, snails, crayfish, lizards, snakes, birds' eggs and nestlings, and mice.

Competitors for food and space seem relatively few, occurring mainly on the Florida winter range, where greater sandhills coexist with the resident sandhill subspecies. Waterfowl, including trumpeter swans, Canada geese, and canvasback ducks, occasionally lay eggs in sandhill nests, as do invading sandhill females in overcrowded marsh habitats. The sandhill's competitors since human settlement have always been the farmer and land developer, whose large-scale drainage of wetlands has deprived sandhill cranes (plus many other species) of crucial nesting and staging habitats.

Sandhill nest predators include foxes, coyotes, wolves, bobcats, American crows, common ravens, and owls.

Focus. The sandhill crane has proven itself a remarkable survivor. Before human settlement, its breeding range was apparently much more extensive than today; presumably it fed mainly in wetland habitats. Habitat depletion—specifically, wetland drainage—plus uncontrolled hunting resulted in near extirpation of the greater sandhill crane over its shrunken breeding range by 1900. Many ornithologists predicted its total extinction. What saved this bird, along with many others, was the 1918 Federal Migratory Bird Treaty Act, which prohibited hunting of most migrants. Recovery was slow; until 1973, the U.S. Fish and Wildlife Service classified greater sandhills as threatened. In the western United States, lesser sandhills recovered much faster, becoming serious grainfield pests by the 1950s. Hunting seasons were reestablished on lessers in 1961; more than 25,000 birds are taken each year with no apparent signs of long-term population decline. Much of the sandhill's recovery owes, no doubt, to its adaptability in exploiting agricultural fields for food plus sanctuaries established for the species and better wetland protection. The fact that this is the oldest living bird species, as Nebraska fossils more than 6 million years old attest, indicates the sandhill's remarkable history of adaptation through tremendous changes in continental geology and climates.

Aldo Leopold wrote movingly of sandhill cranes: "When we hear his call we hear no mere bird. We hear the trumpet in the orchestra of evolution. . . . Their annual return is the ticking of the geologic clock." Leopold would be heartened today by many more crane-occupied marshes than existed in his day. Today the greater sandhill increases in abundance and, in many areas, continues to expand its breeding range. In Michigan marshes, I seldom saw sandhills until the 1960s. Now I see more migrants bugling overhead each year, it seems, than the year before.

Sandhills owe the loud resonance of their calls to a lengthy trachea, or windpipe, that coils deep into the chest cavity, expanding the amplitude of sound. Full voice is achieved at about age 10 months. Typical longevity of adult sandhills may approach 20 years or more. Today the entire continental sandhill population is estimated at about 700,000 birds. Lessers are more numerous than greaters, which number about one-tenth of the total.

Sandhill cranes, biologists hoped, could play an important role in management programs to restore populations of the whooping crane *(G. americana)*, an endangered species. Eggs of the latter placed in sandhill crane nests successfully hatched and eventually produced adult whooping cranes. But the whooping cranes produced by such cross-fostering programs did not breed, probably a result of chick imprinting upon the sandhill crane parents.

Cranes have inspired numerous folk tales and tribal myths because of their size, calls, and ritualistic dancing behaviors. The crane courtship dance has been mimicked in the rites of many tribal cultures. One observer suggests that cranes may "directly or indirectly [have] influenced ballet in much the same way Peter Tchaikovsky was influenced by swans more than a century ago when he composed *Swan Lake.*" Like several other large birds, cranes are reputed to carry small bird hitchhikers during migrations—an extremely unlikely tale.

The English word *pedigree,* from the French *pied de grue,* meaning "foot of the crane," originally referred to a branching family tree (or crane's footprint), as inscribed in genealogy. The word *crane* derives from the Celtic *garan,* meaning "calling" or "crying out"; *sandhill* refers to this bird's staging habitats in the Platte River area of Nebraska.

4

RAIL FAMILY (Rallidae), order Gruiformes

Most members of this large family consist of marsh and waterbirds. They include some of our least familiar avian residents, not because most are exceptionally rare but because of their secretive habits (the gregarious American coot being an exception). Ornithologist S. Dillon Ripley, a rail expert, called them "perhaps the most elusive birds on the continent." Nine North American species exist, and more than 140 worldwide. In addition to the following species accounts and the listed relatives of each, North American rails include the yellow rail *(Coturnicops noveboracensis)*, the black rail *(Laterallus jamaicensis)*, and the purple gallinule *(Porphyrio martinicus)*.

North American rails can conveniently be divided into two general forms. The first group, the marsh waders, are hen-shaped, dark-colored birds. Their laterally compressed bodies ("thin as a rail") are believed to be adaptive for movement in dense marsh vegetation. Other adaptations include flexible vertebrae and a clawlike appendage at the bend of the wing. Most wading rails appear to be weak, awkward, and reluctant fliers, winging only short hops with dangling legs, then flopping down in the marsh

All wading rails have a clawlike hook at the bend of the wing, as seen in this Virginia rail; it is probably a climbing adaptation.

and crouching rather than running elsewhere; this impression is misleading, however, for they travel far during migrations.

The second group, coots and gallinules, are ducklike swimmers with chickenlike bills. Their brown, red, or blue forehead shields extend upward from the base of the bill. Their bodies are precariously balanced on outsize feet; red legs and flexible, splayed-out toes are long in proportion to body size, probably another habitat adaptation.

The vocal repertoire of rails is varied; many utter distinctive clicks, grunts, or cackles more suggestive of frogs or other marsh sounds than of birds. Both sexes in each species bear similar plumage. Hatching is asynchronous, and chicks are precocial.

RAIL FAMILY (Rallidae)

Virginia Rail *(Rallus limicola)*

This 9-inch-long marsh denizen, like its close relatives, has a long, slender, slightly down-curved bill, reddish colored in this species. Distinctive marks include gray cheeks, dark red eyes, black barring on the flanks, and a general rusty color, especially on neck, breast, and wings. Full-grown summer juveniles are blacker. This rail voices metallic "kid-ick" notes, mainly at dawn, dusk, and night, sounds often likened to a telegraph key, sometimes repeated for moments at a time. Other sounds include the "kicker song" ("tic-tic-tic-McGreer") and a ducklike series of descending notes ("wak-wak-wak"). The bird also utters multiple piglike grunts and froglike calls.

Close relatives. North American *Rallus* species include 2 other long-billed species: the king rail *(R. elegans)* and the clapper rail *(R. longirostris)*. Six other *Rallus* species exist, mainly in South America and Africa. The water rail *(R. aquaticus)* of Eurasia resembles the Virginia rail in many features.

Behaviors. One is far more likely to hear a wading rail than see it, for these birds are expert eye evaders, able to fade into the reeds and cattails without a trace and seldom exposing themselves in flight. Only by patient waiting at a marsh edge may you catch a view of this rail as it ventures from cover to forage in the mud. When it

The Virginia rail, more often heard than seen, seldom flies up when alarmed; it usually runs to escape danger.

does fly, usually only to make a rapid escape from danger, it flutters up weakly, with legs adangle and rusty fore-wings conspicuous, and soon drops again. But usually it runs swiftly through the dense marsh cover when pursued, and it can also swim. Long toes enable it to cling to stems and stalks in the marsh. Yet, despite these typical elusive behaviors, it occasionally exhibits startling departures from the norm, sauntering into open areas as if oblivious of its own visibility.

Virginia rail breeding range extends across North America from southern Canada to the middle tier of states and along coastal areas to Mexico. During migrations, the birds fly singly and low at night, often following river courses.

Spring. Usually arriving on their breeding range from mid-April to mid-May (males first), Virginia rails are probably *philopatric,* homing to previous breeding sites and natal marshes if conditions remain suitable in these often fluctuating habitats. Breeding begins in the first year. Territories are relatively small, often overlapping with those of sora rails; several pairs of each may occupy a half-acre marsh. Food and cover availability probably determines both territory size and breeding density. Courtship behaviors consist of bowing, mutual preening, feeding, and male running and tail twitching in front of the female. Grunting duets indicate pair bonding and start of the nesting season. Both sexes construct the nest in May or early June, also building up to 5 dummy nests nearby, which often serve as later brooding and loafing sites.

> EGGS AND YOUNG: typically 8 to 10, laid about 1 per day; eggs pale buff, brown spotted, often wreathed at large end. INCUBATION: by both sexes; begins with laying of first egg; 18 to 20 days for each egg. FEEDING OF YOUNG: by both sexes; mainly aquatic insects, snails. FLEDGING: about 25 days.

Summer. Virginia rails probably produce only 1 brood per year. The sooty black chicks can swim on their first day and feed themselves in about a week, but they continue to be brooded and fed by parents for 2 or 3 weeks. One parent often broods hatched chicks while the other continues to incubate on the nest. Rail researcher S. Dillon Ripley memorably described a newly hatched chick as resembling "a tiny meatball banded with fluff, impossibly skewered on a pair of toothpicks." So secretive are these birds, however, that chicks are a rare sight even to seasoned observers. They move about in the dense vegetation by using their wing claws. Soon after the chicks fledge, the pair bond dissolves, and the birds go off on their own. A pair may, however, return to the same site the following year and pair again.

The annual molt of adults occurs in July and August, producing a somewhat darker plumage than in spring, and the birds remain flightless for a brief period as wing and tail feathers are replaced. Virginia rails sometimes desert marshes in late summer and early fall to feed in upland fields, but they also tend to concentrate in large marshes before migration.

Fall. Migration, again solitary and at night, occurs from mid-September to mid-October. A few birds do not migrate, remaining in isolated, icefree marshes of the breeding range through winter.

Winter. Coastal marshes along the Atlantic from North Carolina south and the Gulf and Pacific coasts are the Virginia rail's main wintering areas. The winter range also extends into Mexico south to

Guatemala. Winter territories exist only loosely, if at all. In March, before northward migration, the birds undergo a partial molt of body plumage.

Ecology. "Vagrancy and generalist habits allow it to exploit a highly ephemeral niche," wrote ornithologist Courtney J. Conway of this species. Its particular niche consists of marshes with fluctuating water levels. Habitat needs include a mixture of open, shallow water, dense cover of aquatic vegetation (usually cattails or rushes); and high invertebrate populations. Virginia rails are most common in marshes larger than 2 or 3 acres that contain 40 to 70 percent erect vegetation interspersed with open water, mudflats, or matted plant materials.

Virginia rails build their nests in dense marsh vegetation, sometimes over water and often near a border between vegetation types (for example, cattails and sedges), but not near open water. The nest is a loosely woven basket fastened to stems a few inches aboveground or on a muddy tussock. Outside diameter is about 8 inches. Materials consist of available dead plant debris—layers of cattails, coarse grasses, rushes—with a live canopy of sedges or rushes arching over the nest, concealing it from above. Often a loosely built ramp projects from the nest rim. Sometimes the nest is lined with leaf fragments, often not. Materials continue to be added as incubation proceeds.

Unlike most birds, Virginia rails have a highly developed sense of smell, which presumably aids their food probing in the mud. Their largely animal diet (about 60 percent insects) consists of larvae, caterpillars, earthworms, snails, amphipods, crayfish, small snakes, and fish. Occasional plant foods include duckweeds and seeds of wild rice, bulrushes, smartweeds, sedges, and other marsh growth.

Little competition apparently exists between Virginia rails and soras; the smaller, related soras often nest in close proximity to Virginia rails. Virginias seem to favor slightly drier habitats than soras and, in contrast to them, consume a diet of primarily animal organisms.

Nest predators include snakes, hawks, short-eared owls, northern harriers, American crows, muskrats, minks, weasels, skunks, and raccoons. Pike, bass, frogs, and sandhill cranes prey on rail chicks. This rail's most sinister foe, however, is the enemy of so many native birds—man. Marsh reclamation and pollution have put an end to rail presence in many areas it formerly occupied. As one ecologist wrote, "The disappearance of a rail seen ambling amid the marsh grasses may be illusory, but the disappearance of high-quality rail habitat is not."

Focus. This rail bears a unique relationship to Virginia in the same sense that Virginia territory once occupied most of the known continent during early American settlement. Thirty-seven states plus Ontario list the Virginia rail as a game species, but hunters take few—mainly from the bird's coastal winter ranges. Despite America's determined attacks on its wetlands, this rail remains a hardy survivor; its numbers appear relatively stable, a tribute to the "vagrancy and generalist habits" aforementioned. Its ability to reestablish itself in wetlands following flooding, storms, and other natural disasters results in its irruptive appearances within habitats that are notoriously unstable; thus a lack of Virginia rails in a given marsh this year may not necessarily bode its absence next year.

Little data exist on this species' lifespan. Many other gaps also exist in Virginia rail life-history information, owing chiefly to its secretive habits and the difficulty of observing this bird in its habitats.

RAIL FAMILY (Rallidae)

Sora *(Porzana carolina)*

This small rail (about 9 inches long) has a short, yellow, chickenlike bill. Its body, like those of other wading rails, looks laterally compressed. Adults of both sexes are gray-brown with a black facial mask extending to the throat. Brown barring on the flanks, yellowish legs, and a short, cocked tail provide distinctive field marks. Most characteristic of its sounds are a rapid, descending whinny (once described as "a tumbling peal of shrill laughter") and a sharp "keek!" when alarmed.

Close relatives. Thirteen *Porzana* rails exist worldwide; the sora is the only North American species. The spotted, little, and Baillon's crakes *(P. porzana, P. parva, P. pusilla)* are Eurasian residents.

The sora, its body laterally compressed, looks ungainly but slips easily through the marsh growth. (From The Atlas of Breeding Birds of Michigan.*)*

Behaviors. Like the other rails, the sora seems all legs and toes as it steps daintily over mud and lily pads, its splayed feet distributing its weight over the unstable surfaces of its habitat. More often, though, one sees it not at all, only hears its startled note, often evoked by a handclap or toss of a stone into the marsh. The whinny call of a sora often heralds an outburst of similar calls across the marsh. Soras lurk deep in the dense vegetation, preferring to slip away elusively in the reeds rather than fly (I once caught a sora in a marsh by running it down). When it does fly up, its legs dangle awkwardly, and it plops down only a short distance away. These weak and rare flight occurrences are highly deceptive, however; most soras migrate almost 3,000 miles each spring and fall. They also swim and have even been observed to walk underwater. The sora is the most common rail in many areas, probably because it tolerates many types of wetland habitat.

Soras breed across most of North America from southern Canada to the middle tier of states.

Spring. Sora life history, like that of most rails, is full of probablys, maybes, and unknowns; these birds were not designed for easy observation, and birds that require more hours of field time than researchers can conveniently schedule are the birds we know least about. Probably most soras arrive on their breeding marshes in late April and early May, when pair bonding occurs. Probably too they are *philopatric,* homing to their natal or previous breeding sites. And again probably they are monogamous only for the duration of a breeding season. Details of all these patterns remain obscure. Facial coloration becomes more vivid at this season, and courtship behaviors include mutual preening and bowing. Territories average about a half acre in size. Listen for the sora's distinctive spring call, often voiced at night; the whistled "per-weep?" with rising inflection sounds somewhat similar to the northern bobwhite's covey call or the call of a spring peeper frog.

Nesting begins in May. The chicks, glossy black, leave the nest soon after hatching, usually in late May and June. As hatching proceeds over a period of days, one parent feeds the mobile chicks while the other continues to incubate the yet unhatched eggs. Nesting associates of soras often include Virginia rails, marsh wrens, swamp sparrows, and red-winged blackbirds.

EGGS AND YOUNG: 10 to 12; eggs glossy tan, brown spotted. INCUBATION: by both sexes; about 19 days. FEEDING OF YOUNG: by both sexes; insects, other invertebrates; chicks are brooded in the nest for up to 3 weeks. FLEDGING: about 4 weeks.

Summer. Soras usually nest only once per year, though second nestings do occur. Nest parasitism occasionally occurs when a sora lays eggs in another sora's nest, in which case the nest owner often buries the eggs of the intruder; how the nest owner can tell the difference between the 2 sets has so far eluded researchers. After the juveniles become independent, they and the adults disperse from the home range to larger marshes or upland fields. In late summer, the birds often frequent the margins of sedge-bordered lakes.

Adult soras undergo a complete plumage molt between July and September; the juveniles also gain adult plumage at this time.

Fall. In late summer and fall, soras congregate, sometimes in large numbers, in wild rice marshes and other prime feeding sites. The birds are winging southward, mainly at night, in September and early October, many in flocks of up to 100 birds. Some researchers believe that temperature controls the timing of sora fall migration; with their low cold tolerance, a hint of frost in the air sends them on their way. Many fly only to the Gulf coast; others cross the Gulf to Mexico, Central America, and northern South America. Many also cross the Caribbean to the West Indies.

Winter. A few soras do not migrate, remaining in ice-free marshes on the breeding range through winter. Most, however, reside in coastal marshes from the Gulf and Virginia coasts southward. Peninsular Florida and Louisiana bayous are areas of the largest winter abundance. A molt of body plumage occurs between January and March.

Ecology. A "denizen of the oozy marsh," as one early observer wrote, the sora may inhabit almost any shallow freshwater wetland site of whatever size, though it favors large cattail and sedge marshes. Highest breeding densities occur in shallow, shoreward sites where changing water levels produce varied plant mosaics. But marshy ponds, wet meadows, bogs, even roadside ditches often host soras too. Soras seem to prefer somewhat wetter sites than Virginia rails, which often occupy the same habitats. Soras, however, seem more opportunistic in habitat use, usually outnumbering Virginia rails in areas where both are present. Several

Prime habitat for both Virginia and sora rails includes marshy ponds and dense border vegetation.

researchers have noted its frequent use of edges or borders between aquatic plant communities for both nesting and foraging. On their winter range, soras often inhabit flooded rice fields and salt marshes as well.

The exceedingly well camouflaged nest often lies a few inches above a water depth of 6 to 10 inches, attached to stems and arched over by surrounding vegetation. Composed of dead cattail leaves, bulrushes, or grasses, the loosely built basket holds a lining of finer plant materials. A path or slight ramp from the nest rim is often seen. Soras occasionally nest on the ground in grassy meadows.

Among rails, soras are probably the foremost vegetarians. Their diet consists mainly of aquatic plant seeds (about 75 per-- cent). Favored seed foods include those of sedges, bulrushes, wild rice, smartweeds, and foxtail grasses; duckweeds are also widely consumed. On the winter range, bull paspalum grass and cultivated rice rank high in the diet. During spring and summer, soras consume many high-protein animal organisms as well, probing in the mud for aquatic insects, spiders, snails, and small crustaceans.

Soras vigorously defend their territories against Virginia rails, but the two coexist in many marshes. Virgina rails favor somewhat drier nesting sites than soras and also feed mainly on animal matter, in contrast to the soras' preference for seeds. Soras also seem more adaptable to varying sizes and types of wetland habitat. Wetland drainage spells the decline of rail populations. Today sora abundance reflects the pattern of marsh habitat loss over the past half century. Thus the sora's present occurrence tends to be more localized and spotty than formerly. Soras also compete with humans in some rice-growing areas of the southeastern United States where the birds winter.

Predators are generally the same as for the Virginia rail. Marsh wrens sometimes prey upon sora eggs, and muskrats are known to climb aboard the nests, using them for feeding platforms. Flooding of nest sites, ingestion of lead shot pellets, and collisions with lighted towers during migration are frequent hazards for this species.

Focus. The source of the name *sora* remains unknown. It may derive from an American Indian term for this bird, which ornithologists once called the Carolina rail. Soras are considered gamebirds and are legally hunted in 31 states and 2 Canadian provinces. Relatively few, however, are taken, though a century ago the bird was shot in large numbers, especially during fall migration in Chesapeake Bay and Atlantic coastal marshes. "Its flight is so slow and steady that it is easily killed," wrote an observer, hardly affording "really good sport." Audubon noted many soras in the market stalls of New Orleans in spring.

Little information exists on sora lifespan or annual survival rates. Spring bird census takers could hardly gain any idea of this bird's abundance without using taped playbacks of its calls, to which soras readily respond. Despite its typically secretive habits, a sora will sometimes approach an observer imitating its calls (or just clicking rocks together), exhibiting itself in full view.

RAIL FAMILY (Rallidae)

Common Moorhen *(Gallinula chloropus)*

This ducklike member of the rail family is about the size of an American coot (13 inches long) and resembles that relative in general form. Moorhens and coots both lack the flattened body shape typical of wading rails. Both sexes have blackish heads and necks, slate gray bodies, brownish wings and tails, and greenish legs and feet. Their red, henlike bills are tipped with yellow, and a red forehead shield extends up from the bill. A white band runs along the body beneath the folded wings. Moorhens utter a variety of froglike croaks, henlike clucks, and plaintive cackles and squawks.

Close relatives. This is the only North American *Gallinula* of 8 species worldwide. The purple gallinule *(Porphyrio martinicus)*, which closely resembles the moorhen, resides mainly in the southeastern United States. (Recently a wild population of purple swamphens *[Porphyrio porphyrio]*, a native of Eurasia closely resembling the purple gallinule, has become established in Florida as a result of escapes from the Miami Metro Zoo during Hurricane Andrew in 1992.)

Behaviors. Moorhens, like coots, are basically swimmers rather than waders, pumping their smallish heads as they swim. Their foreparts often ride lower than their hindquarters, showing their white undertail coverts when seen in profile on the water.

Moorhens also walk on mud and lily pads in this slanted way, lowering the head and jerking the short tail. In habits, moorhens rank somewhat midway between wading rails and coots. Not as secretive as the rails, they are much more easily seen in marsh edges and open water; yet they are hardly as social or gregarious as coots, though they often associate with them. Moorhens also dive for food but fly reluctantly, half fluttering, half skittering barely above the water, suddenly dropping into the marsh again. Like others of its family, however, the moorhen can and does fly strongly and directly when headed for another pond or during migration. It climbs expertly in the marsh vegetation, often peering inquisitively at a passing boat or group of waterfowl from its perch in the reeds.

Common moorhens range globally in warm and temperate climates—in the Western Hemisphere from southern Canada through the eastern United States to Central America. In Europe, they are the commonest, most abundant members of the rail family.

Spring. Moorhens arrive on their continental breeding range in late April and early May, probably returning to natal and breeding marshes of the previous year. Like most of the rail family, they are monogamous only for a season. Marion Petrie's 1986 research on moorhens revealed some previously unknown facts about this bird's reproductive strategies. Pair formation occurs in the winter-spring flock context. Females rather than males initiate courtship, aggressively competing with other females for mates. (Several earlier witnessed accounts of moorhen courtship displays apparently assumed without question the conventional gender roles.) The heaviest females vie for the smallest males—that is, female weight and male size are negatively correlated. Males do not compete for females but for territories, which they vigorously defend against other males. Males also select the nest site, though females do most of the construction. Males perform most of the incubation, and they build several additional nestlike platforms later used as brooding, loafing, and roosting sites.

Courtship behaviors include bowing and open-wing displays. Moorhen courtship calls—harsh "ticket-ticket-ticket" notes—are mainly heard during early morning and evening hours. Moorhens sometimes nest in small, loose colonies, especially in large, undisturbed marshes. Nesting occurs mainly in June and July.

EGGS AND YOUNG: typically 10 to 12 (more than this usually indicates brood parasitism, with more than 1 female laying in a nest); eggs buff colored with brownish speckles. INCUBATION: by both sexes (males about 70 percent of the time); about 3 weeks. FEEDING OF YOUNG: by both sexes, often aided by juveniles when 2 broods are raised; mainly dragonfly and mayfly nymphs, snails. FLEDGING: 40 to 50 days.

Summer. Most moorhens nest only once per year in their northern range, but occasionally a pair nests twice or even 3 times. When this occurs, the birds exhibit *cooperative breeding*—that is, juveniles of the first brood help defend the territory and aid in feeding, brooding, and leading chicks of subsequent broods. (Some 3 percent of all bird species, including American crows and eastern bluebirds, are cooperative breeders.) After nesting, moorhens undergo a complete molt, and yearling birds gain their first fully adult plumage. Moorhens are most readily seen in late summer after nesting—they become less shy and, with juveniles added, more of them exist.

Fall, Winter. Moorhens migrate southward in September and early October. Many travel to Gulf and Atlantic coastal marshes (from North Carolina south), joining year-round resident moorhens, and to Mexico and Central and South America. Local populations also winter in California, Arizona, and Texas.

Ecology. Moorhens favor deep-water marshes with tall, dense vegetation (often cattails) interspersed with open-water pools 1 to 3 feet deep. The birds utilize both large and small marshes plus marshy pond edges and other wetland borders. Grassy banks for foraging also

Moorhens often forage on banks alongside ponds or marshes; red bills and forehead shields make both sexes colorful.

attract moorhens. The moorhen's "taste in habitat," suggests writer Gail A. McPeek, "lies between that of rails and coots, with moorhens spending less time in the reeds compared to rails and less time in open water relative to coots."

Moorhen nests, usually built 4 to 6 inches over water in dense marsh vegetation, are wedged or anchored to plant stems, often sited near open water. In some areas, beds of pickerel-weed are favored nest locales. Dead cattail leaves, rushes, and other plant materials form a shallow-cupped platform about 15 inches in outside diameter, the cup lined with grass and sometimes canopied with surrounding vegetation. The extra platforms built by males lack the nest cup. A sloping ramp of plant materials usually descends from the nest rim (which may be built up higher when flooding occurs) to the water. Moorhen nests strongly resemble those of American coots but are usually slightly smaller. Moorhens occasionally nest in low shrubs or on the ground near water.

Primarily feeders on aquatic vegetation, moorhens consume seeds, grasses, rootlets, and other parts of plants. Duckweed probably is a foremost food item. The birds also eat berries and other fruits as well as aquatic insects, snails, and worms.

Competition with American coots for nesting sites may occur in some locales; both species' habitat needs are similar, though differences in timing of nest construction may preclude most hostile interactions.

Moorhen nest predators are generally the same as for wading rails (see Virginia Rail). Common predators of moorhen eggs include snakes and American crows. Survival of a

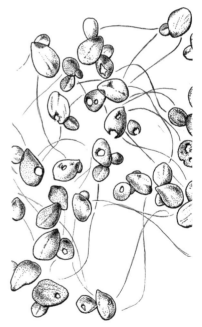

Tiny duckweeds, common food of many waterbirds, including moorhens, grow on the surface of quiet waters almost everywhere.

full moorhen brood to fledging is probably a rare occurrence. Wetland losses have resulted in significant declines of common moorhens in many areas.

Focus. This bird has undergone two name changes in the past few decades. It was once known as the Florida gallinule, then became the common gallinule. British ornithologists had long called it the moorhen, however, and in a bold move to compound confusion (especially since we have no moors labeled as such in North America, and since a gender-specific label for a species hardly exemplifies a scientific ideal), the American Ornithologists' Union officially endorsed the Old World name. Owing to earlier confusion of nomenclature—nineteenth-century and some later observers called both moorhens and coots "mudhens," a vernacular name still heard—moorhen historical distribution in North America remains obscure. Since records became more reliable, moorhen abundance has generally declined—to the point where several northern and midwestern states have named it a threatened or special concern species. The largest moorhen populations today reside in protected marshes of state and federal wildlife refuges. This bird, though once hunted to some extent, was "never considered much of a gamebird," according to ornithologist Arthur C. Bent.

Moorhens have survived in the wild to age six, and probably much longer, since longevity of the closely related coots sometimes surpasses 20 years. Partly because the moorhen is much less common in our marshes than it once was, seeing this colorful waterbird always marks a high point of a marsh outing.

RAIL FAMILY (Rallidae)

American Coot *(Fulica americana)*
With slate black plumage, a short, chalk white bill, and stout, greenish legs with lobed toes, the ducklike coot measures about 15 inches long. A white patch beneath the tail, red eyes, and a reddish forehead shield *(callus)* that extends up from the bill are also prominent features. The coot's galaxy of sounds includes series of harsh "kuk-kuk-kuk" and "ka-ka- ka" notes plus assorted cackles,

croaks, grunts, and babbles—sounds not easily distinguished from those of its relative the common moorhen.

Close relatives. Eleven *Fulica* species exist worldwide. Two species similar to the American coot are the common coot *(F. atra)* and the crested coot *(F. cristata),* both Eurasian birds.

Behaviors. This most numerous and gregarious North American member of the rail family is easily observed at most times of year. Its tendency to flock and associate with waterfowl, along with its highly aggressive territorial behaviors, distinguish the coot from most of its kin. Also distinctive are its lobed toes, adaptations for swimming, weight distribution, and cooling of body temperature in hot climates. Coots pump their heads while both swimming and walking—"like aquatic pigeons," as one observer noted. On land, their posture appears hunched, somewhat like guineafowl. In water, they tip up to feed like mallards and dive like canvasbacks, as deep as 25 feet. An awkward, graceless flier, the coot patters and splatters across the water, beating its wings and creating a great splashing hubbub before becoming airborne. Once up, it usually flies low, no more than 10 or 15 feet above the water, its big feet trailing behind its stubby tail.

In areas where coots remain on their breeding range in winter—generally from the Ohio River southward in the eastern United States— they often defend core areas of their territories year-round. Despite their social habits, pairs do not tolerate territorial invasion; males, especially, fight as if for keeps. The male coot's technique, seen even in 4-day-old chicks, is to sit back on its tail, clutching the invader with one clawed foot while kicking it with the other, also jabbing with its bill. "Apparently the aim is to push the opponent onto its back," wrote one observer team, "and in

Lobed toes aid coots in swimming and in walking on unstable surfaces such as mud or floating plants.

some cases, hold it underwater." Threat displays directed toward almost any intruder, including human, also consist of swelling their forehead shields and erecting their feathers, increasing the bird's apparent size by half.

American coots have an extensive breeding range, spanning most of North America eastward from Alaska, thence to Greenland, and south to Costa Rica, the West Indies, and northern South America. The foremost nesting range, however, lies in Canada's prairie provinces and the northern Great Plains, prime center of most waterbird breeding in North America. Coots migrate from their northern range, but some often winter as far north as open water permits.

Spring. Coots become most abundantly visible during migration seasons, when they swim together in often large flocks. They arrive on their northern range from March through early May, usually hard on the heels of icemelt. Early-arriving coots sometimes die of starvation if open waters refreeze.

Courtship displays include noisy, flapping, male-female chases on the water and elevating and spreading of tails, showing the white patches. A very subtle display is inflation of the white forehead shield. The territory, averaging about an acre or less in size, is mainly defended by the male but also, in his absence, by the female. The bird rushes at an intruder across the water with loud splattering, readily engaging in combat if the trespasser doesn't flee. Some researchers believe that the coot's aggressive territorialism serves more to maintain the pair bond than to protect a given space. Others postulate protection of the brooding sites for chicks. Nesting is often delayed until marsh vegetation has reached a sufficient height to provide concealment (usually June and early July in the northern range). Both sexes build the nest. The male often constructs up to 9 other nestlike platforms, used for resting, copulating, and brooding chicks.

Locomotory behavior—swimming about the territory—also serves to advertise the territory, in which all feeding occurs. Territorial behaviors reach a peak when the brood hatches. Coots often attack grebes, mallards, and ruddy ducks that stray into their territories.

EGGS AND YOUNG: 8 to 12 (more than 12 usually indicates brood parasitism by an invading female); eggs buff colored, densely brown spotted. INCUBATION: by both sexes (male often at night); about 23 days. FEEDING OF YOUNG: by both sexes; aquatic insects, other invertebrates, small fish, tadpoles. FLEDGING: about 50 days or more.

Summer. Many coots are still nesting as summer begins, and the entire season is largely given to brooding and feeding chicks. Coots often nest twice in their southern range, sometimes with overlapping clutches, but only once in the northern range. Nest loss due to predation usually leads to renesting, up to 4 times if losses continue. The chicks, with orange-red heads and bright red bills ("a black ball of down with a fiery head," as an observer described one), soon gain their first juvenile plumage. Until the following summer, they remain paler gray versions of their parents, with dull white bills. Coots undergo a complete plumage molt in August and September. As territorialism lapses in the northern range, coot families begin flocking together; juveniles often unite and form separate flocks.

Fall, Winter. Large rafts of coots, numbering from hundreds to thousands of birds, gather in late summer, often mingling with migrant ducks in large lakes, sewage lagoons, marshes, and river mouths. Fall coot migration is usually a gradual, drawn-out process, with many flocks and individual birds remaining in the northern range far into the season—even into winter where open water permits. Probably most eastern coots that migrate simply shift southward in the fall and do not leave the continent, though the extensive winter range, reaching into South America, hosts large influxes of coots. At least some of the migrators return to previous wintering locales. The birds remain in large flocks through winter in coastal and inland marshes and lakes.

Ecology. The coot resides in freshwater habitats—marshes, ponds, lakes, and rivers—though it also frequents marine bays and estuaries during migrations. For breeding habitat, coots favor deep, open waters surrounded by bog or marsh vegetation.

Coot nests, built in dense marsh vegetation, sometimes exhibit dump nesting by more than one female.

Typical nests lie low in the marsh, often floating atop 1 to 4 feet of water, firmly attached to surrounding cattails or rushes. The cupped platform, about 18 inches or less across, consists of dry marsh vegetation— bulrushes, cattails, grasses. Sometimes coots use muskrat lodges for resting and brooding sites; where such structures exist, coot males may not construct additional platforms in the territory.

Mainly vegetarian, coots consume a large variety of aquatic plants and plant parts, favoring submerged growth. Some 60 percent of the diet consists of algae (including stoneworts) and pondweeds. Duckweeds, naiads, coontail, and wild celery also rank high as foods, as do seeds of wild rice, bulrushes, and others. In some southern reservoir systems, coots provide a useful control on the submerged plant *Hydrilla,* a nuisance species. Coot flocks also sometimes graze on upland grasses or sprouting grain. In summer, the diet becomes about 30 percent animal matter, including aquatic insects, spiders, crustaceans, worms, snails, tadpoles, small fish, and eggs of other marsh-nesting birds.

Coots probably offer more feeding competition (mainly to waterfowl) than they receive. A frequent coot habit is to pirate plant items retrieved by swans or ducks, often seizing the material from the bird's bill. Small groups of juvenile coots sometimes gang up on surfacing divers, quickly relieving them of their greens.

Frequent victims of this harassment include tundra swans, mallards, northern pintails, canvasbacks, and redheads. A few surface-feeding ducks, however—mainly American wigeons and gadwalls—often turn the tables on the pirates, grabbing food from coots as they surface after a dive; interestingly, in such cases, the normally aggressive coots rarely resist the thieves. Coots are also known to victimize the nests of such marsh-nesting birds as pied-billed grebes and red-winged blackbirds. Although some hunters shoot coots on the arrogant notion of helping "fix nature" by eliminating perceived duck competitors, little evidence exists that American coots compete to any important degree with ducks.

Sometimes coots lay eggs in nests of other coots, but coots rarely become victims of brood parasitism from redheads and ruddy ducks, two waterfowl that frequently parasitize nests of other waterbirds. Coots "have somehow evolved a way to circumvent brood parasitism that requires neither the vigilance nor concerted effort seen in many other species," summarizes one report. As many as two-thirds of coot nests may be lost to predators in some areas. American crows, magpies, and minks are common predators, along with those that typically raid nests of rails and other marsh birds (see Virginia Rail). Bald eagles commonly harass coots, often trying to separate an individual bird from the flock, then attacking it.

Focus. No two coots show exactly the same shape of reddish callus on the white forehead shield. Experiments have revealed that shield shape and size are the foremost features by which coot mates recognize

An American coot head profile shows the distinctive white bill and reddish forehead shield, which is slightly different in form for each bird.

each other (the shields also make life easier for researchers trying to keep track of individual birds). Also, the color of the *tarsus* (the straight part of the foot directly above the toes, appearing as the lower leg in most birds) is a useful age indicator during the breeding season: Yearling coots show green tarsi, 2-year-olds yellow-green, 3-year-olds yellow, and older birds yellow-orange to red-orange. These colors fade after the breeding season.

The name *coot* derives, it is said, from the Old English word *soot,* referring to the dark color of this bird (the irrelevant slang version, as in "bald old coot," may have originated from Australia as an abbreviation of bandicoot, a marsupial mammal). A common vernacular name for the coot is "mud hen"; the Toledo Mud Hens, a historic minor league baseball team, are said to have christened themselves after the coots that frequented marshy Bay View Park in 1896.

Though classified as gamebirds in many states, coots are not highly valued by most hunters. Large flocks can become pests on golf courses, where they sometimes graze, deposit droppings, and infuriate golfers. "Since coots appear neither comical, vulnerable, nor inspirational," wrote the authors of *The Birder's Handbook,* "the public is often unsympathetic to their problems. . . . But when coots disappear, they usually toll the bell for other species as well." Records show that coots, though still common in many areas of their breeding range, especially in state and federal refuge wetlands, are less common than they once were. Such declines usually indicate loss of crucial wetland habitats.

The longevity record for an American coot is 22 years. Probably few, however, survive to half that age.

5

Common Snipe *(Gallinago gallinago)*

Sandpiper family (Scolopacidae), order Ciconiiformes. Small (11-inch-long), brownish birds with outsize bills (almost 3 inches long, about one-fifth the bird's total length), snipes have buff-streaked backs and lengthwise-striped head crowns. Rising in a fast, zigzag pattern, often voicing a rasping call note when flushed, snipes have long, pointed wings and show a short, orange, barred tail in flight. The so-called song, whistled repetitions of "wheat" or "chip-a chip-a" notes, is mainly heard in spring. Its aerial territorial flights produce the snipe's most distinctive sounds (see Behaviors).

Close relatives. The sandpiper family, part of the group designated as shorebirds (though not all of them frequent shorelines), consists of almost 90 species worldwide, 33 of which reside in North America. Godwits, curlews, the whimbrel, the willet, and phalaropes—in addition to sandpipers—belong to this family, as do snipes. Other *Gallinago* species (of a total 16) include the great snipe *(G. media)* of Eurasia; the jack snipe *(Lymnocryptes minimus)* is also a north Eurasian species. The snipe is closely related to the long-billed and short-billed dowitchers *(Limnodromus scolopaceus, L. griseus)* and to the American woodcock *(Scolopax minor),* which it closely resembles.

Behaviors. From high over the bog or marsh in spring—sometimes more than 300 feet, so high that the small source of sound can hardly be seen—comes a pulsing tremolo chant, a slowly ascending series of "woo woo woo woo woo" notes that may carry for a mile. This is the flight sound (called *bleating,* or *winnowing*) of the male common snipe, performed over the bird's home range. It is produced not by voice but by feather vibration during fast aerial

143

Common snipe (top) and American woodcock (bottom) head profiles are strongly similar; note the rearward eye placement, enabling the birds to see behind as well as ahead.

dives at a 45-degree angle. The mechanics involve the two strong, pliable outer tail feathers (one on each side), which are spread laterally; their rapid, reverberant oscillations are induced by air speeds of 25 to 50 miles per hour. Male snipes can be distinguished from females at this season by the frayed condition of these feathers; dampened tail feathers are said to produce a greater volume of sound. Although spring is the best time to hear these sounds, snipes also winnow occasionally during migrations and on the winter range. Females also winnow, but only briefly and much less frequently. Another common spring call (called *yakking*) by both sexes is a rapid "jick-jack," usually voiced on the ground.

Snipe anatomy closely resembles that of its close relative the American woodcock, which frequents drier habitats (see *Birds of Forest, Yard, and Thicket*). Snipe eyes, like the woodcock's, are set far back in its head, giving the bird both front and rear vision. Its long, straight bill is likewise sensory and flexible. The snipe feeds by probing its bill deeply into mud or soft ground; it can feel unseen prey by the touch of that amazing sense organ. Spines at the base of its tongue plus backward serrations inside the upper mandible help move food up the long bill length into the gullet. Sometimes feeding snipes stamp their feet, possibly activating prey. Like raptors and many other birds, snipes eject pellets of indigestible food items, and they drink large amounts of water daily. Unlike the woodcock's short, rounded wings, snipe wings are long and pointed, more typical of shorebirds. Snipes can swim and dive, though they rarely resort to open water. Occasionally they perch in trees or on fences in the nest vicinity.

The common snipe resides on all continents except Australia and Antarctica. In North America, its breeding range is northern, extending across Canada and Alaska and south from the tundra to the northern third of the United States.

Spring. Early migrators that fly mainly at night, males precede females on the breeding range by at least 10 days in late March and early April, probably homing to the previous year's sites. Males immediately begin winnowing flights over the breeding area, most often at dawn and dusk but often throughout the day and during moonlit nights as well. Winnowing is a territorial and courtship display, directed both as a warning to other males and as a "turn-on" to a prospective or actual mate. Arriving females wander extensively, often mating promiscuously with any available male. Soon, however, they select a male territory for nesting and the mate that comes with it, switching to monogamy. The display *arena,* where pair formation and courtship displays on or near the ground occur, is not necessarily within the male territory; adjacent pastures or even paved roads may be used. Arenas chosen are always free of high vegetation or obstacles. Aerial displays include chases, acrobatics, and the arched-wing display, in which the male drifts in the air with elevated wings.

Territories range in size from about 20 to 50 acres per pair. Nesting occurs from late April to mid-June. Males winnow and aggressively defend their territories from other calling snipes only during courtship and incubation; after the chicks hatch, they cease territorial defense. Both sexes (especially males) resort to small, individual hideaway sites in the territory, usually areas 25 to 70 feet from the nest with dense sedge or shrub cover; there the birds loiter and shelter when not feeding or when the female is off the nest.

EGGS AND YOUNG: usually 4; eggs light buff or dark brown, heavily brown spotted, especially at larger end. INCUBATION: by female, 18 to 20 days; hatching asynchronous over 1 to 6 hours; chicks precocial. FEEDING OF YOUNG: by both sexes; chicks take food from parent bill during first week, feed themselves thereafter; mainly insects, worms, other invertebrates. FLEDGING: about 15 days.

Summer. Parent snipes divide their brood, feeding and guiding the two groups separately. Snipes raise only a single brood per year. Late nesters in July and August are probably yearling birds nesting for the first time. The annual feather molt begins soon after—or sometimes before—the chicks become independent (about 6 weeks of age) and may last until October. Adult birds tend to become solitary and secretive when they molt. Small groups *(wisps)* of juveniles form, gradually aggregating into flocks of 100 or more by mid-August. Premigratory restlessness builds as flocks of 40 or more birds wander from marsh to marsh, feeding and fattening, deserting localities, then returning days later.

Fall, Winter. In late summer, snipes become gregarious; they begin congregating in wetlands and pond edges in September. Numbers peak in late September and October. Probably all the juveniles migrate in flocks that precede the adult migration, and adult females apparently migrate ahead of adult males. During migration, which lasts through November, compact wisps fly high at night, maintaining contact with low, raucous call notes.

Adult snipes apparently home to traditional wintering areas, which span the central United States south through Central America to Colombia and Venezuela. Most northeastern snipes winter in Gulf and Venezuelan coastal marshes and rice fields. In coastal Louisiana, the snipe is said to rank second in abundance during winter only to the red-winged blackbird. A few snipes linger in the breeding range—I once flushed a snipe during a Christmas bird count in Michigan. One researcher speculates that north-wintering snipes may be older birds. In wintering snipe flocks, the frequency of display behaviors increases as spring approaches.

Ecology. In contrast to rails and some other marsh dwellers, snipes favor relatively open wetlands with low herb vegetation and low, sparse shrubs. Common habitats include grass and sedge fens, leatherleaf bogs with areas of open water or mudflats, and marshy zones in ponds and along streams. The birds tend to avoid tall, dense stands of vegetation, such as cattails and reeds, and thick, brushy swamp growth. Tussock-forming sedges, bluejoint grass, and sweet gale shrubs are dominant plants in many snipe nesting locales. One researcher identified snipe breeding range as closely matching the distribution of eastern tamarack trees.

Common snipe habitats include marshy pond edges and sedge fens with relatively low plant growth.

For nesting, snipes often select a small tussock of sedge or grass or a mound of sphagnum moss. The site, though often adjacent to or surrounded by water, is usually a fairly dry elevation. The female scrapes 4 or 5 depressions in the ground, crouching and turning, molding a cup shape with her body. She finally selects one of the scrapes for the nest, adding grasses or sedges to the slight cup. Nests are sometimes canopied by surrounding vegetation arched over them. Vacated snipe nests can often be recognized by bits of eggshell and egg lining that remain; most other birds remove these items.

Snipe diet is primarily animal matter (about 50 percent or more insects)—larvae (especially crane flies, midges, mosquitoes, and aquatic beetles), crickets, caterpillars, small crustaceans, snails, earthworms, leeches, spiders, and frogs, among others. The birds also consume small amounts of grass, sedge, smartweed, bulrush, and other seeds (about 20 percent of the total diet).

If we exclude humans, with their compulsion to reclaim wetlands, the snipe's competitors are relatively few and insignificant.

Snipe nest predation appears relatively minimal. Flooding after heavy rainfall is likely the biggest hazard to nests. Several hawks prey on snipes; probably foremost is the northern harrier.

Focus. "Jacksnipe" is a common vernacular name for this bird (the actual jack snipe is a smaller, related Eurasian species). Birders once knew it as Wilson's snipe, named after renowned pioneer ornithologist Alexander Wilson. The word *snipe* derives from Germanic forms meaning "snipper" or "snapper," alluding to the bill.

The oldest snipe on record survived at least 12 years; lifespans of 5 or 6 years are fairly common, though the average longevity for a yearling snipe is only about 2 years. Annual adult mortality is about 50 percent.

Historically, snipes were one of the most intensively hunted and harvested—if not *the* single most popular target—of all birds. Nineteenth-century market hunters slaughtered them by the thousands. This popularity reflected their great abundance on the American continent. Although snipe populations have never recovered their former abundance, except in some local areas, the species survived without widespread precipitous declines, probably because of their secretive habits and tendency not to assemble in large flocks. A complete moratorium on snipe hunting existed in the United States from 1941 to 1953. Today the bird is again legal game in many states, but the annual hunter kill probably takes less than 2 percent of the population. The snipe's biggest problem these days is the same one that threatens so many waterbirds—periods of drought and the ongoing loss and contamination of wetland habitats.

"To forecast rain by the intense bleating of snipe, the rain bird, is not very difficult," wrote one prominent snipe researcher. "Erratic bleating at low levels during the day nearly always precedes rain on the morrow." Several Indian tribes attached mythic significance to *patsro* (the Hopi name for "water bird") as a weather or storm maker, often involving some aspect of its long bill. "When the snipe bawls, the lobster crawls," is a maxim of Newfoundland fishermen awaiting inshore arrival of the crustaceans. "Alewife bird" and "shad spirit" also reflect this bird's common vernacular association with fisheries.

Henry Thoreau apparently coined the term *winnowing* ("like a winnowing-machine") for the snipe's pulsing flight sound. The sound fans "the air like a spirit over some far meadow's bay," he wrote.

6

HAWK FAMILY (Accipitridae), order Ciconiiformes

Hawks are hunter-predators, their diet consisting exclusively of meat and animal matter. They number more than 200 species worldwide; 15 are eastern North American residents. Family members include the kites, bird hawks (accipiters), harriers, buzzard hawks (buteos), and eagles. Together with owls, ospreys, and falcons, these birds are collectively called *raptors,* so named from their taloned, *raptorial* feet, adapted to seize prey. The foot is a locking mechanism. In most species, its grasp cannot be released by will. The weight of the prey keeps the talons locked; only pushing against a solid surface can release the tension and cause the bird to let go. If the raptor seizes an animal too heavy for it to carry, it may become the prisoner of its prey until it can shove its load against something solid.

The hawk's eye, its supreme hunting organ, is two or three times more acute than human 20/20 vision. Each eye functions like a telescope, with a long focal length between lens and retina, whose receptors produce a sharp, fine-grained image. Vision is both monocular and binocular, the latter covering about 50 degrees of the visual field. Raptor eyes occupy as much head space as the brain.

Most hawks soar in flight. In most species, females are larger than males. Regurgitated hawk pellets, up to 2 inches long, are spongy soft with corroded bone fragments buried in the mass.

Hatching is asynchronous, and chicks are altricial.

Osprey *(Pandion haliaetus)*

Recognize this kingly bird by its size (almost 2 feet long), its white head with dark eye stripe, bright yellow eyes, dark brown back and upper wings, and white underparts. In flight, ospreys exhibit a crook in the lanky wing, giving the 5-foot wingspread a distinctive M shape; black carpal patches at the wing bend and deeply slotted flight feathers at the wing end are also distinctive. Females, slightly larger than males, often show a slight "necklace" of streaking on the upper breast. Ospreys voice a series of high, yipping alarm notes around the nest.

Close relatives. This is the only *Pandion* species, and no close relatives exist.

Behaviors. "An osprey is a hawk that looks like a gull but is not," according to a school of thought. Although it is probably the easiest raptor to identify in flight, an osprey at a distance might be confused with a bald eagle or large gull. But the distinctively bent wing profile, unlike an eagle's, and the broader wings with slotted ends, unlike the narrow, sharp-pointed wings of gulls, provide useful clues. "A distant osprey seems to be all wing and tail," as a veteran hawk watcher observed.

The "fish hawk," as it is also known, is our largest hawk next to eagles and our only raptor that dives into the water. When hunting, the osprey soars about 60 to 100 feet above the shallows, often circling, retracing, or stalling in a series of "double-takes." When it spots a fish, it hovers with tail spread and wings fanning like a huge butterfly, maneuvering for position. Then it pulls back its wings

Its distinctive plumage and flight patterns make the osprey, North America's only water-diving raptor, fairly easy to identify.

and free-falls headfirst. Angle of the dive ranges from about 45 degrees to almost vertical. Just before hitting the water, it throws out its talons, head bent over them "as if sighting over its toes," wrote an observer. If the bird does not abort its plunge, which often happens, it hits the water with a splash, talons wide open. It often completely submerges and can capture a fish as deep as 3 feet. Then it laboriously flaps to gain altitude, shaking off water "like a wet dog," as one observer remarked.

The osprey's average capture rate is about 40 percent—much higher in some studies—well exceeding the success ratio of most raptors. This ability probably owes much to the uniquely agile talon. The osprey's 4 toes, equal in length, form a cross or "net of talons" when outstretched. Long claws on the toes arc sharply downward and are rounded instead of grooved as in other raptors; the reversible, double-jointed outer toe, as in owls, enables a pincerlike grasp from front and rear. The undertoe pads are sharp and scaly, enabling a tight hold on slippery prey. Yet unlike other raptors, the osprey can shift its prey once grasped; the ungrooved claw may aid this maneuver. Ospreys habitually carry smaller prey with only one foot. The bird always shifts its fish prey headfirst beneath its body, reducing wind resistance as it carries the prey. Sometimes it manages this adjustment in the water before rising aloft, sometimes in midair. A large, firmly snagged fish, however, can drag an osprey underwater, and the bird may drown; thus the foot procedure obviously requires some time and effort to accomplish.

Strong and graceful in flight, ospreys fly with slow, stiff wingbeats. During migrations, however, they mainly depend upon updrafts and thermals, rising columns of air, skillfully soaring and gliding between

The osprey's talon shows unique adaptations—including its rasplike undertoe pads—as a fish-snagging instrument.

them. When perched, ospreys exhibit a characteristic hunched posture.

One of the most widely distributed birds in the world, ospreys occupy every continent except Antarctica in either summer or winter. In North America, their breeding range spans the continent from Alaska eastward in the Canadian boreal forest and northern Great Lakes area. North American ospreys are most abundant—and always have been—in Atlantic coastal areas of the Northeast and Florida. Except for year-round resident ospreys in Florida, all adult North American ospreys migrate.

Spring. Subadult ospreys remain on the winter range for their first year. Two-year-olds usually migrate northward in spring with adults but do not begin breeding until their third year. They may, however, intrude on the nesting of their parents until driven away. About 6 percent of the osprey population in the spring range consists of these nonbreeding 2-year-olds. Sometimes they pair and build nests but do not lay eggs—"just keep house," said one observer.

Male adults precede females by a few days in early April at the breeding site, usually a nest from the previous year or years. Since the birds mate for life but apparently do not associate during winter, their mutual site fidelity to the breeding territory reaffirms the pair bond. Male courtship behaviors maintain and reinforce the bond: the "sky dance," consisting of roller-coaster flights several hundred feet over the nest site, marked by high-pitched squeals and brief hovering at the apex of each upward swoop; hover flights at varying heights; and male feeding of the female in response to her begging behavior. Once on the territory and until the young are fledged, males provide all of the food to their mates and chicks. Second-year ospreys often pair for the first time now and may even begin building a nest, to which they will return the next year to breed. Unpaired or widowed females initiate pairing by selecting a nest site and uttering rapid chirping calls. Any nearby male osprey that responds by bringing a fish usually becomes the chosen permanent mate.

Osprey territory extends only around the immediate nest area, but the birds may hunt food miles away from the nest. Sometimes migrating ospreys are seen "packing a lunch"—that is, carrying a fish, often miles distant from water.

EGGS AND YOUNG: usually 3; eggs whitish or pinkish with reddish brown blotches. INCUBATION: mainly by female except when male brings food and relieves female on nest while she feeds on a nearby perch; 35 to 40 days; downy nestlings are black, reptilian-looking for first 2 weeks. FEEDING OF YOUNG: by female; tears apart fish brought by male into small bits; also feeds regurgitant early in nestling period. FLEDGING: 8 to 10 weeks.

Summer. Males spend many hours of each day hunting, while females rarely leave the nest for 3 or 4 weeks after eggs hatch, brooding and feeding the chicks. Asynchronous hatching often leads to sibling rivalries that may affect nestling survival. The larger oldest nestling may attack its siblings, especially if food is scarce (a brood of 3 requires about 6 pounds of fish daily), sometimes even pushing a younger one out of the nest. Parent ospreys take little notice of such conflicts. The chicks become increasingly active as they age, flapping their wings, jumping, and flopping. Females now move off the nest to a nearby perch, and also resume hunting for brief periods. Fish are no longer fed but simply deposited in the nest, where the chicks feed themselves.

Most osprey young fledge in July. In osprey colonies, fledglings may sail over to other osprey nests, and some interchange of young can occur. Parents at these nests often feed the young intruders, probably not distinguishing them as such. Fledglings roost at the nest (usually their own) each night, remaining in the nest vicinity until, a week or so later, they begin making longer flights. Soon they are diving and catching fish for themselves. Anecdotal accounts suggest that some parent ospreys may teach their young by dropping fish for them to catch, but young ospreys do not require such training. They may linger in the nest vicinity until late August or so, then depart along with the adults. Until about 18 months old, immature ospreys are lighter brown on the back and wings with a scaly appearance due to whitish feather edges. Osprey molting seems more or less continuous except during migrations. The birds gradually drop and replace tail and flight feathers in summer.

Fall. Ospreys migrate singly. "Tracked from a satellite and speeded up in time," wrote osprey researcher Alan F. Poole, "this movement might appear as a broad, braided, south-flowing river." Most migration occurs in September and October; juveniles are usually the last to leave. The birds tend to fly over land in daytime, over large expanses of water at night. Most return to the same wintering areas each year. Atlantic coast ospreys move south to Florida's east coast (joining resident ospreys), the West Indies, and northern South America. Great Lakes ospreys travel to Florida's Gulf coast and through Central America to Colombia and Brazil.

Winter. Ospreys seem much more gregarious on their winter range, often roosting or hunting in small groups. Wintering ospreys apparently hunt more often from perches than at other seasons, perhaps because they have only themselves to feed and can afford to be more leisurely in pursuit of food. Most molting of adult body feathers occurs on the winter range. Spring migration begins in early March for all but yearling ospreys, which remain on the winter range.

Ecology. Ospreys require expanses of clear, open, preferably shallow waters for feeding, whether along the seacoast or inland lakes and rivers. For nesting habitat, the birds are widely adaptable but favor forested or swampy areas near open water. Many ospreys choose inland sites for nesting. The availability of stable, predator-free nest sites seems to be the chief factor controlling breeding densities. Coastal bays, tidal flats, and estuaries are the osprey's chief wintering habitats.

If you see a large, flattish nest capping a dead or topped-off tree, chances are good that you're viewing an osprey domicile. Nests are perennial and are incremental in size, often

A flattish, platformlike nest atop a tall tree in isolated country is most likely an osprey nest.

becoming bulky as the birds add material and repair them annually for as long as they return or the tree stands (usually a decade or longer; the weight of an ever-enlarging nest can finally collapse the tree). Nests average about 5 feet in diameter, 2 to 7 feet in height. The birds collect sticks and branches (averaging about 2 feet long) from dead trees, often breaking them off by landing on them, then carry them to the nest site in their talons. Ospreys are noted for the variety of nesting materials they scavenge; carcasses of birds and mammals, fur, bones, cow dung, seaweed, fishline, and other debris are commonly recycled by the birds. "There is a bit of the pack rat to every Osprey," observed Poole. Females line the inner cup (2 or 3 feet in diameter) with finer materials—inner bark, mosses, sod, grasses, and small twigs. Though the birds favor tall, dead trees (often pines, spruces, or tamaracks) in remote locales near water, ospreys in some areas have adapted to human presence and occupy suburban habitats—light poles near parking lots, busy harbors, transmission towers, channel markers and buoys, even outhouses and duck blinds. They also build at varying elevations (often at ground level on island sites) and not always close to water. Osprey nesting platforms placed on poles in appropriate habitats are widely used by the birds, often in preference to natural nest sites. Usually such placements do not recruit ospreys out of the blue, however; initial occupancy apparently depends upon dispersion from nearby nests. In some places, osprey nesting is loosely colonial, with nests often several thousand

Channel markers are common sites for osprey nests in some coastal areas.

feet apart. Reported nesting associates—smaller birds that find convenient sites for their own nesting in the large osprey structure—include European starlings, house wrens, common grackles, and, in urban nest sites, house sparrows.

Osprey diet consists almost exclusively of fish. The birds favor shallow-water or surface-running species. Suckers, bullheads, catfish, carp, perch, sunfish, and eels are common freshwater prey. Herring, menhaden, mullet, shad, and winter flounders are frequently taken in estuary habitats. Ospreys are opportunists, however, taking whatever fish are most available at the time and place. Occasionally ospreys also consume small birds, rodents, snakes, turtles, frogs, crustaceans, and carrion. Ospreys can, with difficulty, capture and carry a 4-pound fish (about a third of their own weight), but most fish prey averages 14 to 22 ounces and 10 to 14 inches long.

The food competitor most often cited is the bald eagle. Not a diver itself, the larger eagle may pirate a fish capture from an osprey by attacking, causing the osprey to drop its catch, which the eagle retrieves. Such piracy is relatively infrequent; most ospreys and eagles coexist with few encounters between them. Frigatebirds sometimes pirate from ospreys in like manner on the winter range. Canada geese may temporarily adopt osprey nests for their own nesting; usually this occurs before the ospreys return in spring, and the raptors quickly drive them out. But probably the most significant competition occurs between osprey chicks. Of the typical brood of 3, the first and oldest is most likely to survive because of its larger size and greater strength relative to the others. Many researchers regard the last-hatched chick of the brood as essentially a "throwaway" bird, an evolutionary spare in case an older chick is lost. In a full brood, many of these youngest chicks do not survive to fledge, mainly because of food competition within the nest. At fish pond and hatchery sites ("natural magnets for hungry ospreys," said one researcher), ospreys can sometimes compete with human interests, and the birds are often illegally shot in such situations.

Predation on osprey eggs and chicks occurs mostly at night. Great horned owls are significant predators of nestlings and incubating females, especially in the Chesapeake Bay and certain New England areas. Despite the ospreys' vigorous defense, larger heron species, American and fish crows, and raccoons also raid the nests at times. Many researchers believe that the osprey's nest-site preference for tall trees in wetland habitats is a form of defense against predation, especially from mammals. Ospreys that nest in lower, more accessible locales often become victims of fox, skunk, and domestic dog and cat predation.

Focus. The word *osprey* derives from a Latin word meaning "bone breaker," originally applied to the lammergeier, or bearded vulture, of remote Eurasian mountain ranges. As with so many bird names, this one apparently "resulted from a series of mistakes," as *Words for Birds* (1972) author Edward S. Gruson wrote.

During North America's grievously effective attacks on its wildlife (especially raptors) via DDT pesticides (1950s–1970s), osprey populations dramatically declined. This environmental debacle further hastened an already advanced decline caused by human encroachment on estuary and coastal nesting habitats and by random shooting of migratory ospreys by people schooled to regard all raptors as vermin. The toxin (actually DDE, a breakdown product of DDT), acquired by the birds from their fish diet, interfered with calcium metabolism, causing females to produce thin-shelled eggs that broke during incubation. Ospreys became increasingly rare in areas they had formerly occupied; they were well on their way toward total extinction on their northern range before the poison was finally banned in 1972. Since then, osprey populations have shown encouraging recovery rates in many places, often abetted by human placement of nesting platforms.

Ospreys are slow to disperse and colonize new areas on their own, and osprey *hacking*—the introduction of chicks into areas where ospreys once bred—has proven highly promising in many locales. Six-week-old chicks taken from thriving colonies are transported to the new sites, fed (sometimes for an extended period after fledging), and released as fledglings. Hacking is often successful because young ospreys tend to imprint on their fledging rather than nesting sites and return as migrants to the places of release. The species remains in officially threatened status on much of its northern range, however.

Osprey plumage is dense and oily, with a distinctive odor; even the eggshells and museum specimens stored for decades smell rank, and a stray osprey feather found in a swamp is instantly identifiable by its aroma. Ospreys lack the fierce, glowering aspect of eagles and many other birds of prey because they have no pronounced supraorbital ridge, the bony protrusion above the eye. A distinctive feature of osprey head markings, useful for observers and researchers, simplifies the identification of individual birds: The crown of the head always bears subtle patterns of dark spotting; number, size, and shape of the spots vary with each bird, changing only slightly as the osprey ages.

Osprey survival rates, despite chick competition, rank high for raptors and birds generally. Researchers estimate that up to 50 percent of fledglings survive to breeding age and that 85 percent of adult ospreys survive to the following year. Longevity of most adults is 10 to 13 years, but many live for 20 years or longer. Annual mortality ranges from 10 to 17 percent.

HAWK FAMILY (Accipitridae)

Bald Eagle *(Haliaeetus leucocephalus)*

The bald eagle, our largest raptor, measures 3 feet or more long and has a wingspread of 7 or 8 feet. Adults, with their white heads and tails and dark brown wings and bodies, are easily identified. Heavy yellow bills as long as the head plus yellow feet also distinguish them. Females are larger than males, and immature bald eagles (that is, birds less than 4 years old) are larger than adults, owing to longer wing and tail feathers. Immatures look predominantly brown, with whitish linings on the underwing and often whitish breasts. The amount of white on an immature's plumage is age related—the more white, the older the bird. The bald eagle's high-pitched, squealing chirps, often described as "creaking cackles" or "chalk scratching a slate," somewhat resemble gull notes but are quite distinctive.

Close relatives. The bald eagle is one of a subgroup called sea eagles. Seven other *Haliaeetus* species reside mainly in Eurasia and Africa, among them the white-tailed eagle *(H. albicilla)* and the African fish eagle *(H. vocifer).* The only other North American eagle is the golden eagle *(Aquila chrysaetos),* primarily a western species belonging to the booted eagle subgroup and much different from the bald in ecological and behavioral characters. Goldens and immature balds bear some physical resemblance, however; viewed from a distance, they can be confused where their ranges overlap.

Behaviors. In flight, soaring on broad, flat, planklike wings, the bald eagle's profile is distinctive. When not riding high on *thermals* (updrafts of land-warmed air), bald eagles spend much of their lives perched conspicuously, often in the topmost branches of tall trees ("look for white golf balls [their heads] in the spruce," advise the rangers at Maine's Acadia National Park). Sometimes immobile for hours at a time on habitual perches, which usually overlook water, they survey the environs, still-hunting for prey with precision vision or guarding their territory with nest in view.

Mainly fish eaters (but more opportunistic than ospreys in choice of prey), bald eagles are scoopers rather than hover-divers. They drop from a perch, plane low across the water, and pluck fish with their talons from near the surface. Immatures tend to wander and search for food, perching less than adults; they often feed on carrion, whereas adults more frequently perch-hunt for live prey in a breeding or winter territory. Keenly aware of other hunters and predators in their vicinity, bald eagles closely watch gulls, ravens, and crows for clues to feeding locales. Sometimes they soar above flying turkey vultures, taking advantage of the latter's ability to smell out dead fish or a rotting carcass. Eagles also pirate fish, mainly from ospreys, immature eagles, and crows. In territorial conflicts, an eagle often rolls over on its back in flight, grappling talons with those of its opponent.

Yet "in spite of appearances to the contrary," wrote eagle expert Priscilla Tucker, "the Bald Eagle is *not* a strong flier." Flapping flight is labored and relatively infrequent. Instead, as Tucker notes, the eagle is "born to soar." Its three typical flight patterns are ascending in thermals, then gliding down to find another thermal; circling downwind on a so-called "street of thermals," a straight succession of rising air masses; and riding updrafts of wind from cliff faces or land ridges. Landing or launching, eagles invariably face into the wind. Thoreau reckoned that "I have got the worth of my glass now that it has revealed to me the white-headed eagle." He marveled at how the bird became "effectively concealed in the sky."

The bald eagle's fierce "scowl" derives from its *supraorbital ridge,* the bony projection over the eyes that may provide shade from glare or help protect the eyes from wind and dust. Taloned feet, resembling the osprey's but even larger, are raspy-rough on the bottom with sharp projections on the toe pads. The massive bill tears open a fish with ease.

Bald eagle breeding range spans the continent from Alaska and Newfoundland south to Baja California and Florida. Its distribution is uneven, however, localized around the seacoasts and interior lakes and rivers. Only eagles in the farthest northern and southern ranges are truly migratory, though resident eagles in between may wander considerable distances in winter seeking food.

Spring. Bald eagle populations on the breeding range consist of breeding adults (about 50 percent), nonbreeding adults, and nonbreeding immatures. Timing of bald eagle breeding depends much on latitude. In southern regions of the United States, nesting occurs from September in the West to December in the East. In the Northeast (the focus of this account), many eagles are spring migratory, arriving from mid-March to mid-April. The birds apparently travel separately in two stages—adults first, then immatures—flying in daylight and often over ranges of hills and other areas of high relief where updrafts facilitate their movement. They may travel for several days without feeding, usually stopping en route only when weather prevents their progress; daily distance averages more than 100 miles. Males usually arrive several days ahead of females, immatures later than adults. With rare exceptions, adult eagles appear monogamous for life. They spend most of the year together and return in spring to the same nest site vacated the previous year. First-time breeders (usually 5- or 6-year olds) must find suitable habitats and construct new nests. Initial pairing may occur on the winter range or just after spring arrival.

Bald eagle territory consists of the nest vicinity and an adjacent elongated area covering a varying expanse of shoreline or river course. In prime undisturbed habitat, nests may vary from less than a mile to 10 or more miles apart. Home ranges, the undefended areas of pair activity, may overlap. Courtship behaviors in bald eagles are not well defined. High-altitude soaring, cartwheeling, roller-coaster flight, chasing, and diving occur most often in spring, but the pair-bonding function of these actions can only be surmised. A pair often perches together, and mates bill and preen each other—but unlike many raptor species, mate feeding seldom if ever occurs (though females often pirate food from males at the nest); each parent hunts for itself and for nestlings. Northeastern eagles lay eggs in late April or early May, and most hatching occurs in late spring.

EGGS AND YOUNG: usually 2; eggs bluish white, often nest stained, laid 1 or 2 days apart. INCUBATION: by both sexes; about 35 days. FEEDING OF YOUNG: by both sexes; mainly fish, occasionally ducks, torn into small pieces by parent; about 1 fish every 2 to 4 hours, 4 to 8 times per day. FLEDGING: about 80 days, male eaglets a few days before females.

Summer. Eaglets remain downy and quite helpless for their first 5 to 6 weeks. Then they begin growing their first juvenile plumage feathers, preening away the down, which litters the nest and surroundings. They begin feeding themselves at 6 or 7 weeks, grabbing food from the parent birds. By 2 months, female eaglets may be larger than their fathers, and the chicks are rambunctious and aggressive, lunging at and even attacking parent birds, which usually vacate the nest (except when bringing food) for nearby perches during this period. Soon the eaglets are hopping and flapping, sometimes fledging prematurely by falling or jumping from the nest tree. Depending on time elapsed between hatching of eggs, the firstborn dominates its smaller siblings. Sibling age difference, as one research team wrote, "is one of the most profound determinants of the well-being and survival of eaglets within a brood." *Siblicide* (killing of a sibling) is not uncommon. Third hatchlings, if present, are the most frequent victims; few survive, dying not from direct attack, but from starvation, as the older, larger eaglets grab all the food. Such nest mortality usually occurs only during the first 3 or 4 weeks of life; size differences become negligible after that. Eagle banders learn to fear clawing, biting nestlings far more than parent eagles, which seldom do more than swoop and call when a bander invades a nest.

For fledgling eagles, flying from the nest is considerably easier than landing, an exceedingly awkward performance the first few times. They crash into trees, tumble and thrash in the leaf canopy, sometimes end up hanging upside down from a branch as they slowly learn to gauge distance, maneuver, stall, and fine-tune their power. The fledglings probably garner many nicks and bruises, but this klutz period doesn't last long; soon they begin to forage on their own, returning at intervals for a period of 6 to 10 weeks to roost or feed at the nest. Then, about midsummer, they wander off, usually soaring downwind, sometimes for hundreds of miles, often joining small groups of other immatures and nonbreeding adult eagles. Sometimes they return to the nest area before migration begins. These hatching-year juveniles are dark brown in color with whitish underwing linings. Annual plumage molting of adults and subadults is virtually continuous over spring and summer. By age four, after several annual molts that progressively lighten head and tail, immatures look almost identical to adults.

In late spring and early summer, Florida and Gulf coast eagles that have finished nesting travel northward in a reverse migration, moving up the Atlantic coast and Mississippi River. These birds wander and forage, dispersing widely in northern eagle range. They move southward again in September. These are the passing eagles most often seen in fall at East Coast hawk-watch sites.

Fall. Migration of eagles from the northern range generally coincides with the freezing up of lakes. Immatures usually leave first, many in October; adults depart in November or December, each flying separately. Often an eagle will accompany groups of broad-winged hawks during migration. Fall movement is much more leisurely than in spring; the birds may stop for a week or more at prime feeding areas, where they tend to flock in groups of up to 100, also roosting together in trees. Prevailing winds generally govern eagle migration in the fall, affecting routes taken and timing of movements. Thermals are weaker, and the birds must work harder to gain distance than in spring. Thus the fall migratory routes are seldom straight and direct; first-year immatures, making their first southward flight, usually go where the wind carries them. Adults, often in large numbers, home to the previous year's wintering site, mainly along the south Atlantic and Gulf coasts and interior areas.

Winter. Most bald eagles that don't need to migrate in order to obtain food remain on or near their territories, sometimes vacating them to wander if food resources fail. Eagles that have nested south of the upper Great Lakes plus most coastal eagles of the maritime provinces and New England do not migrate, though they may become nomadic for a period. Icy conditions do not drive them out if some open water and sufficient food are accessible; I have often watched eagles in the dead of winter perched on an ice rim feeding on hard-frozen fish carcasses washed up on the ice. (Recent reports have noted a possibly common feeding strategy: The eagles break holes in thin ice, usually near shore, by jumping on it, then catch small fish attracted by the movement.)

Winter is the social season for bald eagles. The birds tend to feed and roost communally, especially along rivers in wildlife refuges and around hydroelectric dams where food is ample. Social hierarchies develop, with the oldest, most aggressive eagles occupying the highest perches. Four- and five-year-old eagles may form durable pair bonds on the winter range, sometimes even building nests that they abandon when spring migration begins in March. In breeding pairs, males are always the subordinate sex, deferent to females, especially at the nest.

Ecology. Bald eagles require habitats with a reliable food supply plus tall trees for nesting, fishing perches, and roosting, usually near clear water—along seacoasts, lakeshores, large rivers. They do not tolerate much human activity in their nest environs, often deserting nests in places frequented by too many boats or birdwatchers. They become most abundant in areas where such disturbance is minimal. Exceptions do occur, however; eagles have nested for years on a National Guard bombing range in Michigan.

Bald eagle nests, often used for a decade or more, are imposing structures, probably the largest constructions made by any North American bird. (The world's largest bird nest—more than 9 feet

across and 20 feet deep, weighing about 2 tons—was built by a bald eagle in Florida.) A typical nest, built in the upper, often broken fork of a large tree (though not necessarily the tallest tree present), is an immense pile of branches and large sticks, measuring 5 feet wide by 3 feet deep. It increases a foot or so in depth each year as the birds add bulky materials throughout the breeding seasons—in effect, building a new nest each year atop the old. Both sexes collect dead branches up to 6 feet long from standing trees and the ground, carrying them to the nest in

Bald eagle nests, often incremental in size over many years, consist of constantly replenished sticks and branches; adult (right) and juvenile (left) eagles show different plumages.

their talons. A center hollow 1 or 2 feet in diameter is packed with a mat of softer plant materials—mosses, sod, weeds, grasses. Like many hawks, eagles also bring sprigs of greenery into the nest, leaves and branchlets of both deciduous and coniferous trees (the birds seem to favor white pine). Such greenery may inhibit nestling parasites (mainly blowfly larvae) or aid nest sanitation (rotting fish often accumulate and are buried in the nest) and, possibly, the birds' digestion (eagle pellets sometimes contain much vegetable matter). Adult eagles are constantly adding and rearranging sticks and digging into the softer nest material, pulling out wads of it, shaking them, dropping them elsewhere—actions that may help aerate and dry the materials. Bald eagles favor nest trees with fairly thin foliage, giving them clear lanes of vision and approach. White pines and large trembling aspens are common sites in the birds' northern range. Bald eagles don't often build in dead trees, though sometimes nest trees die beneath still functional nests. In time, increasing weight of the nest often collapses support branches, or the entire top-heavy tree falls in a windstorm. Eaglets excrete feces from the nest by *slicing*—backing up to the nest rim and shooting out their whitewash. Seasonal occupancy of a nest after the birds have vacated can be confirmed by the ring

Bald eagle nest trees often become top-heavy, sometimes causing collapse of the tree as the nest grows larger.

of whitewash on the ground around a nest tree. In some areas, bald eagles also build one or two dummy nests that remain unused, perhaps as alternatives in case their occupied nest is destroyed or abandoned because of predators or disturbance.

The bald eagle's main food is fish—some living ones hunted from perches, but mainly dead or dying ones scavenged from water, ice, and shorelines. Living prey consists mostly of shallow-water or surface-feeding species such as cisco, suckers, northern pike, and walleye. Size of fish captured varies widely; most average about 1 pound in weight. But bald eagles are also extremely opportunistic feeders ("everything from frogs to fawns," one biologist remarked), rivaling gulls where fish are in short supply and during winter. Carrion of all kinds often ranks high in the diet, and they are "fond of sea lion dung and vulture vomit," according to eagle researcher Bruce E. Beans. In winter, much of their diet may consist of captured waterfowl, rabbits, mice, and snails. Road-killed carrion has also become an important winter food, often exposing the eagles themselves to traffic hazards. An adult eagle must consume 6 to 11 percent of its body weight daily, depending on the type of food and coldness of weather. Fishing perches of territorial adults are usually higher and more conspicuous than those of immatures, which tend to perch in lower, more hidden spots.

Probably the bald eagle's foremost bird competitors are other eagles. At communal feeding sites, much squabbling, aggressive posturing, and food pirating may occur; usually older, larger eagles steal from smaller ones. Eagles sometimes chase gulls and common ravens from carrion sites. Eagle-osprey interactions also occur; bald eagles sometimes pirate fish in midair from these smaller raptors, but "few ospreys can pass up an opportunity to dive-bomb a perched eagle," noted one research team. The later-nesting osprey adapts much more easily to human activities in its habitats than bald eagles do. One eagle researcher, however, believes that "eagles actively exclude ospreys" in the remoter locales favored by eagles. Great horned owls are known to adopt bald eagle nests before the eagles arrive; the eagles usually do not contest with the owls, perhaps withdrawing to a dummy nest. Nesting associates sometimes include great horned owls and mice, which may occupy the lower parts of a deep nest.

Eagle predators are relatively few. Black bears and raccoons sometimes climb nest trees but usually fail to surmount the nest rim or are driven off by the adults. Great horned owls and common ravens are opportunistic nest raiders. American crows sometimes mob and attack eagles, as they do any large raptor, but eagles generally ignore them. The bald eagle's foremost enemy is the creature it serves as national symbol, and it usually avoids proximity to people. Even eaglet banders and others who care about the birds have caused premature fledgings and many an eagle to abandon its nest. Shooting, habitat destruction, and pesticides in aquatic ecosystems have devastated eagle populations in the past.

Focus. Audubon called this bird the "white-headed eagle," surely a more accurate designation than the present one; vultures, condors, and wild turkeys are the only truly bald birds in North America. Audubon favored the wild turkey as the national bird, as did Benjamin Franklin earlier, who called the eagle "a bird of bad moral character." In common with many of their countrymen before and since, they regarded the bald eagle (along with most raptors) as vermin, enemies of poultry, gamebirds, lambs, fisheries, and common decency. But Audubon lauded what he identified as another eagle species, the "Washington sea eagle" or "Bird of Washington," which could qualify as the national bird, he thought. Audubon's favorite turned out to be the bald eagle in immature plumage. Official naming of the bald eagle as national bird occurred in 1782; it won the contest chiefly on its fierce looks, supposedly symbolic of national power, although the bird is actually rather timid.

The largest bald eagles are the immature birds. Tail feathers and wing primaries decline in length with successive molts. But significant geographical size differences also exist. A gradient exists from south to north, with Florida-breeding eagles smallest and Alaska-breeding eagles largest. This gradient exemplifies *Bergmann's Rule,* an ecological principle stating that warm-blooded fauna tend to be largest in the colder parts of the breeding range, a heat-conservative adaptation involving the ratio of body volume to surface area.

Probably no other bird has equaled the eagle's frequency of appearance in the artifacts of human cultures, both official and trivial. Its body and fierce visage adorn moneys, flags, signs, and labels. Eagles help sell ideas, propaganda, merchandise. Long before European settlers arrived in North America, many native tribes worshiped the eagle—both bald and golden—as an intercessor between humans and divinity. Feathers and talons (the latter used for necklaces, amulets, and fishhooks) gave heavy significance to individual status and solemn ritual observance. American patriots, hardly original in their choice for emblem of the Great Seal, had ample precedence from nations and cultures dating back to the beginning of recorded history. The eagles decorating battle standards and coinages of ancient and medieval times all carried the same symbolic message of power and ferocity. The symbol evolved into highly stylized representations on stamps, flags, and seals; into names for scouts and squadrons; into a scary mythology of awesome child-hunting predators and scourges of gentle lambs. The paradox is that, as one researcher wrote, "when you see something named for eagles, it usually means they're not there anymore." In most of the nations that so strongly identify with eagles, including the United States, the birds have been loathed, evicted, poisoned, and gunned down. Our national bird started out considered as vermin and continued to be treated as such until very recent years. Americans have always had difficulty with the idea of predators, and images of this idealized one have evoked strange conflicts in the national psyche. The wild turkey, it seems, would emotionally have been a less troubling choice.

The saga of our enmity with eagles—the shadow side of the archetype, as it were—forms a depressing record. It began almost as soon as the Pilgrims landed, when the estimated bald eagle population numbered some 500,000 birds (a nest, it is said, existed for every mile of Chesapeake Bay, every 10 miles of Great Lakes shorelines), making it one of North America's most abundant birds. Feeding flocks of bald eagles were shot for hog feed in Maine as early as 1668. Homesteaders and sheep ranchers hated all raptors on principle, shooting all they could find. State legislatures hastened to support the hunt by establishing bounties, which remained, in the eagle's case, until 1953, when Alaska still paid $2 per carcass, even though scientists had known since 1893 that eagles killed many more poultry predators—mice, rats, and snakes—than poultry.

By 1900, as a result of enthusiastic shooting and habitat destruction, eagle populations showed significant declines throughout their northeastern range. So rare had the bald eagle become by 1940 that a law was finally passed extending protection to the bird pictured on our dollar bills. Seven years later, however, large-scale use of DDT pesticides began, an insidious threat to the reproductive biology of many birds. Fish-eating birds were most vulnerable, since their prey concentrated large doses of toxic residues in their tissues. Eagle and osprey eggs failed to hatch.

Other contaminants affecting eagles included lead (ingested while eating shot-crippled ducks), mercury, and PCB toxins in lakes and rivers.

By 1970, less than 1,000 bald eagles were raising broods in the continental United States. The species was moving well along on the familiar route paved by passenger pigeon, bison, and wolf. (Some researchers have indeed suggested that major prey and carrion food sources for bald eagles disappeared with the extinction of passenger pigeons and radical loss of bison.) Banning of DDT biocides in 1972 and passage of the Endangered Species Act of 1973 enabled the species to turn a crucial corner. The act constituted official recognition, finally, that a problem existed. It declared bald eagles as endangered below the fortieth parallel and as threatened in several states above that line. In 1978, eagle status was upgraded to endangered throughout most of the nation.

Reintroduction programs by means of hacking (see Osprey) and the establishment of bald eagle refuges in key habitat areas began to address the bird's peril. By the 1980s, bald eagle numbers had increased to more than 10,000, and the bird continues its recovery today in most regions of the country. People are seeing eagles again in places where they have been absent for decades. In 1994, officials downgraded the eagle's continental status from endangered to threatened.

Yet recovery remains far from complete. Even as eagle populations are currently recovering in many areas of their range, many eagles still show high pesticide residues. Reproductive success along Great Lakes shorelines remains virtually nil. The battle for restoration of the species is far from won. It unfortunately remains true, as naturalist Edwin Way Teale wrote several decades ago, that "only a small proportion of Americans today have ever seen the emblem of their country soaring high above them, wild and free." Eagle populations still remain far from anything like the numbers that our patriot forefathers witnessed and slaughtered.

Most eagle mortality occurs during their first year; some researchers estimate that fully 50 percent of all eaglets die within that period and that only 4 of every 10 eaglets survive long enough to breed. Given a breeding adult's typical lifespan of 3 decades or longer, however, these numbers are sufficient to increase eagle populations.

The name *eagle* derives from the bird's Latin name, *aquila*.

Northern Harrier *(Circus cyaneus)*

Measuring almost 2 feet long (about crow size) with a 3- to 4-foot wingspread, northern harriers, formerly known as marsh hawks, cruise low across field and marsh with wings slightly uptilted like a turkey vulture's dihedral. Slim bodied with long, banded tails and long, rounded wings, the northern harrier shows a white rump spot on the back, its most distinctive mark; yellow eyes, bill, and feet; and an owl-like facial disk, which gives the small-billed head a hooded appearance. Males ("gray ghosts") are silver-gray with light buff chest and belly and black wing tips. The slightly larger females are sparrow brown above, streaked brown beneath. Juveniles, darker brown above than adult females, exhibit a copper red chest and belly. (Older immatures and adult females can be hard to distinguish.) Vocal sounds include a shrill, nasal "kee kee kee" and flickerlike notes.

Close relatives. Thirteen *Circus* species range worldwide, but the northern harrier (known as the hen harrier in Eurasia and Africa) is the only North American *Circus*.

Behaviors. A large bird slowly quartering and tilting 7 feet or less above the ground is probably a harrier; its large, white rump patch confirms it. Harriers hunt prey on the wing, dropping to seize a mouse or other prey, relying not only upon superb vision but also on acute hearing. The flattish facial disk is believed to help focus sound, as it does for owls, enabling the birds to hunt in lower light levels than most daytime raptors. Females tend to forage closer to the nest than males. Northern harriers also perch-hunt at times, hover-hunt with beating wings, stoop (dive on prey from aloft), and soar high, often rocking unsteadily in the wind. The wingbeats, often seen even when the bird soars on thermal updrafts, are slow and regular, quite distinctive to observers familiar with harrier flight patterns. Northern harriers have been observed flying as high as 3,000 feet during migrations. This is one of the few North American hawks that show *sexual dimorphism* (that is, male-female differences) in plumage; the only one that is frequently *polygynous* (that is, 1 male mating with 2 or 3 females); and the only one that regularly nests on the ground and in colonies. Northern harriers

A male northern harrier with its prey, a white-footed mouse. Note the facial disk similar to that of owls; unseen in this profile view is the harrier's white rump spot.

are circumpolar, breeding in Eurasia as well as North America. Their breeding distribution spans our continent from Alaska to Newfoundland, south to North Carolina, Texas, and southern California. Only harriers on the northern range migrate; snow cover, and thus food accessibility, probably accounts for this movement.

Spring. Harriers have the most protracted migration periods of any North American raptor, appearing on their northern range from late February through early June. Adult males precede females by days or weeks, and subadults come last. The birds usually travel singly or in small groups consisting of 2 to 5 birds, move both day and night, and favor coastal routes rather than inland thermals along land ridges. Male yearlings' reddish breast feathers are now fading to white, resembling adult female plumage.

Adults that have *successfully* reared broods in a certain site are *philopatric*—that is, they tend, as if imprinted, to return to that site. Site fidelity is low, however, for birds with previous nest failures. Thus many previously mated pairs may reappear in the same nesting areas, but relatively few of the birds—even males that remain monogamous for the season—pair again with the previous mate. "Harriers are like the men of Islam," wrote researcher Frances

Hamerstrom; "most of them have one wife, but if they can afford it, more." Polygyny in local harrier populations seems to be triggered by the combination of a surplus of females (the unbalanced sex ratio typical of these birds), shrinking habitats that crowd the birds, and abundant food supply. In such circumstances, even year-old females may become polygynous partners, whereas year-old males, usually chased out by older breeding males, may breed monogamously with a yearling female. Females apparently select their mates based on the quality of their courtship feeding and display behaviors.

Territory varies with habitat quality and nest density, ranging from less than 1 acre to more than 200 acres in size. Typical territories seem to average about 1 square mile. Home range, mainly undefended feeding areas, may extend 2 miles or more and increase in size as the chicks age; each bird typically has its own habitual feeding site within that area. Although solitary nesting pairs are not uncommon, prime habitat may host loose colonies of several to a dozen or more nests. Nests are rarely spaced less than 300 feet apart, though females of a polygynous harem may nest closer together.

The male harrier's aerial courtship displays, known as sky dancing, are spectacular. They consist of multiple U-shaped loops and barrel rolls high over the territory. (Males also sky-dance during migration.) Females occasionally join in. Males seldom approach the nest after incubation begins, spending all their time hunting or perched. As a male nears the territory carrying prey, the female flies up from the nest. He drops the prey item; she catches it in her talons and returns to the nest with it, usually landing some distance away and approaching the nest on foot. Incubation usually begins by early May on the northern range. The birds frequently abandon nest and territory if disturbed before eggs hatch.

EGGS AND YOUNG: typically 4 or 5; eggs bluish white, usually unmarked, sometimes brown spotted. INCUBATION: by female; about 31 days. FEEDING OF YOUNG: by female, which tears prey (mainly rodents and birds) brought by male into small bits; if female dies, male piles food on nest but does not tear prey or feed chicks. FLEDGING: about 30 days or more.

Summer. Parent harriers vigorously defend their nests when chicks are present, even attacking human intruders occasionally. Female chicks often have a better survival rate than male chicks, producing the skewed sex ratio commonly seen in harriers. *Siblicide* (killing, often indirectly by starvation, of one chick by another), though quite frequent in most hawks, seldom occurs in harriers. "I have noticed," wrote Hamerstrom, "that partly grown harriers tend to scurry away upon hearing the shrill cries of their smaller nest mates," perhaps a mechanism giving the younger chicks an increased chance for survival. The family unit remains together through summer. Even after fledging in July, the juveniles do not begin to hunt but continue until migration time to catch prey dropped by the parents. Juveniles spend much time in play, chasing one another, often pouncing on or manipulating corncobs or other objects. Males and (after young have fledged) females roost solitarily at night (and often during the day) on the ground, usually at some distance from the nest.

Adult birds undergo their annual plumage molt from July to September; females sometimes begin molting their flight feathers while they incubate. Yearling harriers now molt into their first sexually dimorphic plumages though do not gain fully adult appearance until the following summer. Fall migration of immatures usually begins in August or September about 3 weeks after fledging, followed by adult females and, lastly, by males through October and November.

Fall. The birds dally, as during spring migration; most travel singly. Harriers from the arctic range seem to migrate farthest, many to Central America, Venezuela, and Colombia. Most northeastern harriers, however, fan out across the southern two-thirds of the United States. A few remain on the northern breeding range over winter in places where depth of snow cover permits them to find prey.

Winter. Harriers often form temporary individual territories of varying size (averaging about 160 acres) on their winter range, defending them from other harriers from several hours to 15 or more days. But they often gather at communal night roosts, sometimes shared with short-eared owls (also ground-dwelling birds). The roosts are often traditional sites but fluctuate in size as the birds wander; about 20 harriers is an average roost size. Harrier migrants are often moving northward by late February.

Ecology. Northern harriers are birds of open lands, making them relatively easy to spot. They favor wet meadows with rank grasses but also occupy fields, marshes, savannas, and prairies. Probably the most important habitat element is an abundance of voles; indeed, good vole habitat (weedy fields, hayfields, clear-cuts) generally indicates good harrier range. These birds perch low and spend almost 60 percent of their foraging time perched, using fence posts, small shrubs, boulders, or ground elevations in their home ranges for this purpose.

The female constructs the nest, often from materials brought by the male. Females sometimes return to the previous year's nests, adding materials. New nests are often flimsy, built of sticks and coarse plant materials, lined with feathers and finer grasses. In wet ground, the nest may be placed a foot or more above soil or water. Nest outside diameter is 15 to 30 inches. The birds usually select sites in tall, rank sedges or grasses, sometimes hummocks, often in marsh vegetation or sphagnum bogs. One study found willows, goldenrods, and sedges the most important plants in harrier nest sites.

In optimal habitat, the harrier's diet consists of about 95 percent voles (also called meadow mice, *Microtus*). A feeding strategy in some areas is harrier seizure of vole nests, which resemble upside-down, grassy bird nests on the ground; many times the voles are at home when the harrier comes calling. Vole populations rise and plummet in about 4-year cycles, greatly influencing local harrier breeding abundance in any given year. Evidence exists that a floating population of harriers, what Hamerstrom calls a "gypsy cohort," can take rapid advantage of high vole abundance to settle and nest. Vole numbers far exceed harrier appetites in years of abundance. As Hamerstrom wrote, "harriers probably have about the same effect on [vole numbers] that a man has on mosquitoes when . . . swatting them at dusk." But efforts to convince people that rodents would demolish crops if not for raptor predation, she believes, are "primarily propaganda to 'justify' the existence of raptors" as friends of man. The voles' effects on harriers are far more significant. Hamerstrom's research established that abundant vole populations increased the likelihood of harrier polygyny and breeding in brown-plumaged, first-year males. She suggested, moreover, that something in the intestinal flora of voles may stimulate harrier gonads, acting as an aphrodisiac, since the birds consume the intestines of small mammals primarily during onset of the breeding season. Harriers opportunistically capture and consume other prey as well: insects (mainly grasshoppers), snakes, frogs, sparrows, redwinged blackbirds, meadowlarks, ground squirrels, and rabbits. Where voles are in short supply, harriers also feed on carrion, and they occasionally capture ducks and raid poultry yards.

A raptor associate and sometime competitor is the short-eared owl, which often nests, forages, and roosts in habitats similar to harriers. The owl territories may overlap those of harriers, usually with few conflicts. Harriers hunt during the day, whereas the owls hunt both day and night. Both birds are rodent eaters, which could lead to food competition in areas of low prey populations (though the vole-cycle mechanism usually governs bird abundance). Harriers tend to pirate food from the owls rather than vice versa, usually by causing the food carrier to drop its prey. And red-tailed and rough-legged hawks pirate from harriers. The harrier's biggest competitors are humans; drainage and filling of wetlands, fire suppression allowing plant succession to advance and thus shrink suitable habitats, and pesticides sprayed on fields account for the harrier's endangered status in several states.

Harrier predators are fairly numerous, as with most ground-nesting birds. Egg raiders include American crows, northern ravens, skunks, and raccoons. Great horned owls, red-tailed hawks, red foxes, coyotes, domestic dogs, and raccoons devour nestlings; cattle and white-tailed deer sometimes trample nests. Carrion beetles (Silphidae), attracted to meat scraps in the nest, also attack and sometimes kill nestlings. Like most large raptors, harriers are frequently harassed or mobbed by smaller birds—sparrows, European starlings, American crows, blackbirds, swallows, and American kestrels, among others.

Focus. Harrier populations fluctuate widely from year to year in many areas, reflecting cyclic prey abundance. Grassland habitat loss and pesticide contamination have also affected harrier populations, resulting in widespread decline of this once-common species since about 1960. Various recovery schemes have been proposed: reversing the loss of wetland and grassland habitats; placement of perching posts in open field habitats; creating more mouse habitat by increasing hay acreage. ("Few people put their minds on how to maintain good mouse habitat," notes Hamerstrom. It requires periodic ground disturbance, as in burning, plowing, or mowing.)

The name *harrier* derives from a sixteenth-century English word *harien,* meaning "to pillage and torment." British birders call female harriers "ringtails" for the barred tail feathers. "Frog hawk" was Thoreau's frequent name for the harrier, but he thought "kite" would be a better label. Unaware that the harrier nests on the ground, he once spent an afternoon searching for its nest by climbing four pine trees. "The sight of a marsh hawk in Concord," he wrote, "is worth more to me than the entry of the allies into Paris."

Studies have determined that some 60 percent of harriers die in their first year, probably mainly from accident, predation, or starvation. Annual adult mortality is about 30 percent. Harriers sometimes live to age sixteen or more, but mean age at death is about 16 months.

7

Pied-billed Grebe *(Podilymbus podiceps)*

Grebe family (Podicipedidae), order Ciconiiformes. This brown, chunky, ducklike diver, the most abundant North American grebe, measures about 13 inches from its short, blunt, unducklike bill to its negligible tail with white undertail rump. In breeding plumage, this grebe has a black throat patch and a dark ring around its whitish bill (hence its name); in winter plumage, its throat is whitish and the ring is absent. Sexes look alike; immatures show brown facial and neck striping. The pied-bill utters a series of about 10 notes in a distinctive, throaty, resounding call ("cuck cuck cuck cow-cow-cow cowp cowp cow-ah cow-ah"), heard mainly in spring and summer; the sounds somewhat resemble the call of the yellow-billed cuckoo. These grebes rarely vocalize outside the breeding season.

Close relatives. Only one other *Podilymbus* species exists, the Atitlan grebe *(P. gigas)* of Central America. Of 22 grebe species worldwide, only 6 reside in North America. The red-necked grebe *(Podiceps grisegena)* and horned grebe *(P. auritus),* in addition to the pied-bill, are the grebes most often seen in the Northeast.

Behaviors. Awkward on land and seldom seen flying except during migrations, this grebe is supremely adapted to the water, usually escaping danger by diving. The pied-bill not only swims on the surface and swiftly dives—as deep as 20 feet—but also silently and uncannily sinks in place, reducing buoyancy by expelling air from body and feathers as it submerges. Often it swims with only its head projecting above the surface. Its large feet with lobed, partially webbed toes with flattened claws resembling toenails make it a powerful swimmer, but it may also bask motionlessly for hours amid beds of thick algae or stands of bulrush. Shy, solitary, and

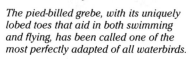

inconspicuous except during migrations, pied-bills seldom associate with other waterbirds. To birders, their loud, infrequent, but resonant calls echoing over the water are often the first indication of their presence. Launching into flight is a major effort, requiring a running start over water; pied-bills cannot take off from land because the rearward placement of their legs and center of gravity prevent a rapid run. In flight, the grebe's short wings and hunched profile with a slight dip in the stretched-out neck are characteristic, as is the near absence of a tail; the birds fly with rudderlike extended feet.

The pied-billed grebe, with its uniquely lobed toes that aid in both swimming and flying, has been called one of the most perfectly adapted of all waterbirds.

Grebes have a peculiar eating habit: In addition to their regular diet, they consume their own feathers—lots of them (up to 50 percent of stomach contents). Biologists presume that the feathers, forming a ball in the stomach, function to cushion the stomach walls from sharp fish bones and to slow the passage of bony material, enabling it to dissolve. Why grebes have not evolved digestive tracts that work without feathers remains unknown. (Many bird species aid digestion by consuming grit and small pebbles.)

Pied-billed grebes breed throughout the continent from central and southern Canada south to the Gulf, also through Central and South America to Argentina. Most populations in upper latitudes are migratory.

Spring. Early to arrive and late to leave, many migrant pied-bills have returned to their northern breeding range by early spring or before, depending on rates of icemelt and the presence of open water; many arrive about 10 days after ice breakup. Pairs are probably monogamous and return to previous breeding sites, though detailed knowledge of these behaviors remains uncertain. Courtship and territorial displays are more vocal than visual; a pair may duet-call, and males in adjacent territories often face off at their boundaries, turning away to call with elevated bills, then turning face-to-face again as if to gauge the effects of their intimidations.

The solitary pied-billed grebe sometimes sits for hours in a clump of floating vegetation.

Territories in ponds large enough to hold more than a single pair average about 30 yards in extent. Both sexes construct the nest over a period of several days. On the northern range, eggs are laid from early April to late May. Parent birds often approach the nest underwater, surfacing at the nest rim. When they leave the nest, they usually cover the eggs with nest debris. Eggshells of this species are more porous than those of most birds; since water must diffuse from eggs during incubation, and grebe nests are often wet, the added pores aid such diffusion.

EGGS AND YOUNG: 5 to 7; eggs bluish white, nest-stained to brownish; asynchronous hatching; chicks precocial. INCUBATION: by both sexes but mainly female; 23 days. FEEDING OF YOUNG: Though chicks are immediately mobile, parents feed them aquatic insects and snails for first week or so; chicks also ingest feathers of parent birds. FLEDGING: information scant, probably 6 or 7 weeks.

Summer. Pied-billed grebes raise only a single brood in their northern range, often two farther south. The downy chicks are black striped down the back and have a red mark behind the eye. Parents often carry one or more chicks on their backs, sometimes even diving when young are aboard; they often return with them to the nest for brooding. About 6 weeks after hatching, chicks develop their first juvenile plumage, which much resembles that of winter adult grebes. By August, grebes are dispersing from their territories to other ponds and feeding areas.

Fall, Winter. Groups of 30 to 50 pied bills sometimes gather during early fall in shallow lakes, the only time of year when these solitary birds seem very sociable. Withdrawal from the northern range is prolonged, with most birds moving southward, mainly at night, between mid-September and mid-November. Some, however, linger until freeze-up makes food inaccessible. Where power plants or sewage lagoons maintain open waters, a few grebes may reside over winter. The majority travel hardly farther than they must to find open water, usually southward of the southern Great Lakes and British Columbia.

Ecology. Pied-bills are essentially pond birds—the more densely vegetated the pond with rushes and reeds, the better, though open water at least a foot deep is also necessary for foraging. They generally avoid open waters of large lakes and bays. A pair may occupy a pond as small as half an acre, but ponds smaller than 10 acres seldom host more than a single pair. Pied-bills also occupy sluggish streams, marshes, and marshy lake edges.

The nest is a more or less floating platform of dead aquatic vegetation at least partially anchored to dead submersed plants—cattails, reeds, sedges. Nests are usually sodden and consequently "cooking" with heat as the wet mass decomposes. Well hidden in standing emergent plants such as

Pied-billed grebes favor habitats of dense rushes adjacent to open water.

spike-rushes or bulrushes, the nest measures about a foot across. The pair often plasters it with algae scum, thus aiding camouflage. Nests are usually sited within 50 feet of an open-water area.

Aquatic insects—mostly various larvae and water beetles— form some 40 percent of this grebe's diet. Crayfish and fish such as minnows, small carp and catfish, and many others also rank high. Other morsels include spiders, snails, tadpoles, and frogs. Recent information indicates that pied-bills occasionally prey on swimming ducklings. The birds also consume small amounts of vegetation and seeds.

Competition seems negligible in this species. Where flocks of waterfowl are present, pied-bills usually stay off by themselves. They do, however, often nest in fairly close proximity to other nesting marsh birds such as gallinules, coots, and rails. American coots, which often pirate food items from diving waterfowl as they surface, rarely pester pied-bills, probably because the items retrieved by the latter are relatively small and less appealing to the coots.

Raccoons, which can indeed swim, are the major nest predators in some areas. Stormy weather and flooding probably account for about half of all nest losses. Wetland filling and drainage and water pollution have destroyed many grebe habitats, resulting in a general, though not radical, decline of this species throughout America. Occasionally grebes land on wet highways, mistaking them from aloft for streams; it is usually their last landing.

Focus. The pied-billed grebe is probably better known by its nicknames—"hell-diver," "dabchick," "dipper," "water-witch"—than by its ornithologically sanctioned label. A duck hunter once identified a grebe to me as a "gurby"; at least he recognized the bird— numerous grebes are shot each fall by gunners who don't know a duck from a dabchick. The name *grebe* is French, obscure in origin, possibly deriving from the Breton word *krib,* meaning "crest" (many grebe species, though not the pied-bill, have head crests). Longevity of this species remains unknown.

8

Double-crested Cormorant
(Phalacrocorax auritus)

Cormorant family (Phalacrocoracidae), order Ciconiiformes. Almost entirely black, like most members of its family, the double-crested cormorant (so named from its ragged, often barely visible head crest) measures almost 3 feet long, with a wingspan of more than 4 feet. Identify this waterbird by its size and long neck, often held in heronlike S-shape when the bird perches erectly on a log; flattish head and long, cylindrical hook-tipped bill; bright yellow-orange chin patch *(gular pouch);* short, black, webbed feet; and long tail. Cormorants often fly in lines or V-shaped formations like geese, with necks outstretched. Sexes look similar; immature birds have brown bellies and whitish plumage on neck and breast. The birds rarely vocalize except in the nesting colony, uttering guttural croaks and grunts.

Close relatives. Of the 36 cormorant species worldwide (all of the same genus, 14 of them called shags), 6 reside in North America, most along the seacoasts. The great cormorant *(P. carbo),* larger than the double-crested, is the only other cormorant likely to be seen in northern Atlantic coastal areas. Western and southwestern cormorants include Brandt's cormorant *(P. penicillatus),* the neotropic cormorant *(P. brasilianus),* the pelagic cormorant *(P. pelagicus),* and the red-faced cormorant *(P. urile).* The cormorant family is related to the boobies and anhingas.

Behaviors. Cormorants, though sometimes solitary, are characteristically gregarious, often seen clustered on rocks, piers, or trees along beaches, harbor islands, and other waterfronts. Typically the birds in this black array stand erect (their feet are placed far back), and several may be holding their wings outstretched and immobile. Some bird species use spread-wing postures to aid thermoregulation by catching some solar rays, but cormorants are simply air-drying themselves; they must do so before they can fly. Cormorants differ from

Cormorants, gregarious birds year-round, may perch almost anywhere near water.

other waterbirds in that water does not run off a cormorant's back, and its plumage is wettable, not waterproof. This owes more to microscopic feather structure, which decreases buoyancy, than to nonfunction of the oil gland. Even so, only the outer feathers become heavy and soaked; an insulating layer beneath the external plumage protects them from chill when swimming underwater.

Like grebes, cormorants can submerge by either diving or sinking, reducing buoyancy by expelling air from body and plumage. Sometimes they swim partially immersed, with only head and neck above the surface. Atop the water, they ride low like loons but with their long bills always tilting upward, a distinctive identity trait. Beneath the surface, their powerful webbed feet propel them as they pursue a fish, their wings held slightly out. Cormorants have been known to dive 75 feet or more. Typically, however, they forage 5 to 25 feet deep, usually remaining submerged for less than 30 seconds, but sometimes longer than a minute. Cormorant eyes, green in most species, are adapted for underwater as well as aerial vision, and the birds can spot fish prey by flying low over the water. They bring their prey to the surface for eating, repositioning it for swallowing headfirst. Alighting on water, cormorants use their tails as brakes, dragging them along the surface. Their short, rear-placed legs impel them to launch into flight by means of a takeoff run across the water; from a tree perch, they usually drop into flight.

Like raptors and many fish-eating birds, cormorants regurgitate pellets of indigestible bones and other material. In hot weather, cormorants may be seen pulsing their throats *(gular flutter)*, a cooling mechanism common to many bird species, which aids evaporation from the body.

This cormorant resides only in North America. Its breeding range covers both seacoasts and the Gulf coast, spanning the continent locally from central Canada and the Great Lakes south to Florida. The bird is a migrator only in its northern range (coastal and continental areas north of Tennessee and Maryland).

Spring. Migrant cormorants move northward up coastlines and watercourses to their breeding colonies *(rookeries)* from early spring through early May, traveling day or night, usually in V-shaped flocks numbering 200 birds or less. Many return to their previous nests, adding materials and rebuilding them. Double-crested cormorants begin breeding at age three. Only during the breeding season does the double crest—several small feathers curling up over the crown—become very visible; the tufts are shed during the nesting period. The nesting period is prolonged, commonly lasting from late April through mid-August, though each pair nests only once per season unless nest failure or disruption occurs, in which case a pair may renest.

Thus in a typical colony during this period, all phases of development, from nest building through incubation, brooding, and fledging, may be seen simultaneously. Earliest breeders are usually the older, experienced nesters. Males bring materials, and females build the nests. Chicks, unable to maintain their own

Adult double-crested cormorants wear their small head plumes only during the breeding season.
(From The Atlas of Breeding Birds of Michigan.)

body temperature for almost 2 weeks after hatching, are brooded by parents almost continuously for that long.

EGGS AND YOUNG: 3 or 4; eggs bluish white with chalky surface, nest-stained; hatching asynchronous; black, downy chicks altricial. INCUBATION: by both sexes; about 27 days. FEEDING OF YOUNG: by both sexes; regurgitant, mainly fish. FLEDGING: 5 or 6 weeks.

Summer. Three weeks or so after hatching, the now mobile chicks wander from the nest, often gathering in groups that range free (apparently unmolested by adult cormorants) throughout the rookery while continuing to be fed. They rapidly take to the water, swimming and diving; they begin flying by accompanying adults to feeding areas. At 2 months of age, they have gained full immature plumage; some 10 weeks after hatching, they are fully independent, roosting in the rookery or else-where, often with other young. Cor-morants molt their complete body plumage in late summer.

Fall, Winter. October and No-vember are the peak migration peri-ods for northern cormorants. The birds winter mainly in southern sea-coast habitats, some as far south as the West Indies, but also inland in the Mississippi valley to Tennessee. In some parts of the winter range, double-crested and neotropic cor-morants associate in the same habi-tats, even on the same perches. Highest-density winter populations occur on Florida's southern tip, but the bird is expanding its winter range northward, now appearing

Juvenile cormorants in subadult plumage are numerous on the birds' winter range.

irregularly in southern New England and the lower Great Lakes, areas where minimum January temperatures usually measure over 30 degrees F.

Ecology. Rugged coastal islands, rocky beaches, and large inland lakes and rivers are this cormorant's breeding habitats, often shared with gulls, terns, and, in the southern United States, pelicans. Double-crested cormorants seem equally at home in both freshwater and marine habitats. They need a reliable food supply (mainly fish) and a lack of disturbance; human or other intrusion may cause entire colonies to vacate. During winter and migrations, cormorants may be seen solitarily or in flocks of various sizes along just about any water area, including harbors, lakes, bogs, river mouths, and sewage lagoons, and near power plants. In recent years, the more numerous their populations grow, the more often cormorants show up in waters where nobody had seen them before.

Most nests are built flat on the ground or amid rocks. Some 30 percent of the population, however, nests in living or dead trees near water. Often 5 to 20 or more nests occupy a single tree at almost any height. These ragged platforms of sticks and rubbish often resemble smaller versions of colonial great blue heron nests. Ground nests, measuring about 2 feet outside diameter, likewise consist of beach drift—short sticks, matted seaweeds, and feathers. Finer materials line the 9-inch-across, 5-inch-deep cup. Repeatedly used nests, often layered, reflect the birds' seasonal repair work; some nests may stand a foot or more above ground owing to more or less continual additions. Such nests often become heavily infested with fleas in spring. The birds typically decorate their nests with bits of grass, cedar sprigs, or other greenery; such additions may help repel insect pests. One reason for infestations probably owes to the cormorant's unsanitary nest habits; nests are often foul, littered with dead fish (and often dead nestlings) and guano deposits (droppings). Cormorants occasionally adopt vacant great blue heron or black-crowned night heron tree nests for their own.

Primarily fish eaters, double-crested cormorants prey on small schooling species such as alewives, smelt, yellow perch, sticklebacks, and many others likewise captured by underwater pursuit. An adult cormorant eats about a pound of fish per day; relatively few of them are game species of commercial value. Other prey items include mollusks, crustaceans, snakes, and salamanders. Cormorants sometimes compete (usually successfully) for nesting space with gulls and terns. Dramatic increases in cormorant numbers since the 1970s have also brought the birds into conflict with fish farmers and commercial fishery interests. Maintaining that cormorants severely deplete fish stock, despite many studies showing that the birds' overall impact on fisheries is minimal, they advocate the reduction of cormorant populations. Catfish farmers in the Mississippi delta region, where many thousands of cormorants winter each year, are said to lose 3 to 7 percent of their annual stock to the birds. Opponents of population reduction argue for more effective and economic methods of predator control; these include long-needed reengineering of fish hatcheries and commercial fish farms to reduce or eliminate the problem of fish-eating species. To cormorants and other fish eaters, such as gulls, herons, many ducks, and kingfishers, most fish farms as presently laid out are open invitations, and the presence of fish predators in such places hardly makes them vermin.

Cormorant predators, given the birds' size, are few. Herring gulls are frequent raiders of cormorant nests, devouring eggs and chicks. Northwestern crows and glaucous-winged gulls harass cormorant colonies in the West. Studies have shown that nests on the colony edges are much more vulnerable to predation than centrally located nests. Island-nesting cormorants remain relatively safe from mammal predation. The major cormorant predators, both historically and currently, are humans. In addition to being illegally shot, many cormorants become snagged in fishnets and on bait hooks.

Focus. Dramatic declines that followed widespread DDT contamination of our waters (especially its metabolic product DDE)—and equally dramatic resurgences following the prohibition of DDT pesticides in the early 1970s—have marked the double-crested cormorant's history of the past 50 years. Before that, cormorant populations existed locally in fairly stable numbers across North

America. Human settlement, however, brought increasing conflicts between the birds and both commercial and sport fishermen. Until 1966, the Ontario government waged effective war on cormorant rookeries by gunning and on cormorant reproduction by systematic spraying of eggs with a lethal formaldehyde and soap solution. The birds continued to sit on the unhatchable but intact eggs, thus suppressing any replacement clutches they would normally lay. Actions such as these, plus PCB and DDT contaminants, to which these birds are highly vulnerable, almost succeeded in extirpating cormorant rookeries from eastern North America. Cormorants with pesticide-deformed bills were fairly common sights. The birds were never officially listed as endangered, but Great Lakes populations, which had thrived from the 1930s, had all but disappeared by the late 1950s.

The resurgence of cormorant populations, now increasing at a rate of about 5 percent annually, has revived controversy involving fishery and wildlife interests. Whereas the return of the cormorant is a welcome indicator that our waters are recovering from toxic contaminants, the birds' breeding success has renewed competitor concern in many areas. Decline of the Great Lakes perch fishery, for example, has been attributed, along with other factors, to spring cormorant raids in perch spawning bays. In 1998, it appeared likely that the U.S. Fish and Wildlife Service would issue unlimited depredation permits for cormorant shooting in 33 states.

Similar controversy has erupted over cormorants in England, where one observer attributes the problem to the fact that cormorants "are simply better at catching fish than the anglers." In the meantime, strong evidence both here and abroad shows that cormorants offer negligible competition to fishery interests. Many researchers believe that except in rare instances, cormorants are scapegoats for another problem that fishermen don't like to discuss: human overfishing of large fish stock. Lacking control by large fish predators, small fish populations explode, attracting cormorants and contributing more to their abundance, some believe, than DDT absence. Also aiding resurgence is the cormorant's early breeding age (2 or 3 years), its relatively high percentage of fledgling survival, and its longevity, which may approach 2 decades. This bird's remarkable resilience in the face of poisoning, systematic slaughter, and rookery disturbance speaks for itself.

Much of the world's supply of guano fertilizer comes from Peruvian islands, where huge rookeries of guanay cormorants *(P. bougainvillii)* have deposited it for centuries. The word *cormorant* (accent on first syllable) derives ultimately from the Latin *corvus marinus,* meaning "sea crow." The latter is still a colloquial name, as is "shag," among East Coast fishermen. Early settlers also called them "crow ducks."

9

HERON FAMILY (Ardeidae),
order Ciconiiformes

Sixty-five heron family species exist worldwide. Long necks, usually tucked back in S-shape when the birds fly, and long, spearlike bills characterize this family of wading birds. Many species exhibit plumes on the head, back, or chest during the breeding season; in most, the sexes show identical plumage.

Herons feed primarily in wetland and shoreline areas. Some often nest, however, in woodland areas far from these sites. The birds are strong fliers, with broad, rounded wings and short tails. Steady, flapping, crowlike flight is characteristic. Many (though hardly all) species are long-legged, and the feet are unwebbed. When feeding, herons may stand motionless in the water for long periods or walk with slow, stately grace. Occasionally they may stir the mud bottom with a foot or suddenly dash in pursuit of swimming prey. Some herons spear prey with their bills, but most usually grasp and swallow it whole. They regurgitate pellets of indigestible materials.

Herons carry their own "dust baths" used in cleansing and preening their plumage. This substance exists in the form of modified feathers *(powder down)* that grow close to the skin. The small, brittle feathers continually disintegrate from their tips into a fine, whitish, talclike powder that absorbs and helps remove fish slime and other residues. Almost all birds have some powder down plumage, but herons develop more of it than most species. Heron chicks are altricial, and hatching is asynchronous.

The word *heron* derives from the Old German label for the bird, *heiger.* This family includes the egrets and bitterns. Most egrets are white; bitterns are chunkier, brownish, and shorter-legged. Twelve North American species exist. In addition to the following four accounts and the close relatives of each noted, other eastern family members include the reddish egret *(Egretta rufescens)*, tricolored heron *(E. tricolor)*, little blue heron *(E. caerulea)*, and snowy egret *(E. thula)*; the cattle egret *(Bubulcus ibis)*; the yellow-crowned and black-crowned night-herons *(Nyctanassa violacea, N. nycticorax)*; and the least bittern *(Ixobrychus exilis)*.

HERON FAMILY (Ardeidae)

Great Blue Heron *(Ardea herodias)*

The largest, most common North American heron, the stately great blue stands up to 4 feet tall (males are slightly larger than females). Gray-blue back and wing plumage, white head and neck feathers, and a black eye stripe extending into a black, swept-back plume or crest identify adults in the breeding season. Cinnamon-colored neck plumes drape over the breast, and the golden-yellow eyes are distinctive. The 6- or 7-foot wingspread shows black primary feathers; in profile, the black bend of the wing ("shoulder") appears as a crescent-shaped mark on the side. In flight, the S-curve of the neck

A great blue heron profile shows its spearlike bill and head plume. (Courtesy of Kalamazoo Nature Center.)

and the long legs trailing behind are also distinctive. Immatures have black crowns and no head plume. Great blues utter deep, raucous croaks ("craank craank"), usually only when alarmed or defending a territory.

Close relatives. The great white heron *(A. h. occidentalis)*, an all-white subspecies, resides in marine habitats from Florida to South America. The so-called Wurdemann's heron is probably an intermediate color morph between great blue and great white subspecies, its white, crested head lacks a plume. Eleven other *Ardea* species include the great egret (see next account) and, in Eurasia and Africa, the grey heron *(A. cinerea)*, which much resembles the great blue.

Behaviors. Colonial nesters in crowded tree rookeries *(heronries)*, great blue herons usually favor solitude when they feed. Their shallow-water feeding areas are often located miles from the heronry. Great blues exhibit several feeding strategies. When foraging in streams, they usually stand or walk against the current; most fish prey are likewise aligned as they forage, enabling the bird to approach from the rear. In still waters, a heron may stir up prey action by stretching a wing and flicking its tip rapidly in the water, scattering hidden prey. Foot stirring is another occasional strategy. The "dead duck" technique involves floating with current or wind in deeper water, the heron's wings cupped on the surface, its head extended beneath the water as if

A slow, methodical stalker, the great blue heron forages in just about any water area or wetland.

trolling. About 90 percent of foraging, however, consists of standing and walking, sometimes in upland fields as well as in water. Seizing a prey creature (usually a fish) with a quick head thrust, the bird often kills its victim by spearing before flipping and aligning it head-first for passage down the gullet (herons occasionally choke to death trying to swallow oversize prey).

Great blues may feed both day and night but are most typically *crepuscular,* feeding in the twilight hours of dawn and evening. Their eyes are highly adapted for night vision. In feeding locales used by many great blues, the birds maintain temporary feeding territories independent of season. These territories may range in size from a few to several hundred yards in diameter, depending upon availability of food.

The great blue's long-toed foot (3 toes forward, 1 rear) is not entirely webless; a short stretch of skin between first and second front toes aids the bird's footing in soft mud. The middle front toe has a hooklike comb on the bottom surface of the claw, which the bird uses to preen its plumage. Great blues spend much time preening and grooming, typically when perched on a tree branch or atop a muskrat lodge after feeding. Oiling its plumage from its preen gland above the tail, and raking its feathers with its "comb toe," it also spreads a dusty bloom over itself from 3 invisible patches of powder-down feathers. When it launches into flight after a long preening session, it sheds a dusty cloud in its wake.

The great blue heron's noted grace in flight and its stately bearing in the marsh do not extend to certain actions. It more or less crash-lands in the congested heronry, for example, where it appears an exceedingly angular, awkward, and gangly creature, all legs, neck, and joints. One wonders that the birds do not sprain their necks in these tight quarters. I have also watched great blues take off from small ponds hemmed by trees, allowing too short a space for them to gain quick altitude; frenzied flapping is not enough to prevent a collision with topmost branches or to clear them over the barrier.

Great blue heron breeding range spans most of the continent south of about 54 degrees N latitude (southern Canada) to the Gulf states and into Mexico. Most great blues that nest north of about 38 degrees N are migrants.

Spring. Migrant northern great blues have usually arrived at their colony sites by mid-March to April. In some areas, the birds first assemble in staging areas before entering the heronries. Few yearling birds apparently return to the native heronry. Here pairing occurs among first-time breeders (usually birds in their second spring), and previous breeders reestablish monogamous pair bonds. Courtship displays are often intricate and impressive, most occurring on or near the nest site: head stretching with bill pointed straight up, erection of head plumes, the head-down stretch angled below body level, head swaying in unison with bill tips interlocked, plus bill clapping, twig shaking, mutual preening, stick transfers, and other rites in a large repertoire. Most conspicuous is the circle or nuptial flight of either mate over the perched mate, lasting about 30 seconds and spanning a diameter of 50 to 75 yards before the bird lands on a branch near the mate. At times several birds may circle at once over a colony. This flight is the only occasion when great blues fly with outstretched necks.

Nest fidelity is weak; most pairs probably select an old nest they have never occupied before or build a new one. Territory consists of the immediate nest area, which is vigorously defended, mainly by threat displays, from neighboring or encroaching herons. Territories often closely abut, sometimes two or more on the same tree branch. In northern heronries, nesting begins in April or May.

EGGS AND YOUNG: typically 4, increasing with geographic latitude to 5; eggs pale bluish green; hatching asynchronous; downy chicks altricial. INCUBATION: by both sexes; about 4 weeks. FEEDING OF YOUNG: by both sexes; regurgitant. FLEDGING: 7 or 8 weeks.

Summer. Chicks vary in size because of their sequential hatching over a period of days. Often the youngest ones, unable to compete for a parent's regurgitant, do not survive to fledge. Sheer force of numbers in a heronry, plus the birds' "uncouth syllables," as Audubon described the incessant noise of a colony, inhibit most would-be predators, but the chicks have their own defense. Threatened by an intruder from below, they lean out and regurgitate food in a discouraging aromatic shower. Leg bones of the gangly young are pliable for the first few weeks, enabling shifting and movement in the confined nest space. Not infrequently, chicks are accidentally crowded over the edge before they can fly, or a windstorm tosses them out. The victims of such events lie injured or starving on the ground until they die, often becoming a predator's meal.

Birds in an active heronry can exhibit all stages of breeding behaviors; some may be courting, others quietly incubating or loudly squabbling over territory, still others feeding chicks. Human observers should not approach a heronry during breeding season, as some of the birds may desert their nests or disrupt brooding or feeding activities. Heronries subjected to repeated intrusion by observers will soon be vacated.

Fledged herons, now almost adult size, remain in the parental vicinity for 2 or 3 weeks, then disperse to feeding and roosting areas, often in loose association with other immatures. Herons progressively molt all their feathers in late summer and early fall. With the increase of heron numbers following fledging, local feeding areas often become insufficient, and herons tend to disperse widely. This is the time of year when one or several vagrant herons may suddenly appear in areas north—sometimes far north—of their breeding range. Immatures often travel farthest.

Fall, Winter. Premigration activity consists mainly of nomadic feeding in dispersal areas, often many miles from the largely vacated rookery. Migration begins in September, with many birds lingering into October. Great blue herons travel singly or in small flocks (usually fewer than a dozen birds), mainly in daytime. Their destinations are widespread. Many northeastern great blues move down the Atlantic coast; numerous midwestern birds migrate to the Gulf coast, Mexico, and Central America. Occasional wintering herons remain near open water in the northern breeding range, but relatively few winter farther north than about 38 degrees N latitude.

The migrant herons may join roosting flocks of local resident herons at night, separating during the day as the birds fan out to solitary feeding territories. In late winter, the birds replace their body feathers in another molt. Spring migration often begins in February.

Ecology. Great blue herons require water or wetlands for feeding and isolated stands of trees for colonial nesting (although in some parts of their range, the birds nest in shrubs or on the ground). Islands are favored heronry locations, as are lowland trees standing in water. Distances from heronry to feeding sites may range up to 6 miles.

Typically heronry trees are tall, holding one or more large stick nests in the tops or on upper side limbs, up to 100 or more feet high. An entire heronry usually holds several hundred nests. Both deciduous trees and conifers are used; stands of birch and aspen are frequent sites in the northern range. Heronries may last for decades, but their longevity often depends on the trees' response to heavy overfertilization of the ground beneath. Heron droppings coat the ground during breeding season in the heronry, and cumulative *phytotoxic* effects of the guano sometimes kill the heronry trees in less than a decade (depending on soil characteristics and tree species), making the trees vulnerable to blowdown and breakage. Thus herons indirectly but quite often

A great blue heron rookery, best seen after the leaves fall, is full of noise and activity in spring.

deplete themselves of heronry habitat. A heron nest usually measures about 2 to 4 feet across. Male herons gather sticks a foot or more long from the ground, from trees, or from old or active nests and bring them to their mates, which build the nest (or add to a previous one) by interweaving the sticks into a flimsy or compact platform. Nest building may take only a few days or a few weeks. The birds line the platform with grass, leaves, and finer twigs. In the southern range, heronries may exist among other nesting heron species, ibises, cormorants, and pelicans. Other birds, including Canada geese, great horned owls, and house sparrows, sometimes adapt great blue heron nests for their own.

Great blues feed mainly on small fish (typically 2 to 11 inches long) but also consume a variety of other aquatic creatures: insects, crayfish, snakes, salamanders, and frogs, among others. Occasionally the birds prey on rails and other marsh birds; rob red-winged blackbird nests; and capture shrews, voles, mice, and ground squirrels. In areas where double-crested cormorants are present, great blue herons sometimes benefit by catching fish driven shoreward by the cormorants. Herons also occasionally pirate fish from gulls.

The great blue's chief competition is for wetland habitat and heronry space. Land development and human disturbance are the greatest threats to heronries. Anything that reduces their isolation and remoteness—house construction, recreation, logging—usually proves detrimental to them. Occasional heronries do coexist with human activities—I know of one almost alongside a busy Michigan highway—but these are rare exceptions.

Nest predators include crows, ravens, red-tailed hawks, bald eagles, raccoons, and black bears. People with guns still claim an annual toll of the large birds, though shooting them is nowhere legal except by permit under special circumstances.

Focus. Unlike some other water predators, such as ospreys, great blue herons are blinded by water surface reflection *(specular reflectance);* studies have shown that their foraging success is greater on cloudy, overcast days than in full sunlight.

First-year mortality in many heronries approaches 70 percent, whereas annual adult mortality is about 20 percent. The oldest banded heron lived to age twenty-three, but such longevity is probably uncommon.

Although these birds are probably not as abundant as they were in presettlement times, a great blue heron plowing across the sky remains a relatively common sight. Researchers always hold the great blue's heavy, spearlike bill tightly closed when banding or handling the birds; it is quite capable of inflicting a fatal blow.

My most astonishing encounter with a great blue heron occurred around a campfire in an open area far from water one windless evening before dark. I looked up when a movement caught my eye; 15 feet above, angling straight at me with wings ballooned and legs dangling, came the heron, set to land. When my startled movement turned it aside, it circled me widely twice, then perched in a treetop some 300 feet away. Equally astonished, I think, we eyed each other for 10 minutes before it finally launched away. This heron, passing overhead, had probably been attracted by the smoke column of the fire and came down for a closer look.

HERON FAMILY (Ardeidae)

Great Egret *(Ardea albus)*

Standing slightly more than 3 feet tall, this largest American egret is all white except for its long, yellow bill (orange during the breeding season) and black legs and feet. Flowing white breeding plumes extend back over the tail in spring. Its 55-inch wingspan and hoarse, croaking notes also typify this egret. Males are slightly larger than females.

Close relatives. The closest North American relative is the great blue heron *(A. herodias;* see previous account). Ten other *Ardea* species range worldwide. American egret species *(Egretta)* include the reddish egret *(E. rufescens),* tricolored heron *(E. tricolor),* little blue heron *(E. caerulea),* and snowy egret *(E. thula).* The cattle egret *(Bubulcus ibis),* a native of Africa, is now cosmopolitan.

Behaviors. Stately and almost as large as its great blue heron cousin, the great egret (formerly called American or common egret) is much more conspicuous in the marsh because of its swan-white plumage. Its characteristic posture when foraging is a forward lean, neck held straight or slightly bent, as it stands or slowly walks in the water, sometimes flicking its wings. Like great blues, great egrets tend to feed solitarily or in small groups, but unlike them, they feed exclusively in the daytime, returning at night to populous tree roosts. Egrets also share the great blue's foot and powder-down feather adaptations. Egrets, however, are sometimes more active feeders, hopping, flying after insects, pouncing on prey from shore, leapfrogging over other feeding waterbirds, even hovering over the water surface. Great egrets commonly associate (at a distance) with other herons and egrets, in both their feeding areas and nesting rookeries. Sometimes they feed commensally (deriving benefit without cost) from the feeding of other water-birds, following in the wake of mergansers, cormorants, white ibises, and others that stir up bottom-dwelling organisms. Occasionally they pirate food items from smaller waterbirds and, like cattle egrets, fol-low cattle in fields.

Probably the most widespread (though per-haps not the most abun-dant) egret/heron of all, great egrets reside on every continent except Antarctica. In North Amer-ica, their breeding range extends locally from southern Canada to the Gulf. Populations with-draw in winter from their northernmost breeding range.

Spring. The great egret breeding season

A great egret stands in typical foraging posture; note the breeding plumes once so highly valued for hats.

varies by months depending on latitude of the rookery. Southeastern egrets usually nest from December into May or June. Northern populations arrive on their breeding areas about mid-April, nesting generally at the same time as great blue herons. At the onset of breeding, adult egrets undergo hormonal changes that turn the bill orange and the *lores* (area between eyes and base of bill) yellowgreen; both sexes develop the flowing, white, capelike plumes for which these birds were once hunted almost to extinction. Egrets that remain yellow billed at this season are probably yearlings, which do not breed until their second year. Most egrets probably home in spring to their previous or natal rookery. Pair formation begins when males claim a nest site—often an old nest not necessarily occupied before by the same birds—and stand on or near it, erecting and fanning their plumes, swaying from side to side, in a stance called the *ausgangs position*. The number of unmated males in a rookery can be judged by counting the birds maintaining this posture.

Territorial and courtship displays—some 17 of them—include vertical neck-stretches, bill snapping, bowing, and twig shaking, most done by males as females land nearby or other males intrude. Display bouts may last up to 10 minutes. Females often launch into extended-neck circular flights in the male vicinity. Male territory size in a densely populated rookery averages about 50 square feet, but this area is vigorously defended only during initial pair bonding. A trial pair bond of several days often occurs before egg laying begins. One study indicated that up to 20 percent of pair bonds dissolve during this initial, highly active phase, the birds deserting one partner to seek another. Displays between mates also decrease once the final pair bond exists.

Both mates collect and add sticks to the nest. Unlike great blue heron ceremonies, however, no elaborate stick transfers or divisions of labor occur; the whole breeding procedure, once the birds are mated, seems much less formal and less driven by ritual behaviors. Nesting in northern rookeries usually begins in April or May.

EGGS AND YOUNG: typically 3; eggs light bluish. INCUBATION: by both sexes; about 25 days. FEEDING OF YOUNG: by both sexes; regurgitant (frogs, crayfish, fish). FLEDGING: about 45 days.

Summer. Comparative studies of great egrets with great blue herons indicate that egret chicks suffer higher mortality from predation than from starvation, whereas the reverse is true of great blue heron chicks. Egret chicks, for whatever reason, seem more vulnerable to nest raiders, especially during their third week; after 5 weeks, however, survival rates are high. Adults, which quickly lose their plumes during nesting, continue to bring food to the gangly chicks until they fledge. Adult molting has usually begun before the egrets abandon the rookery in summer (egrets that remain in the area may continue to use it for night roosting). Egrets are noted for the frequency and distance of their nomadic drifting and wandering—usually solitarily or in small groups—after breeding. An egret can turn up almost anywhere in summer; southern egrets often travel hundreds of miles north from their spring rookeries at this season.

Fall, Winter. The birds remain nomads until harsh fall weather drives northern egrets southward. Most of the northeastern migrants fly to the southeastern United States, some to Mexico and Central America. The pattern of foraging in small groups and roosting in large flocks at night continues on the winter range. The birds probably form at least temporary feeding territories similar to other herons.

Ecology. Nesting and feeding habitats closely parallel those of great blue herons. Great egrets sometimes nest solitarily but more often in small clusters amid the tree rookeries of other herons (especially great blue herons and black-crowned night-herons) and waterbirds. Egrets tend to build lower or in smaller trees (beech and red maple are common northern-range sites) than great blues. Cormorants, anhingas, and pelicans associate with egrets in southern-range rookeries. Great egret nests, about 2 feet in diameter, consist of sticks and twigs and may or may not be lined with leaves and finer materials. As with the herons, egret whitewash (feces) is often toxic to their nest trees and the vegetation beneath them; where soils are coarse or thin, rookeries may last only a few years before the trees die and begin to collapse.

Great egrets are opportunistic marsh, mud, and lowland feeders; common prey includes insects, crayfish, fish, snakes, frogs, mice, occasionally small birds, and fragments of vegetation.

The egret's aigrette, human demand for which almost exterminated the species in America, is worn by both sexes only in spring.

Somewhat more aggressive "walker-stalkers" than great blue herons, great egrets feed in the same habitats, but probably neither bird significantly competes with the other for rookery space or food. One researcher identified several specialized foraging techniques used among 9 species of herons and egrets feeding in Florida Bay, behaviors tending to reduce competitive interactions. Size variation among the species also dictates territorial dominance when feeding.

Nest predators are generally the same as for great blue herons. The egret's deadliest predator was the plume hunter.

Focus. Desirability of the egret's filmy back plumes, called *aigrettes* (sprays) and much valued by the nineteenth-century millinery industry, led to the bird's near extinction on this continent (though it was never slaughtered in numbers equal to the related snowy egret, which bore even more coveted plumes). Publicity by the fledgling National Audubon Society and a few other conservation organizations, along with a changing fashion market, saved the egrets in America. Protective federal legislation, first established about 1900, bore immediate results, but egrets suffered another bout of avicide during the pesticide poisoning of our country from the 1950s to 1970s. Since 1972, when DDT was banned in the United States, the birds have trended toward recovery, showing larger brood sizes and northward population expansion. Slowness of this species' recovery may owe to the fact that relatively few nests fledge more than 2 young; some 76 percent die in their first year. The youngest often falls prey to *siblicide* (killing by an older nest mate), which the parent egrets do not prevent. Thus great egret populations hang on in most places with quite thin margins of stability. Great egret lifespan is probably comparable with that of great blue herons, with a maximum of over 2 decades. The words *egret* and *heron* derive from the same French root *hairon* or *aigron,* referring to these birds.

HERON FAMILY (Ardeidae)

Green Heron *(Butorides virescens)*

Recognize this small (18- to 22-inch-long), dark heron by its usually squat posture, shaggy crest (not always visible), and dark chestnut-colored neck and sides of head. Its dark, glossy, greenish back (often appearing bluish), dark bill, and greenish yellow or (in spring) orange legs are also distinctive. Immature birds look heavily brown streaked on neck and breast. The most common note is a loud, sharp "skewk!" or "kyow!" higher pitched than the larger herons' croaks.

Close relatives. Only 2 other *Butorides* herons exist—the striated heron *(B. striatus)* of South America and Africa and the Galapagos heron *(B. sundevalli).* Few biological or morphological differences exist among all three.

Behaviors. Some authors claim this species, rather than the great egret, is the most widely distributed American heron. Next to the least bittern, the green is the smallest. Feeding both day and night, the green crouches in the marsh or pond margin, its neck drawn in, waiting for prey to swim by. Or it walks stealthily, catlike, sometimes raking the bottom with a backward drag, then examining the scraped area. Or it perches on a branch or stump over the water, flicking its stubby tail or erecting its ragged crest. Sometimes it dives headfirst from a branch into deep water, submerging completely. A unique feeding adaptation of *Butorides* herons (also of black-crowned night-herons) is bait fishing—dropping a small item (feather, insect, twig, leaf, bread crumb) on the water surface, then

A green heron sometimes stands immobile for long periods; unlike the larger herons, it extends its neck infrequently.

striking at any small fish that rises to investigate it. The birds have been seen to carry and reposition their floating lures, even trimming twigs to size. (Other birds that use tools, at least occasionally, include brown-headed nuthatches, green and blue jays, and several others.) Small fish, caught crosswise in the bill, are tossed and swallowed headfirst.

In flight, green herons resemble tailless crows, moving along with slow, plodding wingbeats (their wingspan is almost 2 feet). Thoreau noted "a sympathy between its slug-gish flight and the sluggish flow of the stream." Flying away from dis-turbance, this heron often lets loose a stream of white defecation, hence the vernacular labels "shitepoke" and "chalkline."

Green herons breed throughout the eastern continental United States from southern Canada to the Gulf, and along the Pacific coast and south to Central America and the West Indies. Northern popula-tions migrate.

Spring. Moving northward in late winter and early spring, often in flocks and usually at night, most green herons arrive on their northern breeding range in April. Researchers believe that fidelity to previous breeding sites *(philopatry)* is probable, but solid evi-dence for it remains lacking. Adult bills turn glossy black, legs bright red-orange in spring. Most first-time breeders are probably 2-year-olds. Green herons are only seasonally monogamous. Pairing probably begins during migration, with both mates arriving on the breeding area about the same time. Males establish and defend nesting territories of unknown size marked by song-post perches, where they utter low-pitched "skow!" calls. Courtship displays include exaggerated flapping, erected crest and neck plumage, bill snapping, neck stretching and swaying, bowing, and hopping.

Nesting on the northern range usually begins in May. Males may sometimes begin nest building before pairing; after pairing, they bring materials to their mates, which do most of the construction. The birds sometimes renovate or raid previous nests for materials, and they continue to add sticks through the nesting period. As nesting proceeds, territory shrinks, often to only the nest and its immediate area. Nesting is often solitary, but green herons also nest in rookeries with other greens or other heron and waterbird species. Common grackles, whose clamor may warn nesting herons of intrusion or danger, are also common nesting associates.

Green heron chicks begin to wander on branches outside the flimsy nest when 2 or 3 weeks old.

EGGS AND YOUNG: 3 to 5; eggs greenish blue, becoming nest-stained. INCUBATION: by both sexes; about 3 weeks. FEEDING OF YOUNG: by both sexes; regurgitant. FLEDGING: about 3 weeks.

Summer. Chicks begin to crawl outside the nest when about 2 weeks old, continuing to fly back to the nest for feeding up to a few days after fledging. Soon, however, they accompany parents to feeding areas. By 1 month of age, they are largely independent.

Green herons in the northern range usually raise only a single brood, though they often renest if the first nest fails; those in the southern range raise 2 broods. Molting in this species remains poorly understood, but adult birds progressively replace all plumage from late summer into winter, and yearling birds molt into their first fully adult plumage. Like most herons, greens wander widely after the breeding season; summer fledglings banded in Maryland and Virginia have been retrieved months later in Wisconsin, Nicaragua, and Puerto Rico.

Fall, Winter. For northern greens, the fall dispersal merges gradually into southward migration, and most green herons are gone by early October, though a few may linger through winter where ice-free marshland exists. Most winter migrants end up in peninsular Florida, others along the Gulf coast and southern ocean coasts and into Mexico and Central America.

Ecology. Green herons require brushy freshwater or marine wetlands, swampy thickets, marshes, pond edges, shallow ditches, or mudflats for foraging. The birds usually hug the banks and thicker plant growth, tending to avoid the open flats frequented by larger herons. They seldom wade in water deeper than 4 inches. These birds are highly adaptable, however, in nesting habitat; although nests are often placed near or over water, I found the nest pictured in the accompanying illustration in a small plantation of red pines at least a half mile from the nearest stream. Islands and tree stands in marshes are common nest sites, as are orchards and groves away from water.

Green herons favor dense-foliaged trees or shrubs for nest sites, usually building 10 to 20 feet high beneath a branch overhang. The structure, often a flimsy platform of sticks about a foot in diameter, may be relatively solid or so thinly laid that the eggs are visible from beneath. Plenteous droppings usually coat the nest edges and the ground beneath—nest sanitation is not a heron forte. The birds often nest solitarily, though sometimes they do so in loose colonies or at the margins of larger heronries.

Primarily fish eaters (about 45 percent of the diet, mostly minnow size), green herons also consume many aquatic and other insects (24 percent, often dragonflies and pygmy grasshoppers), crayfish and other crustaceans (21 percent), and other inverte-brates including spiders, earthworms, leeches, and snails. They also may capture frogs, lizards, snakes, and mice.

Competition is negligible. Greens establish and defend feeding territories from other greens and from intruders such as American coots.

Egg predators frequently include snakes, American crows, and common grackles. Territorial greens often attack just about any smaller bird that ventures close. Raccoons probably capture chicks, causing some nest failures. Because the nests are flimsy, many are probably blown down. Recreational boating along rivers discourages green heron presence, but the birds make ample use of backwaters and side pools seldom penetrated by channel traffic.

Focus. This little heron is "a taxonomic yo-yo," in the words of one researcher; it has complicated the lives of numerous birders seeking something authoritative to call it. Before it was "green," it was "little green," then "green-backed" heron. "Green bittern" is also a popular vernacular name. The confusion results from the presence of various geographical *Butorides* populations (mainly in the global tropics and subtropics), which differ slightly in size and coloration. Opinions vary about the precise connections among them; the current wisdom is that our North American green heron stands distinctly apart. The adjective itself seems questionable to describe this bird, whose greenish tinges are not easily seen in most field conditions; the dominant impression is rather of brown shades. As we know, of course, official bird namers relish the descriptively obscure or nonexistent; "swamp squaggin," another of this bird's vernaculars, has always seemed to me a vastly supe-rior label in every way.

This heron is apparently not as long-lived as its larger relatives; the record age is almost 8 years. Data on its historical abundance appear scant. It was once hunted for food and has at times been subject to predator-control programs at fish hatcheries, but in nei-ther case very extensively. Green herons seem much less suscepti-ble to pesticide effects than many waterbirds. Their populations are increasing in many areas, and their range is also expanding, especially along midcontinent rivers and impoundments.

American Bittern *(Botaurus lentiginosus)*

Recognize this brown, almost 2-foot-long heron by its streaked underparts, black neck stripe, yellow or greenish legs, and (in flight) its blackish outer wings. When alarmed, it typically stands in a stiffly vertical, bill-up posture. Its distinctive, resonant call is a tri-syllabic gulping sound ("oonk-ka-choonk," a kind of mechanical, metallic grunt), uttered in a series of two or more phrases, that may carry half a mile. No other bird sound resembles it.

Close relatives. Sixteen herons worldwide are called bitterns, generally identified by shorter legs, stockier bodies, and more cryptic, concealing coloration than other herons. Of the 4 *Botaurus* species, only the American bittern resides in North America; the great bittern *(B. stellaris)* of Eurasia, though larger, closely resembles our native bittern. The only other North American bittern is smaller, the least bittern *(Ixobrychus exilis)*.

Behaviors. Unlike most herons, which often exhibit themselves in open-water and wetland edge areas, the bittern is a shy, furtive marsh dweller that frequents tall, dense growth and rarely perches in trees. Its stealthy habits and inconspicuous coloration (if not its bold spring "thunder pumping") aid its survival strategy of blending into its background. This strategy extends to the bird's alarm stance as it freezes rigidly, feathers compressed, its body and bill aligned with the vertical rushes and reeds; it even sways slightly as wind rustles the stems around it. Its vertical, frozen pose is not adaptive in all situations, however; occasionally I have seen an alarmed bittern stand rigidly and sway after it has emerged from surrounding vegetation, thus making it quite conspicuous. The bittern's eyes are placed very low in its head; even standing with bill straight up, it can see forward and down.

All herons are stealth hunters to greater or lesser degrees, but probably the bittern stands and waits motionless for longer periods than any other. When it walks, it moves slowly, deliberately, but it can also run when disturbed or pursuing prey. As it spots a prey item, it stretches its neck so slowly that movement is almost imperceptible, then suddenly darts and seizes its prey, kills it by biting or shaking, and swallows it headfirst. Bitterns feed both day and night but most often in the dim light of dawn and evening. This bird's cryptic coloration, researchers believe, primarily aids its foraging behaviors rather than its own protection from predators. When flushed from cover, bitterns often flop awkwardly, voicing hoarse, croaking notes. Like green herons, they frequently drop a string of feces as they fly up. These birds are solitary

The American bittern's characteristic alarm posture and brown coloration mimic marsh growth, often camouflaging the bird. (From The Atlas of Breeding Birds of Michigan; *courtesy of Russell Schipper.)*

most of the time, even when nesting. Their pumping or booming sounds are products of great effort, preceded by a number of clicks and gulps as the bird, with violent contortions, inflates its esophagus.

The American bittern's breeding range spans the continent from Canada's treeline to the northern states (it breeds the farthest north of any heron), and discontinuously south to the Gulf, California, and Mexico.

Spring. Because of this bird's secretive nature, many aspects of its migratory and breeding behaviors remain to be discovered. Bitterns are probably nonmigratory in their southern range, but northern populations arrive at their breeding marshes mainly in April—whether alone or in small groups is uncertain. Pair bonding occurs shortly after arrival, with aerial chases between males and display fluffing of small, white, fanlike ruffs on the back and sides (perhaps the source of folk tales that the bittern can project light from its body, enabling it to find prey at night). Courtship feeding may also take place. Apparently the birds remain monogamous only for a single season, but the proximity of 2 or 3 nests in some male territories suggests that *polygyny* (1 male breeding with 2 or more females) occurs at least occasionally in this species. Territory size remains unknown. Females apparently choose nest sites and build the nest; the male's parental role seems to end with copulation.

EGGS AND YOUNG: 4 or 5; eggs buffy brown, unmarked. INCUBATION: by female; about 4 weeks. FEEDING OF YOUNG: by female; regurgitant; animal matter. FLEDGING: unknown, probably about 50 days.

Summer. Bittern nests become rank and foul with droppings and rotting food after a time. Chicks leave the nest when about 1 to 2 weeks old but remain brooded and fed in the vicinity for 2 to 4 weeks, sometimes extending into July on the northern range. All association between family members apparently ceases after fledging. Like most herons, bitterns disperse widely in summer. The annual plumage molt begins in August, sometimes lasting into November.

Fall, Winter. Information is skimpy on the timing of bittern migration. Presumably it occurs mainly in September and October, is mainly nocturnal, and follows major river systems and coastlines. The winter range encompasses the southern breeding range (mainly southern Atlantic and Gulf coastal areas) plus the West Indies and, rarely, Central America. The highest winter concentrations center in the Everglades and California's San Joaquin River marshes. Another molt, of body feathers only, may occur in late winter, extending into spring.

Ecology. American bitterns favor freshwater wetlands, mainly large marshes with tall, dense vegetation, as well as lake and pond edges thickly grown with cattails, sedges, or bulrushes. The birds inhabit wet areas of all sizes but dwell most abundantly in wetlands larger than 25 acres with a water depth of about 4 inches. Thus it may qualify as an *area-dependent species* (that is, a species scarce or absent in small habitat areas). Beaver-created wetlands seem favored over those of glacial origin. The birds use brackish coastal marshes in winter and also forage occasionally in dry grassland habitat.

The nest, a thick platform of dry vegetation lined with grasses, measures 10 to 16 inches across. It may be placed atop a slight mound or a dry piece of ground some 3 to 8 inches above the water or mud surface, becoming increasingly well hidden as surrounding vegetation grows.

Bittern diet consists of large insects (about 25 percent: dragonflies, water beetles, water bugs, grasshoppers); small fish (about 20 percent: eels, bullheads, pickerel, sunfish, suckers, perch); plus crayfish, frogs, tadpoles, salamanders, snakes (mainly garter and water snakes), and meadow voles.

Little information exists on bittern competitiors. Its habitat preferences (plus some of it habits) seem similar to those of rails, perhaps a fruitful area for investigation. The least bittern, whose breeding range overlaps, occupies more restricted wetland habitats than the American bittern.

Predators probably include hawks, owls, snakes, minks, and raccoons.

Focus. American bitterns have suffered significant population declines, especially in the northeastern and north-central states, since the 1960s. In many local areas where bitterns once flourished, none have been spotted for many years. The major reason for this decline is probably the widespread loss of freshwater wetland habitats and fragmentation of those that exist into smaller, less ecologically productive areas. Concurrent declines in frog populations over much of North America—likewise reflecting loss or contamination of habitats—may be another factor. American bitterns are currently listed as an endangered species in several states, as species of special concern in others. A latitudinal trend in abundance is evident—the farther north, the more numerous the bitterns. Some researchers suggest that this may be a *relict species* (that is, an ecological "leftover" from an earlier period of more favorable climatic and environmental conditions) over much of the United States, and that its primary range has shifted northward as retreating continental glaciers left cold, northern wetlands in their wake. "Population declines in the U.S.," according to one research team, "may represent a hastening of an ongoing northern retreat by the species, in part because of habitat destruction in the southern portion of its range."

"Stake driver" and "thunder pumper" are only two colloquial names reflecting this bird's unique call. The sound fascinated Thoreau: "It sounds the more like wood-chopping or pumping, because you seem to hear the echo of the stroke or the reverse motion of the pump handle." He further noted its ventriloquial nature: "It does not sound loud near at hand, and it is remarkable that it should be heard so far." (His friend Minott said, "I call them belcher-squelchers. They go *slug-toot, slug-toot, slug-toot.*")

Because of its strange call from the deep marshes, the bittern has gained a somewhat sinister reputation in folklore. Biblical prophecy began the bittern's negative image, making it a symbol of doom and desolation; the bittern resided in the abandoned cities leveled to wastelands by the vengeful Old Testament deity. The bittern's call was an evil sound, an affront to the Sabbath in New England, where a large gang of men invaded the swamps around a Connecticut town in 1786 to rid themselves of such sacrilege. Greed and idleness were other qualities symbolized by this mostly unseen though often heard waterbird (though such mythology did not prevent roasting it as a table delicacy in Britain). Audubon reported the American bittern as common in market stalls during the 1800s, but the bird has never been hunted as a game species.

Longevity information is lacking. One banded bittern survived at least 8 years, and many probably live longer. The word *bittern* derives from a Latin term for the great bittern of Eurasia, specifically its deep, bovine call.

10

Common Loon *(Gavia immer)*

Loon family (Gaviidae), order Ciconiiformes. This large (up to 3 feet long), ducklike waterbird has a stout, daggerlike bill, red eyes, and patterns of black and white plumages that vary seasonally. Breeding plumage includes black head, checkered white collar, white underparts, and checkered black and white back. In winter plumage, the birds are dark on top, whitish underneath (including chin and neck). Sexes look alike in both plumages. Loud, tremulous calls, wails, and yodels mark the loon's presence.

Close relatives. All 5 *Gavia* species occupy the Northern Hemisphere, most of them worldwide. In addition to the common loon, they include the red-throated loon *(G. stellata),* the Arctic loon *(G. arctica),* the Pacific loon *(G. pacifica),* and the yellow-billed loon *(G. adamsii).* Taxonomically, loons are currently ranked between penguins and petrels.

Behaviors. Their plumages, profiles, calls, and behaviors make common loons among the easiest of waterbirds to identify. Loons ride low in the water, their buoyancy modified by high specific gravity. Loon skeletal structure is much denser and heavier, less porous, than that of most birds; loon bones are primarily adapted for an aquatic rather than aerial existence, enabling them, like grebes, to sink without a ripple by expelling air from the body. Usually, however, they dive. (In Europe, loons are called divers, and this species is the great northern diver, an altogether fitting name for this magnificent bird.) Powerful swimmers, they forage by chasing and capturing fish, propelling themselves both on and beneath the surface with large, webbed feet. They can dive deep (at least 100 feet, also recorded much farther) but probably seldom do, since most small fish prey swims near the surface; they remain underwater normally about a minute, but up to three. Another loon feeding strategy is "peering"—swimming along with bill and eyes immersed. Loons are said to spot their prey in most cases before they dive. Crucial to underwater foraging is the loon's superb vision, which filters out yellow, red, and orange light; the red pigment of the iris aids the bird's night vision.

The loon's legs and feet, superbly adapted for water locomotion, are set so far back on its body that the bird shuffles awkwardly on land. Anybody who has watched loons for an extended time is familiar with the one-foot waggle, when the bird preens on the water, rolls over, and floats with one big foot sticking up. To gain flight, a loon requires a long running start on water, about 90 feet; it cannot rise from land on its relatively small, pointed wings. Some observers have described the loon as a "flying anachronism" because of its almost absurdly high wing load (that is, ratio of bird weight to wing area). In flight, the birds look hump-backed, head thrust forward and down, legs projecting beyond the tail. Loons typically fly fairly low over the water, sometimes at speeds of 75 miles per hour or more. During migrations, however, many fly much higher, up to several hundred feet.

Four types of loon calls may be heard day or night year-round, though most frequently in spring. All except the yodel are voiced by both sexes. The *wail* is a long, drawn-out "wolf howl," sounded as a contact call between mates over long distances or when an adult and chick become separated. The *tremolo* is a quavering, laughlike call, typically voiced when a bird is disturbed or alarmed, the only call also sounded during flight. (This call is a favorite background sound effect of many TV lake and river scenes, sometimes used ludicrously out of habitat or range context.) The *yodel* is exactly that, a loud, complex series of undulating phrases, given only by males establishing or defending a territory. The *hoot,* rarely heard unless the observer is quite close, is a soft, one-note call given between mates and between adults and chicks, also within loon flocks.

Common loon breeding range roughly coincides with northern boreal and hardwood forests in northern North America and Europe, in America extending from tundra ponds of the far north to the northern Great Lakes and several northern states. The birds are migrators.

Spring. Common loons arrive as ice breaks up on northern inland lakes, usually from late March into May. They typically travel in daytime flocks of 2 to 15 birds but at night often settle by the hundreds to sleep on waters en route, usually along the seacoasts and Great Lakes. The flight northward is gradual, following the icemelt. Seacoast migrants may travel up to 25 miles offshore, often just above the water. Inland, however, migrants often fly 1,000 to 2,000 feet high. Migration routes appear scattered, with few identifiable flyways. Males usually arrive a few days before females.

Loon pairs apparently mate for life, returning each year to the previously used territory and often the same nest (though data on loon *philopatry,* or site tenacity, are slim). Allegiance is not to the partner, however, but to the previous year's nest site, which attracts both mates separately and where they re-pair in the spring. One study found that about 20 percent of the returnees find new mates and 13 percent establish new territories. Pair formation rarely occurs before age two or three, however, and the younger, prebreeding population does not migrate in spring, remaining on the winter range until fully adult. The pair bond probably dissolves after the chicks fledge. If one mate fails to return in spring, the other remates on the same or a different territory. Presumably 3-year-old males migrating north for the first time do not return to their natal sites but search out other likely areas. In any given spring, many loons (perhaps 20 to 30 percent of adults) fail to find a mate or find one but for some reason don't breed. These loons socialize, feed, and wander throughout the season.

Loons exhibit a variety of courtship and distraction displays. Most courtship actions are relatively subdued and unspectacular—bill dipping, short dives, ritualized preening. One mid-May day I observed a placid loon pair cruising just offshore in a small lake. The birds would face each other, then one would dive quietly and surface behind the other in a repeated series of turnings, dives, and bill dips—no loud splashing or calls. The scene struck me as one of intense, peculiar intimacy; though the birds must have detected my near presence on shore, they gave no hint of it, or that it mattered.

Loons can be excitable, however, when threatened or disturbed on their territory. Treading upright in the water with spread wings, showing the white belly and voicing the yodel call—or raising upright without spreading the wings—are common territorial displays known as "penguin dancing." The penguin dance is a sign of extreme agitation. The crouch-yodel, when a male flattens itself on the water and yodels, is also a threat. Other common displays include splash-diving and a noisy rush across the water with flapping wings. Territories vary in size from 15-acre bays to entire lakes of 100 to 200 acres, averaging about 40 to 70 acres. Nesting usually begins in May.

EGGS AND YOUNG: usually 2; eggs olive-brown. INCUBATION: by both sexes; about a month; hatching asynchronous (up to a day apart); black, downy chicks precocial. FEEDING OF YOUNG: by both sexes; small fish of an ounce or less. FLEDGING: 2 to 3 months.

Summer. Nesting success of common loons, based on a number of studies, averages about 40 percent, and most hatched chicks survive because of constant parental care. Many pairs that hatch 2 eggs, however, end up with only a single chick, owing to aggressive attacks of the older on the younger. Yet a 2-egg nest has double the chance of chick survival than a single-egg nest, perhaps because 2 eggs receive more attentive care. The nest is abandoned as soon as the last chick hatches and dries off, and few loons venture ashore again (unless to brood the chicks) until another nesting season. Chicks often ride on a parent's back for their first 2 or 3 weeks. Since chilling threatens chick survival more than predation, this perhaps is an adaptation that conserves their energy and 95-degree F. body temperature (in contrast to the adults' 102 degrees F.). Parent loons continue to feed their chicks for about 11 weeks, long after the chicks have begun to dive and feed themselves. Juveniles are almost all black during their first summer.

An important part of the nesting area is the nursery pool, which may be located up to several hundred yards from the nest

A just-hatched loon chick rides on its parent's back; another egg soon to hatch remains in the lakeside nest.

site. The nursery is typically a food-rich shallow cove well protected from wind, waves, and predators. Chicks, led by adults, swim to the nursery when less than 2 days old and remain there most of the time until they fledge. Loon researcher Judith McIntyre believes that imprinting of chicks on the parent loon occurs during this first long swim.

Later in summer, the flocks of nonbreeding loons that have socialized all summer enlarge as postbreeding adults and juveniles join them, often congregating in flocks of 100 or more.

Fall. Timing of plumage molts in loons appears highly variable. Most loons are molting into their gray winter plumage by mid-September but do not replace wing feathers until they have completed migration or just before spring migration. At this time they are flightless for 2 to 3 weeks. "After the late fall molt," wrote author Tom Klein, "the northern postcard loons just aren't the same"; thus the "loon mystique" is not a feature of southern wintering areas. Head and body molt may continue into December.

September and October are the main months of loon migration, though many linger into November. Adult loons usually depart first in the fall, with juvenile flocks following. As in spring, loons migrate in small groups but often form large roosting flocks of hundreds on stopover lakes en route. On such lakes, flocks usually break up into feeding groups of 10 or so birds, then regather in the afternoon to form large offshore rafts. Fall is the only time of year when loons consistently feed in flocks. From the Great Lakes and other interior lakes, common loons head for the seacoasts, where most actual southward movement occurs. The large volume-to-surface-area ratio of a loon's body tends to overheat the bird during flight, especially during warm-weather fall migration. Migrating loons frequently fly with their bills gaping wide open, probably reducing body temperature by so doing.

Winter. Wintering loons enter the annual maritime phase of their existence (juveniles, as aforementioned, for 2 or 3 years); exceptions include a few loons that remain on the Great Lakes over winter. Like other families of maritime birds, loons possess a nasal "salt gland" that enables them to secrete excess salt from the body. The highest concentration of wintering loons in the East occurs along the South Carolina coast; abundant populations also winter along the Atlantic coast in New England and the Gulf coast in Florida. Many wintering loons maintain individual feeding territories of 10 to 20 acres, often in coastal bays and inlets, during daytime hours. At evening, they abandon this spacing and flock together in rafts of 100 or so, usually in protected coves. Loons seldom vocalize during winter, remaining mostly silent. In February, as adult birds begin flocking preparatory to migration, they molt into their black and white breeding plumage; the adult wing molt and flightless period apparently also occur at this time in many populations. Many spring migrants show transitional plumages.

Ecology. Common loons have several habitat needs, some of them increasingly scarce in our world: clear, relatively nonacidic lakes that contain a stable food supply; protected nest sites at the water's edge; shallow nursery coves for feeding of the chicks; and low levels of human activity on both water and shoreline. The latter requirement is especially vital in May and June, when loons, if even slightly disturbed, are likely to abandon their nests. Loons favor small islands or bog mats for nesting sites. They also occupy lakes with no islands, however, and shallow as well as deep lakes (shallow, warm-water lakes with emergent vegetation are more food-productive than many northern wilderness lakes, which often necessitate larger loon territories). Lakes smaller than 120 acres are usually occupied by only a single loon pair; larger lakes may host several pairs. Feeding areas, however, may extend beyond the residential lake. Inflow and lack of clear water resulting from human uses and practices may be a factor in the common loon's withdrawal to the northern portions of its historical breeding range.

Both sexes help build the nest at the shore edge (an average of 16 inches from nest to lake, in one study), using whatever dead plant materials lie within reach. The result is a more or less shapeless, thrown-together pile of debris, 2 feet or more in diameter with a slight center dip. The nest is often continuously wet and quickly deteriorates when vacated. Many loons build in heavy, shore-edge cover, but many also nest in the open, on gravel bars or rock ledges, with no apparent concern for camouflage. Thus incubating loons, sitting so close to the water's edge, can often be spotted rather easily with binoculars. If nesting on an island, the birds usually select the side away from prevailing winds and wave action.

Mainly fish eaters (about 80 percent of the diet), common loons consume minnow-size to much larger fish, up to 10 inches or more, but mostly small ones such as suckers, perch, and shad. Breeding loons with chicks may easily consume more than a ton of fish over the entire season. The birds also capture aquatic insects, crayfish and other crustaceans, snails, leeches, and frogs. In lakes where fish are few or lacking, these items make up the entire diet. Chicks consume fragments of green vegetation as well. Winter diet consists of such saltwater fish as rock cod, flounders, sea trout, herring, and others. Loons consume most of their prey underwater. Loons have also been known to prey on ducklings.

The common loon's only significant competitors for lake habitat are humans. The speedboater, the shoreline builder and developer, and the intrusive fisherman are the banes of loon lakes. "Lakes without a necklace of summer homes are hard to find these days," noted one observer, except in Maine, Minnesota, and Canada. Not only human noise and activity but also the more subtle contamination of lakes with toxins, acid rain, and fertilizers have driven loons from much of their former range. Today the ancient wilderness call of the loon seems a signal of retreat in this habitat contest. The loon's only hope appears to lie in putting distance between itself and its chief competitors, which it has done and continues to do. Herring and ring-billed gulls increasingly harass and compete with loons for nesting sites, again an indirect result of human activities. As more people visit wilderness areas, gull food supply—especially fish remains placed on rocks near shore, as some Canadian park officials instruct fishermen to do—increases. "While this practice keeps campsites clean," an observer wrote, "it also creates fast-food stands for gulls," ultimately expanding their populations in loon country.

Loon predators, as for any ground-nesting bird, are fairly numerous. Foremost is probably the raccoon, though nests on islands are relatively safe from these raiders. Skunks, minks, otters, and possibly muskrats and beavers also consume the eggs, as do gulls, ravens, and crows. Once in the water, chicks are vulnerable to large fish, such as northern pike and muskellunge, and snapping turtles. A common migration hazard is pavement, which the birds often mistake for water; once landed on a road or paved lot, they cannot run into flight launch. Ongoing research shows that many loons carry high levels of PCB and mercury contaminants, obtained in concentrated form from fish and reflecting widespread infusion of these deadly pollutants into the environment. Type E botulism causes periodic loon die-offs, especially in the Great Lakes, and many loons also drown in fishnets. One of the most serious loon threats in eastern North America is acid rain pollution; fish in lakes with pH levels fallen to 5.4 cannot reproduce, resulting in crystal-clear "dead" lakes. Loon chicks typically starve to death in these lakes, but parent loons continue to nest on them, as the adults can fly elsewhere for food.

Focus. The loon's image is virtually synonymous with remote lakes and wilderness sunsets. As everybody's favorite bird of the North, the common loon decorates everything from T-shirts and trinkets to coffee mugs. Its icons, always presented in breeding plumage, commercially symbolize the wild places probably more often than even the eagle and the wolf.

The word *common* in its name is a decidedly qualified adjective; loon populations remain *common* only in areas away from motors, boaters, and voters—increasingly far north, in other words, though some loons do habituate to the presence of people. Pristine lakes once characterized most of North America above 40 degrees N latitude or so, and even until about 1920, breeding loons remained as far south as central Pennsylvania, northern Indiana, Illinois, and Iowa, plus most of New England. Since then, loons have been in general decline and withdrawal so that today, in the United States, their distribution is an uneven mosaic—mostly marginal populations, where any exist at all, with rare locales of abundance. Though the species is not on the federal endangered list, many states now label it endangered, threatened, or at risk. Canada's loon populations remain substantial—Ontario loons alone far outnumber the total population in the United States. Many public and private organizations have devoted themselves to protecting and preserving loon habitat in recent years. The North American Loon Fund is probably the most prominent.

Until the last decade or so, biologists ranked the loon as phylogenetically the most primitive North American bird, a ranking primarily based on its physical resemblance to the fossil toothed diving bird *Hesperornis*. Such resemblance, however, results from convergent evolution. Recent DNA research has revised the evolutionary and taxonomic status of many birds, and loons were found to rank considerably higher in the evolutionary bush than previously placed—higher than waterfowl, gamebirds, and even raptors.

Such a solitary, conspicuously voiced bird figures heavily, as might be expected, in many Indian myths and legends. The Ojibwa claim a special affinity to the loon as the first creature of creation, and the bird identifies a tribal clan. Likewise, loons are pervasive in the tradition and art of the Inuit, who have more than 30 different names for them. Loon masks, totems, icons, and carved images of every size and degree of realism long ago established the pattern for modern "loonacy" in the souvenir trade. Some observers maintain that the loon's call evokes a deep psychic or "racial memory," inspiring feelings of mystery and mystique. Recreational loon shoots were amusements of our forefathers, who tested their skills by treating the birds as clay pigeons. Certain Indian tribes harvested them for food (as some in Quebec still do); others sternly prohibited killing them. Minnesota claims the common loon as its state bird.

Sources differ on the derivation of the name *loon*. Some say it comes from the Scandinavian word *lom*, meaning "clumsy," supposedly referring to the loon's awkwardness on land; from the Norse words for "diving bird" or "waterbird"; or from the Old English word *loom*, meaning "track (wake) of a fish." The simile "crazy as a loon" and the adjective "loony" may have derived from the loon's tremolo call.

Adult loon longevity is estimated at 15 to 30 years. Loons that survive their first 2 or 3 maritime years have excellent chances for living 2 decades or longer.

11

Alder Flycatcher *(Empidonax alnorum)*

Tyrant Flycatcher family (Tyrannidae), order Passeriformes. Flycatchers introduce the order of perching birds, or *passerines,* about 60 percent of all bird species. Passerine birds show a distinctive *anisodactyl* foot, in which 3 toes point forward and 1 backward, all joining the foot at the same level—a foot adapted for perching. The passerine foot also relates to many behavioral characteristics, enabling these birds to specialize in certain ecological slots, or *niches,* that might otherwise remain unexploited by birds. Except for flycatchers, most passerines are classified as songbirds *(oscines).* Flycatchers, though many do sing, possess fewer syrinx (voice) muscles than true songbirds and are therefore labeled *suboscines.*

North American flycatchers show somewhat flattened bills bearing *rictal bristles,* or whiskers, at the base. Strong ligaments connecting upper and lower jaws snap the bill shut, as if spring loaded, on a flying insect. Flycatchers use a sit-and-wait strategy, launching forth in brief, looping flights from a perch to capture insects.

Several North American flycatchers—the willow, the yellow-bellied, and the olive-sided—typically reside in wetlands, but the alder is one of the most common swamp dwellers of its family. About 6 inches long, the alder has brownish olive upper parts, olive sides, a white throat, and a whitish belly. Two whitish bars mark each wing, and the bird shows variable whitish eye rings. Its song is a raspy, accented, 2- or 3-note expletive. "While the traditional rendering . . . is 'fee-bee-oh,'" wrote ornithologist Raymond J. Adams, Jr., "I have never heard one sound this way; the translation 'rrree-beea,' with the accent on the second syllable, gets my vote." "Knee-*deep!*" is another description.

The alder flycatcher, like many insectivorous birds, shows rictal bristles—hairlike, tactile feathers that presumably aid in sensory functions— around its bill.

Close relatives. Positive species identification of all *Empidonax* individuals ("empids") by sight alone is usually impossible; trust no birder who claims otherwise. Most empids are plain, grayish little birds tinged with olive, brown, or yellow. Four of the 5 northeastern empids look so much alike that the only sure way of identifying each is by habitat and song. In addition to the alder, these include the willow flycatcher *(E. trailli)*, the Acadian flycatcher *(E. virescens)*, and the least flycatcher *(E. minimus)*. (See discussions of these species in my *Birds of Forest, Yard, and Thicket.*) The fifth empid, the yellow-bellied flycatcher *(E. flaviventris)*, has more distinctive field marks. Ten other empids reside in the western United States and Central America. All empids are exclusively New World birds. Sexes look alike in all species.

Behaviors. Alders exhibit typical flycatcher feeding behaviors, darting from a perch to snap up insects, then returning. This is a wet-thicket flycatcher, and the perch is usually a shrub. Alders are most easily confused with willow flycatchers, which often occupy adjacent, perhaps slightly drier habitats; the only reliable way to distinguish them is by their distinctive songs and call notes. The songs of both species, unlike those of most songbirds, are innate rather than learned from adult birds, and unlike different geographical populations of most songbird species, they exhibit little variation in their songs across their breeding ranges.

The alder's breeding range extends farther north than the willow's, though considerable overlap occurs in the alder's southern range. Alder range spans the continent from western Canada to the Maritimes and south to the northern Great Plains, the Great Lakes, and the Appalachians. They are migrators.

Spring. Fairly late migrants, alder flycatchers usually arrive on their breeding range in mid-May or early June, after the first large insect hatches appear; the timing of their travel probably closely matches the rate of hatch occurrence along the way. Alders can show up in just about any sort of habitat during migration and do not seem very particular about where they stop. Males arrive first, probably returning to the same territories each year, and sing through the morning hours. Courtship chasing begins when females arrive. Alders are apparently monogamous, but whether for a single breeding season or longer remains unknown. Territory size also remains largely unknown but probably encompasses only a fraction of an acre. Nesting usually begins in June, extending through that month into mid-July. Females probably construct the nest, as with other flycatchers. As nesting proceeds, the birds vocalize less, singing mainly at dawn.

EGGS AND YOUNG: 3 or 4; eggs white, brown spotted at large end. INCUBATION: by female; about 13 days; hatching synchronous; nestlings altricial. FEEDING OF YOUNG: by both sexes; insects. FLEDGING: about 2 weeks.

Summer. Summer nests may be renestings by pairs whose first nesting attempt failed, probably because of predation. The birds sometimes remain on their territories into August. By late summer, alders are looking very drab and worn; wing bars and eye rings have sometimes faded almost completely. Empid identification problems make migration timing statements uncertain (the birds are mostly silent now), but probably most are traveling southward by late August through mid-September.

Fall, Winter. Again, problems of empid field identification impair precise descriptions of wintering areas beyond the generalized locales of Central America and northern South America. Most alders likely have departed the continental United States by early October. Soon after their arrival on the winter range, alders molt, replacing all plumage. Before migrating northward, they may undergo another molt of body feathers in late winter.

Ecology. Alder flycatchers require shrubby wetlands, dense thickets (often in standing water), sometimes occupying bog, marsh, and stream-edge thickets, occasionally wet meadows. In some areas, veeries and golden-winged warblers are frequent bird associates.

The nest, usually built 1 to 3 feet high in an upright or slanting fork, is often placed in dense stands of buttonbush, wild rose, red osier or gray dogwood, shrub willow, or speckled alder, all common swamp shrubs. Loosely constructed of grasses, rootlets, and other plant materials, the nest looks untidy, often dangling bark or plant strips from the bottom. Outside diameter is 3 to 4 inches. The nests, though similar to those of willow flycatchers, are typically placed lower and, unlike the willow's nest, contain few cottony materials and no feathers in the nest rim.

Alder flycatchers are mainly insect eaters, capturing many kinds in flight, though flies rank rather low in the diet. Foremost items include beetles (some 65 species), bees, and wasps (together about 40 percent of the diet). They also eat almost any other flying insect plus caterpillars, grasshoppers, and spiders. The birds also occasionally consume small fruits such as blackberries and elderberries.

The main competitor of the alder flycatcher is often the closely related willow flycatcher. Both species nest together in many areas where their breeding ranges overlap, and they defend their territories from each other. The willow, however, has a somewhat more southern distribution and inhabits not only wet places similar to the alder's haunts but also more open, drier upland areas. Some researchers believe that the willow is expanding its range northward, displacing alders.

Little information exists on predators. Like other open-nested flycatchers, alders occasionally become victims of brown-headed cowbirds, which parasitize many nests by laying their own eggs in them (see *Birds of Forest, Yard, and Thicket*).

Focus. Until taxonomists finally decided in 1973 that alder and willow flycatchers were actually separate species, both nondescript little birds were known as the Traill's flycatcher—and before that, both were called the alder flycatcher. When precise identity of alders and willows cannot be pinned down, as is often the case, birders often lump them as the "Traill's flycatcher complex." The two birds, so alike in appearance and (often) habitats, are not known to hybridize with each other (though how could one tell?). They provide an example of *sibling species*—extremely similar species that nonetheless maintain reproductive isolation. Sibling species perhaps result from relatively recent evolutionary separation.

One banded alder flycatcher survived at least 7 years, but how typical such a lifespan may be remains unknown.

12

Marsh Wren *(Cistothorus palustris)*

Creeper, Wren, and Gnatcatcher family (Certhiidae), order Passeriformes. All wrens are brown; have slender, slightly down-curved bills; and often cock their tails upward. Identify the marsh wren, about 5 inches long, by the white stripe over the eye and black and white streaking on the back. Underparts are whitish. Its song begins with a few scraping notes followed by reedy, gurgling notes, ending in a short, musical trill. Sexes look alike.

Close relatives. Three other *Cistothorus* wrens exist: the sedge wren *(C. platensis)* of eastern North America, and the Apolinar's and merida wrens *(C. apolinari, C. meridae)*, both of the Andes. Other North American wrens include the cactus wren *(Campylorhynchus brunneicapillus)*, the rock wren *(Salpinctes obsoletus)*, and the canyon wren *(Catherpes mexicanus)*, all of the western United States; and the Bewick's wren *(Thryomanes bewickii)*, Carolina wren *(Thryothorus ludovicianus)*, winter wren *(Troglodytes troglodytes)*, and house wren *(T. aedon)* in the East. The majority of the 75 wren species are native to South or Central America. The winter wren of North America is the only species that also resides in Eurasia, where it is known simply as the wren. Family members include the American tree-creeper (brown creeper, *Certhia americana*) and the blue-grey gnatcatcher *(Polioptila caerulea)*.

Behaviors. This small dynamo of noise, darting energy, and double-duty sex inhabits the dense marsh growth. Unless you plunge bodily into such places, you may hear the marsh wren but probably won't see it unless it is advertising its territory by song-flight display. Marsh wren males sing both day and night and, as in many wren species, are often *polygynous* (that is, breed with two or

more females). They are
also aggressively intolerant of other bird species
nesting in or near their
territories.

Marsh wren breeding
range spans the continent
from southern Canada
and New England south
to central Mexico and the
Gulf. The birds reside
year-round in their west-
ern and southern ranges
but migrate to and from
the northern portions.

Spring. Marsh wren
migrants arrive on their
northern breeding range
from late April to early
June, depending upon
latitude. Many have just
completed a partial molt
of body feathers. Older

Although only a few inches long, the marsh wren is an exceedingly aggressive species, intolerant of other birds anywhere in its vicinity.

males arrive before older females, which are followed by yearling
males and females. Unlike the closely related sedge wrens, marsh
wrens exhibit site fidelity *(philopatry)* from year to year, usually
returning to their home marshes. If fidelity to one or more mates
lasts beyond a single breeding season, however, it is probably a
function of territory attraction rather than individual recognition.

Spring is the best time to observe the full range of marsh wren
behaviors. Arriving males establish their territories by frequent
singing—sometimes 10 times per minute—first on one side of the
territory, then on the other. Watch for males flying straight up 5 to
15 feet, then fluttering down at an angle while voicing song; this is
the song-flight display over the territory. Typical territories are
about a quarter acre in size, and song interactions between adjacent territorial males become quite intricate. Many versions of the

basic marsh wren song are heard, and countersinging—in which one bird apparently tries to imitate its neighbor's precise song accents—commonly occurs. On territory borders, male wrens also display by fluffing out their feathers and quivering their wings at each other. While keeping careful track of neighbors and being as exhibitionistic as possible, a male wren dashes about in a flurry of activity within his territory. This activity consists in building num bers of globular nests—up to 27, but usually only 5 or 6. These courting, or dummy, nests are usually grouped in small areas called *courting centers,* several of which may exist and eventually overlap as the season advances. Most male song is voiced from a courting center. Males may work on several dummy nests at once, taking up to 3 days to complete each (actually, they remain incomplete, since they consist only of outside nest "shells"). When a female arrives and pairs on a male territory, the male escorts her to the various dummy nests. She may select one of them for actual nesting, adding layers and lining, or build an entirely new nest herself.

Female marsh wrens tend to be attracted to the highest-quality territories (usually in the densest marsh growth), whether or not a female is already resident and even if bachelor males reside nearby in lower-quality habitat. Most males become polygynous in such circumstances, but rates of polygyny seldom exceed 50 percent (and are usually much lower) in most areas. Usually a male tries for a new mate, resuming song and dummy nest building, when his first mate begins egg laying. Often the second mate's nest is located at the opposite end of the territory, and the two females rarely come into contact but may fight when they do. Nesting occurs from mid-May into July or August.

EGGS AND YOUNG: typically 4 to 6; eggs dull brown, brown speckled, often capped or wreathed. INCUBATION: by female; about 2 weeks; hatching asynchronous (over 2 days); nestlings altricial. FEEDING OF YOUNG: by both sexes; insects. FLEDGING: about 15 days.

Summer. Even monogamous pairs usually raise 2 broods per nesting season, beginning the second nesting in a newly built nest a week or more after the first brood has fledged. Sometimes males, occupied perhaps with another mate during the first nesting, help feed only second-brood nestlings. The parents also continue feeding fledglings for 12 days or so. At night, adults and fledglings often roost in one or more of the dummy nests previously built by the male. As summer progresses and the juveniles become independent, they often flock in groups of 25 or 30, feeding near the water and moving about together. Annual molting of all plumage also occurs in late summer. Northern-range migrants may begin moving southward in late August or early September; these are mostly adults and first-brood juveniles.

Fall, Winter. Second-brood juveniles, some still molting, follow in migration, usually from mid-September to mid-October. Marsh wrens travel to the southern states, the Gulf and Pacific coasts, and into Central America, joining the year-round resident populations of marsh wrens in many places. A few often linger on the northern range through winter in areas where they can find aquatic insects or cocoons. Marsh wrens often move around in small, nomadic groups during winter, remaining mostly silent and hidden.

Ecology. Dense marshland vegetation, primarily narrow-leaf cattail or cord-grass (the latter mainly in coastal salt marshes), is the marsh wren's favored habitat in all seasons. Bird associates may include red-winged and yellow-headed blackbirds.

Marsh wren nests are distinctive, oval-shaped globes of woven cattails, reeds, and grasses. The nest, lashed to standing cattails, is about 7 inches high, has an entrance hole in the side, and typically stands 1 to 3 feet above the water. The entrance hole usually faces south or west. A short tunnel at the entrance hole projects into the nest. The female lines the interior with wet cattail down (which dries to form an insulating layer), feathers, and fine plant materials. The only other nest that resembles it is the smaller, rounder nest of the sedge wren, usually found in sedge marshes. Some of the dummy nests built earlier by the male may later be used as roosting areas by fledgling or adult wrens. Later frequent users of the brood nests include bumblebees, which load up the cavity with cattail down and raise their insect broods inside.

Marsh wrens feed mainly on aquatic insects—dragonflies, crane flies, mosquito larvae, and caterpillars. Spiders, snails, and

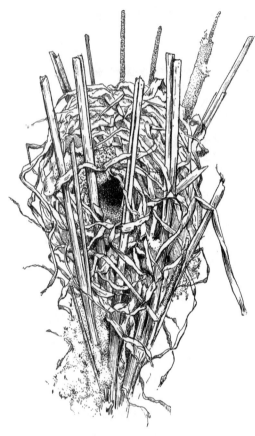

Globular marsh wren nests, usually built amid cattail stems, often host bumblebee nests after the birds vacate.

small invertebrates are also consumed. Winter diet consists mainly of homopterans (planthoppers, leafhoppers, aphids) plus a variety of other insects and invertebrates.

Sedge and marsh wrens (formerly called short-billed and long-billed marsh wrens) do not often compete, because their differing habitat preferences generally keep them apart. Foremost marsh wren competitors include other marsh wrens, red-winged blackbirds, and, in the Midwest, yellow-headed blackbirds; these birds often attack marsh wren eggs. The marsh wren does likewise to blackbird eggs and nestlings—these species are all at war—and also raids other marsh wren nests. One study showed a strong correlation between blackbird nesting success and distance from marsh wren territories. And the bird is a virtual Nazi among its own kind—not really a predator, as such, but a highly aggressive competitor that may raid and destroy nests far outside its own territory. A 1987 study concluded that almost 10 percent of all marsh wren nests fail owing to attacks by outside marsh wrens, and many others suffer partial loss of eggs or nestlings. But virtually any passerine bird in the vicinity becomes a perceived threat. Wrens are the paranoiacs among birds.

Other predators are uncommon. Probably raptors, raccoons, and minks take a certain toll.

Focus. Conspecific egg destruction (that is, by other marsh wrens) is so prevalent that marsh wren eggs have apparently evolved certain defensive features that may protect many egg clutches from complete ruin. A 1996 study found that the eggs have significantly thicker and stronger shells than those of most passerine birds.

Researchers have discovered that two basic song populations of marsh wrens exist, one in the East, one in the West. The western group exhibits more polygynous behavior and has a larger and quite different vocal repertoire from eastern wrens. These populations are separated by the Great Plains, and minimal contact exists between them; some researchers have suggested that they may actually be separate species.

This is a species that has suffered and declined as a result of wetland filling and habitat loss. In many areas, the birds have withdrawn into the large, dense cattail marshes, where much of the eastern summer population is concentrated today. This distribution indicates that the species may be *area sensitive,* scarce or absent in smaller habitat tracts.

The word *wren* in Middle English not only identified the bird but meant "lascivious" (a reference to its polygyny?). Most of the ample wren mythology and folklore refer to the wren of Europe ("Wrens make prey where eagles dare not perch," wrote Shakespeare in *Richard III*). Marsh wren longevity is unknown.

13

FINCH FAMILY (Fringillidae)

This is the largest bird family, comprising almost 1,000 species worldwide, some 150 in North America. It includes the rest of the species accounts in this book. This family lumps several large groups that not so long ago held family status in their own right (and still do in some taxonomic classifications). In the Monroe-Sibley DNA classification system used in this book, however, they have been "demoted" to tribes.

Common traits of the entire family are difficult to generalize; kinship has been established by DNA similarities rather than by physical or behavioral likenesses. Most finches are seedeaters with stout bills adapted for seed crushing; wood warbler bills, however, are slender and sharp pointed, adapted for insect foraging.

Remaining species accounts in this book all belong under the subfamily heading Emberizinae, which includes the tribes Emberizini (sparrows, buntings, juncos, towhees), Parulini (wood warblers), and Icterini (orioles, blackbirds, meadowlarks). Young of all species are altricial; hatching may be either synchronous or asynchronous.

FINCH FAMILY (Fringillidae)

Swamp Sparrow *(Melospiza georgiana)*

Recognize the swamp sparrow by its chunky form, generally rusty color, reddish cap, white throat with sharply marked borders, and grayish underparts. Sexes are alike, though juveniles have striped crowns and less distinct markings. Its metallic trilling song is slow and even-pitched ("weet-weet-weet-weet-weet"), sometimes delivered on two pitches; it somewhat resembles the sound of a squeaky wagon wheel. The bird measures 5 to almost 6 inches in length.

Close relatives. The only other *Melospiza* sparrows are the song sparrow *(M. melodia)* and the Lincoln's sparrow *(M. lincolnii),* both native to North America. (As this book goes to press, a taxonomic split of the swamp sparrow into 2 species—*M. georgiana* and *M. nigrescens*—seems imminent; the latter was classified as the coastal plain race of swamp sparrow from the Chesapeake and Delaware Bay areas.)

Behaviors. Swamp sparrows sing mainly in the morning and occasionally at night during the breeding season, usually from an elevated perch in their territories—sometimes a tree, often the top of a tall cattail or sedge plant. These sparrows are mainly ground and water feeders. They often forage at the water's edge like a sandpiper, either on land or wading in the shallows. Longer leg bones (femur and tibiotarsus) than its *Melospiza* relatives facilitate such wading, and its smaller bill mass reflects its predominantly insect diet (in contrast to most sparrows). It also scratches in the ground litter and climbs mouselike up and down stalks and stems. In flight, swamp sparrows pump their tails much like song sparrows (see *Birds of Forest, Yard, and Thicket),* but they seldom fly high or far except during migrations. Usual flight consists of short, direct hops between song perches a few feet above the marsh vegetation. In escape or alarm behavior, however, the bird is as apt to run away in the dense growth as fly. Swamp sparrow tails frequently look ragged and worn, probably from abrasion in the coarse marsh vegetation.

Swamp sparrows are migrators, though some may winter in southern portions of the breeding range, especially during mild winters. Breeding range extends through much of Canada, from the Northwest Territories, Hudson Bay, and the Maritimes south to the central tier of states east of the Great Plains.

Spring. Migration peaks in April, with males arriving 1 to 3 weeks before females. The birds travel mainly at night. Most swamp sparrows exhibit high site fidelity *(philopatry)* to the previous year's breeding area. Returning males often occupy the same territories they previously occupied, and older males establish them earlier than returning yearling males. Returning females usually settle in the same area but not in the same territory as in the previous year. Thus monogamy is usually no longer than seasonal with a single mate.

Swamp sparrow territories vary greatly in size, from less than an acre to about $1^1/_2$ acres. Average density of birds is probably slightly less than 1 per acre. In large areas of optimal habitat, however, swamp sparrow nesting can become loosely colonial, with up to 15 or so nests per acre. One study found no relationship between territory size and habitat composition; presence or absence of surface water, however, may influence territory size. Males sometimes shift their territorial bounds to accommodate nest-site selection by females. Regular singing by males signals territory establishment, usually before the females arrive.

Count yourself lucky if you happen to hear a male swamp sparrow's flight song in early spring shortly after his arrival. This song, rarely delivered, is an irregular jumble of notes leading into the typical trill song, voiced as the bird flies up and flutters down over his territory. Males also voice this song over open water in areas where song perches are lacking.

Females are extremely secretive, and little is known about the actual pairing process. The only courtship behavior thus far observed in swamp sparrows is the female's copulation-readiness display, elicited by male song; she sits on a conspicuous perch, flutters her wings, and utters soft mewing notes. Females also invariably voice a characteristic call when leaving the nest, a series of short chipping notes; they return to the nest silently. Nesting usually begins in May.

EGGS AND YOUNG: typically 4 or 5; eggs greenish with heavy brown spotting. INCUBATION: by female, which is often fed by male; 12 to 14 days; hatching asynchronous (about 1 egg per day). FEEDING OF YOUNG: by both sexes; dragonflies and damselflies, other insects. FLEDGING: 9 to 11 days.

Summer. Fledglings hop and flutter on the ground near the nest for several days, continuing to be fed by the female for up to 15 days. Swamp sparrows that nest in the northeastern and north-central United States (that is, the southern breeding range) usually raise 2 broods, the second extending into July or August. Females build new nests, beginning a week or so after parental care for the first brood ceases. The complete annual molt occurs in August or September after second-brood birds fledge. As habitat use shifts in summer to drier and upland areas, adults and young forage together in mixed groups, also loosely associating with song sparrows and marsh wrens.

Fall. Fall migration, more prolonged than spring movement, may begin by late August in some areas, usually peaking from late September to mid-October. Birds en route may stop for a week or more at prime feeding areas. "In fall migration," ecologist Donald L. Beaver writes, "individuals can be seen in a variety of habitats, including old fields, pastures, fencerows, and dry uplands." Swamp sparrows that winter in the southern breeding range are probably migrants from the north, replacing the summer resident swamp sparrows that migrate farther south.

Winter. Swamp sparrow winter range extends from the southern Great Lakes to the Gulf and into Mexico, also along the Atlantic coast from the Maritimes south. Highest winter concentrations occur in the Louisiana bayous. Banding studies reveal that members of this species show strong winter philopatry.

Swamp sparrows may maintain loose associations with other sparrow species at times but form only small foraging flocks of 6 to 10 birds. Large roosting flocks of 50 to 60 swamp sparrows may assemble at night. Since winter singing is rare, swamp sparrow presence is often hard to detect. Before and during spring migration, which begins in mid-March, the birds undergo a partial molt, mainly of crown, chin, and throat feathers.

Ecology. Swamp sparrows more typically reside in open marshland than in swampland (the latter has a woody shrub or tree component). The bird has three basic breeding habitat requirements: shallow, standing water; low, dense cover (but not uniformly dense—usually sedges, grasses, or cattails); and a few scattered,

Swamp sparrow nests, bulky and unkempt on the outside, usually lie concealed over shallow water in dense marsh vegetation.

elevated song perches. Bogs, marshes, pond edges, and mixed bog-fen-swamp habitats are good places to look for swamp sparrows. Winter wetland habitat is similar but often more variable, sometimes extending to broom-sedge fields or to shores and fields overgrown with brush and briers.

Males may bring nesting materials, but females select nest sites (often near the edge of the territory) and do all the construction. Nests are usually built about a foot above water (occasionally on the ground) in dense grass clumps, cattails, sedges, or shrubs such as leatherleaf or sweet gale. Most nests are well concealed, lying unattached between stalks 1 to 2 feet below the top of the cattail or sedge canopy and over water about 2 feet deep. The bulky exterior consists of dry grasses or sedges, lined with finer grasses and plant materials. Outside diameter is about 4 inches. Sometimes nests are arched over with grass or sedge, showing an entrance on the side.

Swamp sparrow diet during the breeding season consists mainly of insects (88 percent), both adults and larvae, many of them floating or on aquatic plants: dragonflies, damselflies, beetles, ants, bees, aphids, grasshoppers, crickets, and caterpillars. In summer, as nestlings fledge, the diet becomes granivorous (84 to 97 percent), remaining so through winter. The birds consume seeds of sedges, smartweeds, vervains, docks, panic grass, and various other grasses, plus blueberry fruits.

Swamp sparrow competitors appear relatively few. The swamp sparrow territories rarely overlap with those of other species.

Where swamp and song sparrows
are both present, the latter are
dominant and may chase swamp
sparrows, but song sparrows generally favor somewhat drier breeding
habitats, so little contact ordinarily
occurs. Likewise, marsh wrens,
viciously intolerant of other nesting
species, are usually segregated by
their preference for higher-density,
more uniform marsh vegetation
than swamp sparrows favor.
Swamp sparrows almost always
chase marsh wrens and common
yellowthroats that land in their
territory.

Predators are fairly numerous,
sometimes destroying a large proportion of swamp sparrow nests;
the birds usually renest within a

*Sedge plants in many marshes include
several nut-sedge* (Cyperus) *species;
swamp sparrows plus waterfowl and
rails consume the seeds, especially in
winter.*

few days. Blue jays are frequent nest raiders; others include common grackles, minks, short-tailed weasels, voles, and raccoons.
Garter and water snakes also consume swamp sparrow eggs. Fledglings that fall into the water are sometimes captured by fish, turtles,
and frogs. Brood parasitism by brown-headed cowbirds is fairly
common in some areas (usually near human residences), rare in
large, open marshlands. Flooding destroys many nests, and storms
during migrations can kill hundreds of birds in one night.

Focus. Although nobody has claimed that the swamp sparrow
is an *area-sensitive* species (that is, a species favoring habitat areas
of a certain minimal size for successful breeding, scarce or absent
in small patches of habitat), many swamp sparrow populations
appear to thrive best in extensive, nonfragmented wetland areas,
away from cowbird parasitism and human disturbance. Filling or
drainage of these areas represents critical loss of wetland habitat,
and thus of many bird species in addition to swamp sparrows. The
birds are adaptable, however, often moving into fragmented

wetland habitats, such as ponds, ditches, or reservoirs, but these "fallback areas" cannot entirely offset the loss of the larger wetlands in terms of long-range population maintenance. Although census data indicate stable or increasing densities in this species since the 1960s, it is uncertain how accurately such data reflect the actual status, since extensive wetland tracts are seldom efficiently censused. The figures may only reflect the bird's increasing appearance in fragmented tracts, as a result of loss of larger habitats. Yet, as biologist Gail A. McPeek writes, swamp sparrow populations "are apparently holding their own, which is much more than can be said for most species reliant on wetlands."

Song development has been well studied in this species. From a basic series of unstructured note components and syllables, the birds learn full or *crystallized song* from imitation of adult males. Two song-learning peaks occur: between 15 and 25 days of age and between 225 and 300 days of age (that is, during the bird's first spring). Song structure somewhat varies geographically, but the different "dialects" are all recognizable swamp sparrow songs.

Swamp sparrow longevity is at least 6 years, based on banding records. The average adult survival age is probably considerably less.

WOOD WARBLERS (TRIBE PARULINI)

Birds of the tribe Parulini—about 115 species—all reside in the Western Hemisphere. Forty warbler species (most in the genera *Dendroica, Vermivora,* and *Oporornis)* breed in eastern North America, but most of these reside for all but a few months of the year in the tropics. Small in size (4 to 6 inches long), they have slender, sharp-pointed bills. In the spring, most (though not all) show brilliant yellow plumage on some part of the body. Songs are distinctive for each species. Warblers "lisp, buzz, hiss, chip, rollick, or zip," wrote one observer; few actually warble, a trilling song description better ascribed to sparrows.

Migrant warblers are usually among the last bird arrivals in spring. Seldom remaining still for long, they hyperactively forage in well-defined *niches*—specific subdivisions of a habitat particular to a species. Warbler niches range from ground surface to treetops; certain warbler species may also prefer particular stages of plant succession, from transitional edges to mature forest. Warblers can be classified by foraging sites into three broad categories: those that feed primarily in trees (most warblers), in brush, and on the ground.

Today many wood warbler species are profoundly at risk, showing steadily decreasing abundance in areas where not so long ago they thrived. Severely affected by habitat fragmentation in their breeding range and probably by Neotropical rain-forest destruction as well, our dwindling warbler populations are alarming indicators of environmental decline.

FINCH FAMILY (Fringillidae) - WOOD WARBLERS

Northern and Louisiana Waterthrushes
(*Seiurus noveboracensis, S. motacilla*)

Plumage of these two warblers that frequent wet woods and streamsides is drably thrushlike, with brown upper parts and striped breasts. The two species look much alike. Each is about 6 inches long and has a light eyebrow stripe and pinkish legs. Northern waterthrushes often show a yellowish cast on the breast and

External differences between the two waterthrushes are not easily seen; this Louisiana waterthrush appears in typical streamside habitat.

eyeline plus spotting on the throat; these areas in Louisiana waterthrushes are white. The birds also differ in distribution, behaviors, and song. Song of the northern is a loud, distinct series of musical phrases ("twit twit twit twee twee twee chew chew chew"), or sometimes double-note variations. Louisiana song is also ringing, usually introduced by 3 to 4 clear, up-slurred whistles ("seeup seeup seeup"), followed by a jumbled series of descending notes ("this song, more than that of any other warbler," opined researcher Hal H. Harrison, "exemplifies wilderness"). Subtle differences between the two species in size, plumage, and leg color are not easily recognized in the field. Sexes are similar, and both species migrate.

Close relatives. The only other *Seiurus* species is the ovenbird *(S. aurocapillus),* a ground resident of woodlands (see *Birds of Forest, Yard, and Thicket).*

Behaviors. Both waterthrushes look much like woodland thrushes, act much like sandpipers, and sound little like other warblers. They bob and teeter on their legs, wag their tails up and down, and walk, occasionally hopping over objects or between perches. Both are ground and water feeders, but foraging strategies tend to differ: Northerns feed mainly at the water's edge, often walking on partially submerged logs; Louisianas more frequently feed *in* the water, flipping submerged leaves, strolling or dashing around on the rocks. Both species also hawk and hover for insects on occasion. Flight is bounding and direct. Males sing from mid-canopy tree perches in spring, and Louisianas also sing from the ground while foraging. Both species, however, spend most of their lives below shrub level on the ground and in low growth. Waterthrushes bathe by darting into the water, immersing briefly, then return to shore, flicking their wings.

Northern waterthrush breeding range spans the continent from Alaska to Newfoundland, extending south to Washington, the Great Lakes, and New England. Louisiana waterthrushes have a more southern distribution, primarily in the eastern United States. They breed from Nebraska, the southern Great Lakes, and southern New England to eastern Texas and inland in the Gulf states. The two species overlap breeding ranges in a fairly narrow band across the Great Lakes and parts of New England.

Spring. Louisianas are, along with black-and-white warblers, among the first warbler migrants in spring, usually traveling alone and arriving on their breeding range from late March through early May. Northern waterthrush movement, more typical of warbler migrants, peaks about the second week to the latter part of May, usually in small, loose flocks. Both species travel mainly at night. The few studies on the subject indicate that both also show strong fidelity to previous breeding sites *(philopatry).* Data for Louisiana fledglings, however, seem to indicate that they may not return the next year or, if they do, perhaps to a nearby vicinity rather than the natal site.

Males, arriving a day or so before females, immediately establish territories and begin singing, and pairing occurs as females arrive. The birds are monogamous only for the season but are territorial year-round on both summer and winter ranges. Territories along streams are linear (about 1,000 feet but highly variable); those in swamps are rectangular in shape (2 to 3 acres).

Northerns sing less frequently after nesting begins. Courtship in northerns occurs as males perch and sing above females feeding at the water's edge, following them overhead and vibrating their wings. Louisianas almost stop singing after pair formation but continue intermittently through nesting; mates face off on the ground while voicing call notes, flying up and chasing briefly. Both species utter flight songs, often at dusk; males begin with a finchlike twittering, then fly upward above the tree canopy and sing modified portions of their typical songs.

Northerns nest in June and July, Louisianas earlier, usually late May to mid-June.

EGGS AND YOUNG: typically 4 (northern), 5 (Louisiana); eggs white, spotted, or blotched with reddish brown markings concentrated at large end. INCUBATION: by female; 12 to 13 days; hatching asynchronous over 24 hours; nestlings altricial. FEEDING OF YOUNG: by both sexes; insects. FLEDGING: 9 to 10 days.

Summer. Females brood their young in the nest for about 5 days. Parent birds remove the fecal sacs of the nestlings, sometimes dropping them in the water within a few feet of the nest. Both sexes, dividing the brood, continue to feed the fledglings for about 4 weeks, but territorialism lapses a few days after fledging, and the birds begin to wander over much larger areas. Waterthrushes nest only once per season, renesting only if the first nest fails or is destroyed. Family groups split and disperse when feeding of juveniles ceases, each bird becoming solitary.

Molting of all feathers in adult birds occurs mainly in June and July. Both species resume singing briefly before migration. Louisiana waterthrushes often begin migrating southward in July, with movement peaking in August. Northern waterthrush movement peaks in September. Both species fly at night across and around the Gulf to Mexico, Central America, and the West Indies.

Fall, Winter. Northerns travel farther southward, many to Colombia, Venezuela, and northern Brazil and Peru. Louisianas rarely go as far as northern South America; most stop in Mexico, Central America, or the Caribbean region. A few of both species may winter in the southern United States. Both species maintain and defend individual feeding territories of variable size in winter; where both species are present, these territories seldom overlap as they may in breeding areas. Northerns sometimes sing during fall migration and on the winter range; Louisianas are not known to do so.

Ecology. Northern waterthrushes generally favor swamps, wet woods, bog thickets, or streams with dense shrub (willow, alder) margins. They prefer thicker cover, quieter water, more mud than Louisianas. Dense ground-level cover near water is apparently the major habitat requirement for northerns. Louisiana

Louisiana waterthrushes favor rapid streams with relatively open banks, as shown here; northern waterthrushes prefer quieter water with denser cover.

waterthrushes tend to reside along more open, fast-flowing, gravel-bottomed streams. "Territories of Northern Waterthrush," wrote researcher Stephen W. Eaton, "have significantly more moss cover, hummocks, and conifers, and greater total shrub density . . . than do those of Louisiana Waterthrush." Considerable territorial overlap occurs, however, where the two species occur in the same locality. Although winter habitats correspond to summer ones, habitat differences seem more marked on the winter range, where the two species seldom overlap territories. Coastal mangrove forests in Panama are key habitats for northerns, as is gallery forest (woodland strips along streams through open land). Louisianas are rare in mangroves, favoring higher elevations than northerns on the winter range. Louisianas often occur with the ecologically similar buff-rumped warblers *(Basileuterus fulvicauda)* in mountain forests.

Both waterthrushes are cavity nesters in earthen banks, steep streambanks, upturned tree roots, stump hollows, or beneath fallen logs. Northerns favor the root mats of wind-thrown trees in swamps; the root system, resting at right angles to the ground, often has a pool of water at its base where the tree once stood. They also nest in sides of fern clumps and beneath overhanging banks. Females build the basic bowl, using moss and liverwort plants, bark strips, and small twigs. Lining consists of moss sporophytes, fine grasses, and skeletonized leaves. Outside diameter, usually 3 to 4 inches, depends much on the size of the cavity. Louisiana waterthrush nests, about the same size, are more typically placed near running water in the same sorts of shelters, hidden by

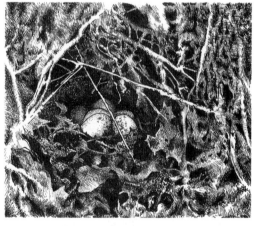

This nest in the niche of an upended tree root, drawn from a photograph, could belong to either waterthrush species; in this case, it was a Louisiana nest, and a cowbird egg was present.

overhanging roots or grasses. Apparently both sexes construct the nest of wet, muddy leaves, pine needles, and small twigs, lined with rootlets, fine plant stems, mammal hairs, and mosses. Louisiana nests typically show an apron of dead leaves in front of the nest cavity, a sort of pathway from the nest, often leading toward a stream below; some nests of northerns also show aprons. Several studies note that Louisiana nests are placed mainly in south- and west-facing ravines or streambanks.

Both species feed mainly on insects. Northerns consume many caterpillars plus aquatic larval and adult insects, occasionally spiders and snails. A 1987 study found that Louisianas fed predominantly on caddisfly larvae and on larger average prey than northerns, which fed mainly on fly larvae. Louisianas also feed on other aquatic insects and invertebrates, including some flying insects such as mayflies. Louisiana foraging habitats appear to change as the breeding season advances. Until eggs are laid, most prey is taken from the water; during incubation and brooding, water foraging declines while ground and foliage foraging increases. Other studies indicate that almost 80 percent of spring foraging for both species occurs in shallow water. The winter diet broadens to include beetles, ants, flies, and small crustaceans. Both species occasionally consume small fish.

Competition appears minimal. Even where both species are sympatric and territories overlap (which is relatively infrequent), interactions are few, and hybridization is not known to occur. Northerns respond as strongly to songs of the rare Kirtland's warbler, studies found, as to songs of other northerns; these songs also sound similar to many birders, but ordinarily the birds' differing habitats would not bring them into song proximity. Researchers in 1967 discovered a northern waterthrush–blackpoll warbler hybrid— certainly an anomaly, since these species' habitats are vastly different and they would not normally compete, much less hybridize.

Nest predators include a variety of snakes plus blue jays, shrews, red squirrels, raccoons, and opossums. Sharp-shinned and other bird hawks sometimes capture adult waterthrushes. Louisianas are more frequently brood-parasitized by brown-headed cowbirds than are northerns, probably owing to the latter's thick understory habitats and more northerly range, much of which lies outside cowbird range.

Focus. Like waterthrushes, several other birds that frequent shore and water habitats and share similar plumage patterns—spotted sandpipers, pipits, and wagtails—also teeter and wag their tails. Some researchers suggest that the habit serves as visual communication to mates or flock members or enhances cryptic patterns of the birds against moving water. These "reasons" sound labored at best; nobody really knows why waterthrushes and other birds teeter.

Maximum longevity for both species, based on banding returns, is about 8 years. Annual survival of northerns averages about 70 percent; survival data for Louisianas are lacking. Both species have expanded their northeastern ranges into New England within the past 60 years. Recent population census trends show general increase of northerns, regional increases and decreases of Louisianas. Researchers emphasize that little of the abundance data is statistically significant, however. Early ornithologists often failed to distinguish the species, thus confusing the historical population range and status data. Wetland filling on breeding ranges and tropical rain-forest depletion on winter ranges seem the most important potential threats to waterthrushes.

In the bird's case, the name *Louisiana* refers not to the present state but to the old French territory sold to Thomas Jefferson and explored by Lewis and Clark—more than half of the continental United States, in other words.

FINCH FAMILY (Fringillidae) - WOOD WARBLERS

Common Yellowthroat *(Geothlypis trichas)*

Olive-brown upper parts and bright yellow throat and breast mark both sexes of this 5-inch-long warbler. The male, masked like a bandit, has a glossy ribbon of black extending down the sides of the head. The loud, rhythmic, chanting song consists of several repetitions, typically "witchery-witchery-witchery-wit." Harsh chattering and a husky "chip" note are also commonly heard.

Close relatives. Eight other *Geothlypis* species reside mainly in the Neotropics. Bahama yellowthroats *(G. rostrata)* and grey-crowned yellowthroats *(G. poliocephala)* venture occasionally into the southern United States. The similarly named yellow-throated warbler is of another genus *(Dendroica dominica).*

Behaviors. Pairs of these common, lively warblers are easily detected, if not always readily seen. A birder's pishing or squeaking sounds usually arouse any yellowthroats that are present, causing great commotion among them. Yet a loudly singing male can be almost impossible to spot in the brushy tangles of its habitat. Females are even more elusive, usually seen only in transit as they dart and disappear in the shrubbery.

Although yellowthroat song is more distinctive to human ears than that of many other warblers, numerous dialect variations occur across this bird's extensive breeding range. One researcher classified 138 overlapping song-phrase types, each spanning up to 300 miles cross-country. Yet the basic pattern of yellowthroat song remains essentially similar wherever you hear it, though an observer may learn to identify an individual male by learning his subtle but consistent variations in song phrasing. This species also shows minor plumage variations in some 10 subspecies throughout the continent.

Common yellowthroats have one of the largest contiguous breeding ranges of any North American warbler, spanning the continent from southern Canada to the Gulf and into Mexico. It is probably our most abundant warbler. All but the extreme southern continental populations migrate.

Spring. Males arrive on the breeding range in late April and early May and immediately begin loud, frequent singing. Many probably return to the previous year's site. Territorial size varies widely, averaging $1/2$ to 2 acres. Sudden silence occurs when females arrive some 2 or 3 weeks later. Few courtship displays are evident, but male singing resumes as females begin building nests in late May or early June. Later in the nesting cycle, watch for males performing song flights, often in the afternoon; they arch over the territory as high as 100 feet, voicing a sputter of notes at the apex of flight, then drop silently to a low perch. *Polygyny,* in which the male mates with two or more females, sometimes occurs, but pairs usually remain monogamous for the season, and some pairs for successive seasons. Experiments suggest that the black facial mask of males is more important in signaling and defending territory from other males than as a sex recognition device in pair bonding, which seems to depend less upon visual than upon vocal or other cues.

EGGS AND YOUNG: usually 4; eggs white, brown spotted, especially at larger end. INCUBATION: by female; 12 days; hatching asynchronous; nestlings altricial. FEEDING OF YOUNG: by both sexes; insects. FLEDGING: about 10 days.

Summer. Although they become highly excited if an intruder approaches the nest, yellowthroats do not perform distraction displays. Second broods may extend the nesting season into early August but are uncommon north of the Great Lakes. Fledglings can fly about 3 days after leaving the nest, but parent birds continue to feed them for about 20 days, a longer dependency period than for most warblers. Family groups range freely, ignoring territorial bounds, which may shift and become reestablished if and when second nestings begin. In early August, as singing declines, the annual plumage molt replaces and duplicates the breeding plumage. Parent birds may still be feeding juveniles as migration time approaches in August. Southward migration extends through September.

Fall. Northern yellowthroat populations move in a leapfrog migration pattern, bypassing the permanent resident yellowthroat populations of the Gulf and southwestern United States. Flying at night, the birds probably suffer their heaviest mortality during migrations. Many perish in stormy or foggy weather by colliding with transmission towers, tall buildings, and lighthouses, becoming disoriented by lights on these structures.

Winter. Most migrant yellowthroats winter from the West Indies and southern Mexico through Central America. Points of highest winter concentration on the continent include southern Florida, southern Texas, and the Louisiana coast. Not uncommonly, however, a few yellowthroats remain on their northern breeding range through winter, usually in extensive marshland or brushy swamps.

A common yellowthroat nest, low and well camouflaged in marsh vegetation, is bulky but not very durable.

Ecology. Sometimes termed our only true wetland warblers, yellowthroats favor both freshwater and salt marsh edges, shoreline thickets, roadside ditches, and brushy or open areas near water. They also inhabit drier upland thickets, dense grass and shrub mixtures, overgrown fields, hedgerows, and woodland edges—basically any area of tall ground vegetation that provides thick cover (see *Birds of Forest, Yard, and Thicket).* Density of low-growing vegetation rather than presence of water is apparently the key habitat factor. Their adaptability to both wet and dry sites gives yellowthroats a much greater habitat range than most warbler species. In their winter range, yellowthroats occupy the same general habitat types as in the summer range.

The bulky nest, usually placed just above ground surface and well concealed in rank vegetation, is supported on all sides by cattails, weed stalks, or grass tussocks, though not attached to them. Skunk cabbage leaves sometimes hold yellowthroat nests in their central hollows. Coarse grasses, sedges, and dead leaves frame a cup lined with fine grasses, bark fibers, and sometimes hair. Second-brood nests or renestings that result from early-season failures tend to be placed slightly higher.

Almost entirely insectivorous, yellowthroats forage mainly in brush vegetation but also glean from bark and occasionally from the ground. Caterpillars, including cankerworms and gypsy moth larvae, aphids, and spiders rank high in the diet. Small grasshoppers, dragonflies, moths, butterflies, and ants are also common food items.

Competition is probably negligible in both wet and dry habitats, given the adaptability of this species. Swamp sparrows and marsh wrens are frequent yellowthroat associates in wetland habitats.

Snakes and mammal predators raid yellowthroat nests, but this bird's foremost enemy is the brown-headed cowbird. Cowbirds may parasitize some 40 percent of early-season yellowthroat nests, often resulting in nest desertion or almost an entire brood of large, demanding cowbird nestlings. Occasionally yellowthroats, like yellow warblers, bury cowbird eggs under a new nest lining. Later-season nests are less frequently parasitized; perhaps most yellowthroats that survive to adulthood are summer offspring.

Focus. Successively named the Maryland yellowthroat and northern yellowthroat before receiving a more cosmopolitan adjective, this species is also known as the ground warbler. Today its abundance appears to be increasing over its breeding range, probably because of its adaptability to both wet and dry edges. Adult annual survival rate in yellowthroats is estimated at about 50 percent. Banding recoveries reveal longevity up to almost 11 years, but few probably survive beyond 4 or 5 years.

FINCH FAMILY (Fringillidae)

Red-winged Blackbird *(Agelaius phoeniceus)*

One of our most common and familiar wetland birds, the redwing (7 to 10 inches long) is easily identified. Males are glossy black except for a red shoulder patch (epaulet) bordered by a lower yellow strip. Females and juveniles are brown and heavily streaked with a light line over each eye. Redwing sounds are also distinctive: the male's gurgling "konk-kee-ree" song and shrilly whistled "cheee-er" alarm call, and the harsh "chack" note of both sexes. Female song is a chattering "spit-a-chew-chew."

Close relatives. Still listed as a separate family (Icteridae) in some classifications, the blackbirds are included as a subordinate tribe (Icterini) of finches in the Monroe-Sibley DNA classification scheme. Almost 100 species exist, all in the Western Hemisphere and most in South America. Twenty-one species reside in North America—orioles, meadowlarks, and grackles, among others—and 11 breed in the Northeast. Other *Agelaius* species include the tricolored blackbird *(A. tricolor)* of the western United States and 9 residents of tropical South America and the Caribbean.

Behaviors. Many ornithologists believe that the red-winged blackbird is the most abundant bird in North America. It is probably also the most widely studied; every aspect of its biology and behavior has been inspected and analyzed repeatedly, and more research accumulates each year. This attention owes not only to its abundance but also to its easy accessibility, observability, and conspicuous actions. It is, in biologist Robert W. Nero's words, "an ornithological white rat." Yet many facets of its life history still pose interesting problems.

Vital to behavioral interactions of the red-winged blackbird is its most distinctive feature, the red epaulets (lesser wing coverts) of the male. Males fully expose and display them during their so-called "song-spread," in which the perched bird leans forward, partially spreads his wings, flaunting the red shoulder patches, spreads his tail, and utters his liquid "konk-kee-ree" song. Song-spread is mainly a threat and advertising action, aimed at other males and at arriving females. Aggressiveness in redwings, the ability to establish and hold a territory or successfully challenge a territory holder, is also a function of badge display and apparently is proportional to epaulet size and conspicuousness—the bigger and gaudier the epaulets, the more belligerent and successful the bird. Yet actual combat and fighting are rare; most boundary disputes are settled by threat displays alone.

Redwing males often stray when seeking food or vacant territories, frequently trespassing onto occupied territories. When they do, they cover their red badges with black scapular feathers of the wing so that only the lower yellow margins of the epaulet show, thus reducing chances of being attacked by the territory holder.

Casual observation might indicate large amounts of variation in size of red patches among male redwings. The fact is that all males have epaulets of about the same size but, unless displaying, the birds often cover them to greater or lesser degrees. The epaulets form only a single component of the threat display complex; others are the bird's vocal sounds and movement patterns.

Redwings, like several other blackbirds, are polygamous breeders; indeed, this is one of the most highly *polygynous* of all bird species. Males may mate with 1 to 6 females (average of 3, but up to 15 have been recorded), and male competition is intense. "Polygyny," as Robert W. Nero wrote, "is related to the fact that first-year [that is, second-summer] males do not usually breed, whereas first-year females do, thus providing . . . a surplus of females." Many males, called "floaters," never gain territories or mates.

Redwings forage frequently, though not exclusively, on the ground. Like many blackbirds, they walk and can double-scratch in a quick hop-skip backward like juncos and towhees. A flock of redwings foraging in a field often appears to "roll" across it, as birds in the rear continuously leapfrog over their flock mates to the front of the flock. "The advantage of the system," wrote redwing researcher Gordon H. Orians, "is that each bird has exclusive use of foraging sites that have not yet been visited by other flock members, and yet has to make only short flights between feeding locations." A feeding adaptation common to many blackbirds including redwings is *gaping*—inserting the closed bill into crevices or vegetation or beneath rocks, then forcibly opening it (the jaw muscles work in reverse fashion, snapping open rather than shut), exposing insect larvae or other prey unavailable to most other birds.

Redwing flight is strong, with bursts of wingbeats followed by slight pauses, producing a slightly undulating course. Large winter flocks tend to fly in long, strung-out columns; during migrations, however, the birds usually fly side by side.

Redwings are highly gregarious for most of the year, not only with other redwings but also with other blackbird species (common grackles, brown-headed cowbirds, rusty blackbirds), European starlings, and sometimes American robins as well. An important element of redwing social dynamics is the roost, or sleeping area, where thousands of birds gather in the evening after foraging all day. Some roosts are used almost year-round; others are seasonal. Males and females tend to roost apart, and most roosts are also age segregated. Spring roosts are mainly occupied by subadult, nonbreeding males. Age and gender components of roosts, however, may change seasonally. Roost numbers and occupancy dramatically increase in late summer, often reaching peak size in winter. The birds establish dominance hierarchies in roosts and maintain them by the same sorts of song-spread displays and aggressive behaviors they exhibit during the breeding season. Adult males, for example, are dominant to younger males, which remain at the roost periphery.

Red-winged blackbirds breed across most of North America, from the arctic tundra to Costa Rica, the Bahamas, and Cuba. Breeding redwings in Alaska, Canada, and the northern United States are migratory, but most lower-latitude breeding populations remain resident year-round. Fourteen races or subspecies are currently recognized; these vary in size and, to some extent, plumage and behaviors. The redwing subspecies occupying almost the entire eastern continent (thus the main focus of this account) is *A. p. phoeniceus.*

Spring. In southwestern Michigan, I can usually count on seeing the first returning redwings about mid-February. All-male flocks continue to pass, arriving throughout the northern breeding range through March. Arthur A. Allen, in his classic 1914 study of the redwing, divided spring migrants into 7 classes, beginning with "vagrant" birds and ending with resident immature females. Probably the movements are not this distinct or easily seen in many cases; many noisy male flocks that settle temporarily in the marshes are en route to distant breeding areas. Site fidelity to previous territories *(philopatry)* is strong in both sexes, though some dispersion of previous territory holders to nearby marshes occurs each spring. Almost all redwings breed within 30 miles of where they hatched, most at much shorter distances than that. Subadult males (yearlings) do not often breed, though many do establish territories and *can* breed if replacement males are needed.

Arriving adult males immediately establish territories (rarely *exactly* the same in size and locale as in the previous year) by means of song and display behaviors. In addition to song-spread displays, they also engage in territorial song-flight, a slow, stalling flight between perches as they flare their epaulets and sometimes sing. Sex chases—rapid, acrobatic flights over the marsh—occur between males and females. Two birds at their territorial borders often exhibit the bill-tilt display: Both birds elevate their bills and flare their epaulets but remain silent.

Male territory size varies greatly. Territories are usually fairly small, averaging $1/8$ to $1/4$ acre in size. Intense competition for territories in good habitat often results in *territory compression—* that is, the squeezing of many small, adjacent territories into optimal sites.

Red-winged blackbird males (top) are highly territorial; a female (bottom) may become part of a harem on a polygynous male territory.

Most food foraging, however, is done off territory. Usually a male territory holder retains a territory from the time he first establishes it until his death (about 2.6 years, on average). Territorial boundaries may shift within a breeding season and from year to year, but the site generally remains stable. Each year a small proportion of males change territory locations or are evicted by competing males. Most males do not begin breeding until their second year (that is, their third summer), though they incessantly try to invade and establish territories. They wander nomadically for most of the summer. Redwing floaters often include many former territory holders that have been displaced.

Females, which arrive several weeks later than males, also exhibit song-spread and bill-tilt displays. Researchers disagree on whether females also establish and defend subterritories within male territories. Female display perches overlap considerably in male territories. Evidence indicates that females choose a desirable male territory rather than a specific male. Thus a female occasionally ends up with the same polygynous mate 2 years in a row but not because of any durable pair bonding beyond a single breeding season.

The *harem,* which consists of all females nesting within a male territory, exhibits both cooperative and competitive aspects. Dominance hierarchies apparently do not exist as such in harems. Harem members seldom operate at the same stage of breeding; one may be building a nest, another incubating eggs, another feeding young. Harem females may help defend each other's nests; they also compete for male paternal care of nestlings. Complicating the parental situation is evidence that female residence on a male territory does not necessarily indicate exclusive mating with the territory holder; thus *polyandry*—the mating of two or more males with a female— may also occur. Most nesting occurs from mid-May through mid-June.

EGGS AND YOUNG: 3 to 5; eggs bluish green, streaked and blotched with brown. INCUBATION: by female; about 11 days; hatching asynchronous, within 12 hours to 2 days; nestlings altricial. FEEDING OF YOUNG: mostly by female; variable feeding also by male (little in some populations, up to 90 percent frequency in others; male tends to feed fledglings with greater frequency than nestlings); insects (mainly dragonflies and damselflies in marsh habitat, caterpillars in upland habitat). FLEDGING: 11 to 14 days.

Summer. Most northern redwings nest only once per year, though double brooding does occur. Anybody who walks the marshes in late spring and early summer knows the protocol of red-wing defense. One's distance from a nest becomes obvious from the male's behavior. As one approaches a territory, he voices his piercing "cheee-er" calls from a perch and utters harsh "check" notes. Then, as one nears the hidden nest, the bird's excitement increases; he dives or circles and hovers just above one's head. The female often joins in, both hovering just behind or at the sides of one's head ("like earmuffs," reported a researcher). The commotion often attracts other redwings, eliciting mobbing behavior. Intensity of redwing attack is unpredictable. In many years of checking redwing nests, I have seldom been actually struck, but many other observers have been, usually from behind by the diving male; typically he twists in the air, striking one's head with his feet, not his bill. A broom or jacket on a stick held above one's head often deflects the focus of attack. Perched fledglings just out of the nest also elicit strong defense behavior by adults.

Parents continue to feed fledglings for up to 2 weeks on the territory, up to another 2 weeks off territory. The independent juveniles then join flocks of adult, postbreeding females, which they strongly resemble. Flocks often feed in upland fields during the day, roost in cattail marshes at night. From late July through early September, however, redwing flocks seem to vanish quite mysteriously. This is the annual molting period; the birds secrete themselves deeply in secluded marshes, becoming relatively quiet and inconspicuous. Juvenile males emerge with variable plumages; some have brown streaking like females, others look quite black, and most show orange-red shoulder patches. Yearling males (that is, in their second summer) develop their first full adult plumage. Adult males wear new black plumage, much of it edged with brown and buff (this edging wears off before the next spring), and red shoulder patches.

Fall. Redwings on the northern range congregate in dense premigration flocks in the marshes. Sources differ on whether adult males depart before or after the females and young. Migration begins in force by mid-October, continuing through November. The day-flying flocks are often joined by flocks of common grackles and brown-headed cowbirds. Migrant flocks vary in size but tend to number less than 100 birds. They stop en route to feed in grainfields and often do not arrive at wintering areas for several weeks. A few migrants from farther north may remain on the northern breeding range through winter but seldom linger where snow cover prevents ground feeding. Most northern interior redwing populations use the Mississippi flyway, fanning out to join year-round resident redwings in the central areas of Kentucky, Tennessee, and Alabama. Atlantic and Gulf coastal marshes also hold many migrants and permanent residents.

Winter. The lower Mississippi valley holds the largest concentrations of wintering redwings on the continent—upward of 200 million redwings and starlings, often roosting together. At least 150 major blackbird roosts exist in the southeastern United States, each containing a million or more birds—some as high as 20 or 30 million. Individual birds may be site-faithful to certain roosts during a winter but not often to the same one over succeeding winters. Redwings sometimes travel up to 50 miles between roosting and foraging areas. Most northern-range redwings are migrating by mid-February.

Ecology. Red-winged blackbirds are highly adaptable to both wetland and upland habitats, accounting in large part for their abundance. Common wetland habitats include swamps, freshwater and salt marshes, and wet meadows. Cattail marshes are probably the places most associated with redwings. Within such habitats, however, a few song perches are necessary, sometimes on trees outside the marsh. "It's important to be able to perch above the tops of the cattails," wrote Robert W. Nero. Hayfields (especially alfalfa) are also frequent nesting habitats, and the birds forage extensively in grainfields. Redwings in presettlement America (and until the 1940s) apparently dwelt almost exclusively in wetland habitats; forest clearing, agricultural development, and wetland shrinkage resulted in habitat shifts so that today the birds thrive in both environments.

The redwing nest is a 4-inch-deep, sturdy cup usually attached to and suspended from surrounding stems. Inside nest diameter is about 4 inches. In marsh vegetation, nests typically hang some 2 to 4 feet above the ground or water surface. Cattails, bulrushes, sedges, *Phragmites* reeds, and bur-reeds are typical nest-cover plants in wetlands, as are willow, alder, and buttonbush shrubs. Nests in fields are commonly on the ground or a few inches above it. Tree or swamp-shrub nests may sometimes be placed 14 to 20 feet high. Tall grasses provide dominant cover for upland nests. Nest materials consist of dried cattail leaves and other marsh vegetation, grasses, willow bark, rootlets, and mud or soft, decayed wood fragments molded for the inner cup and lined with fine grasses. The birds often use the silvery inner bark of swamp milkweed, if available, for the suspended hammock of fibers upon which the nest is built. Female redwings often immerse cattail and other leaves before weaving them into the nest structure. "Often," wrote Nero, "a peculiar sound heard on the marsh in spring is the tearing sound made by female Redwings as they pull off a strip from a wet cattail blade."

The red-winged blackbird nest is a sturdy, suspended cup attached to adjacent stems.

Redwing diet largely consists of insects in spring and summer, seeds in fall and winter. It captures many insects by gaping (see **Behaviors**), by gleaning from vegetation, occasionally by fly-catching on the wing. "Arguably the most critical attribute of marshes for redwings is their role as insect reservoirs," wrote researcher Les Beletsky; "redwing breeding in many regions is tied to marsh insect emergence." These insects—primarily mayflies, caddisflies, dragonflies, damselflies, midges, gnats, and mosquitoes—are sequentially abundant for limited periods, which coincide with redwing nesting. This high insect productivity ensures that a single parent (usually the female) can capture sufficient prey to feed nestlings, in effect freeing males to court additional mates ("Monogamy almost certainly would prevail if redwing young could not survive without feeding assistance from males," wrote Beletsky). The birds seem to take whatever insect offers in greatest abundance. Early-spring arrivals often feed on cattail moth larvae within cattail heads; redwing feeding activities "serve, in part, to bring about the characteristic puffing out of portions of cattail heads as spring advances," wrote Nero. As calorie needs decrease after nesting, redwing diet turns to seeds of weeds and farm crops: corn, rice, wheat, oats, millet, foxtail-grass, smartweed, and sunflower seeds, among others. Corn provides some 75 percent of the August-September diet in agricultural areas. Ragweed and cocklebur seeds are common winter foods, as are seeds of crotons (doveweeds) and docks.

Male redwings compete intensively for territories. Size of the floater population—itinerant, unmated, often second-summer males that constantly challenge older, territorial males through the breeding season—determines competition levels. Actual fights between competing males are rare; intimidation by song or display is the rule. Another foremost competitor, where its range overlaps with those of redwings, is the yellow-headed blackbird, also a marsh dweller. Each species defends its territories from the other where both are present. Larger than redwings, yellow-heads arrive after redwings are on their territories; yellow-heads compete directly for the redwing-occupied areas, often displacing them to the landward marsh periphery. They do not always evict redwings, however. Yellow-heads favor bulrush over cattail habitat, deeper water over shallow areas, more productive over less productive lakes and marshes. Thus both species can and do coexist, not only on the same range but often in the same wetland area. Even though yellow-heads dominate redwings, redwings seem more adaptable to habitat variability, thus far surpassing yellow-heads in abundance and distribution. Redwings and tricolored blackbirds are also mutually territorial in the latter's narrow western range. Common grackles compete with redwings for territorial space in some marshes; the redwings usually succeed in restricting grackle movement near or across redwing territories. Redwings, however, will mob or attack just about any bird or mammal that ventures too close to a nest.

Foremost redwing nest predators include black-billed magpies, American crows, marsh wrens, raccoons, and minks. Redwings are especially hostile to marsh wrens, which puncture eggs and kill nestlings, and they chase them vigorously. The two species seldom nest in proximity. Brown-headed cowbirds may parasitize almost 75 percent of redwing nests in some areas, usually in peripheral sites. Hawks and owls capture adults and fledglings. Mobbing behavior, in which several redwings from adjacent territories may jointly harass or assault a large predator, is a typical defensive action.

Focus. "Unfortunately," as Nero wrote, redwings "are one of the major agricultural pests and nuisance birds over much of the eastern and central United States, California, and southern Canada." Flocks of redwings may strip husk and kernel from entire fields of standing corn. Late-summer crop damage may also extend to oats, barley, flax, sunflowers, rice, and others. Migrating flocks consume much unharvested as well as waste grain, but local flocks probably account for most crop damage. Although redwings and common grackles inflicted considerable losses on even colonial farmers, losses for farmers swelled with agricultural development and increases in cropland acreage, consequent increases of redwing populations, and the addition of grain-feeding European starlings to our avifauna. Commercial rice crops in Louisiana and Texas are often hard hit, though less so today, with mechanized harvesting and drying, than formerly. In cornfields, it is male redwings that apparently do most damage; females, with slightly smaller bills, favor smaller grains and seeds. Even in colonial days, redwings showed adaptability for nesting in hayfields when marsh habitat was unavailable, and this versatility in habitat use further increased their abundance (the dearth of tribal lore about redwings makes one wonder how abundant they really were in America before European settlement). Today in the Midwest, most redwings now nest in upland habitats owing to the decline and loss of so many wetlands.

Redwings provide ample demonstration that introduced species from abroad do not bear exclusive blame for achieving pest status in our environments; native organisms such as redwings, brown-headed cowbirds, some gull species, and many irruptive insect species can also burgeon when habitats are changed. Their numbers not only cause economic losses to humans but, in many cases, compete with and threaten less adaptable native species. Yet agricultural authorities recognize that redwings also consume large amounts of crop-foraging insects at the time of year when these services are most vital to farmers. The redwing's heavy consumption of periodical cicadas and corn rootworm beetles, for example, has been well documented.

Efforts to control blackbird and starling populations—especially mass destruction at winter roosts, where the birds gather in greatest numbers—have met with unspectacular success. An amendment to the 1918 Federal Migratory Bird Treaty Act, which protects all nongame migratory species, allows American farmers to kill redwings that threaten crops. They remain wholly unprotected in Canada. Cost-benefit analyses, however, indicate that control of redwings may be cost effective only where crop damage is heaviest.

Annual survival of adult redwings probably averages about 60 percent. About 6 percent of eggs fail to hatch, and losses to nest predators can range from 30 to 50 percent. The longest wild redwing lifespan is 15 years, but mean life expectancy ranges from about 2 to 4 years. Highest mortality probably occurs during migrations and in winter cold. Like many if not most American birds, redwings were once market-hunted—"few could distinguish them from bobolinks," wrote ornithologist Arthur C. Bent—and sold as "reedbirds." The "four-and-twenty blackbirds baked in a pie," however, referred to the Eurasian blackbird *(Turdus merula),* which is actually an all-black thrush.

Selected Bibliography

In addition to listed references and others, basic sources include Arthur Cleveland Bent's classic multivolume series, *Life Histories of North American Birds* (U.S. National Museum Bulletins, 1919-1958), and Bent's modern counterpart, annually produced monographs in the series *The Birds of North America: Life Histories for the 21st Century* (American Ornithologists' Union and Academy of Natural Sciences of Philadelphia, 1993–). I have also frequently consulted relevant research articles in *The Auk, Wilson Bulletin,* and *Journal of Field Ornithology,* among other professional ornithological journals.

Allen, Hayward. *The Great Blue Heron.* Monocqua, WI: NorthWord Press, 1991.

Beans, Bruce E. *Eagle's Plume: The Struggle to Preserve the Life and Haunts of America's Bald Eagle.* New York: Scribner, 1996.

Beletsky, Les. *The Red-winged Blackbird: The Biology of a Strongly Polygynous Songbird.* San Diego: Academic Press, 1996.

Bellrose, Frank C., and Daniel J. Holm. *Ecology and Management of the Wood Duck.* Mechanicsburg, PA: Stackpole Books, 1994.

Brewer, Richard. *The Science of Ecology.* 2nd ed. New York: Saunders, 1994.

Brewer, Richard, Gail A. McPeek, and Raymond J. Adams, Jr. *The Atlas of Breeding Birds of Michigan.* East Lansing, MI: Michigan State University Press.

Carpenteri, Stephen D. *Osprey: The Fish Hawk.* Minocqua, WI: NorthWord Press, 1997.

Clark, William S. *A Field Guide to Hawks of North America.* Boston: Houghton Mifflin, 1987.

Cruikshank, Helen, ed. *Thoreau on Birds.* New York: McGraw-Hill, 1964.

Dunne, Pete. *The Wind Masters: The Lives of North American Birds of Prey.* Boston: Houghton Mifflin, 1995.

Dunne, Pete, David Sibley, and Clay Sutton. *Hawks in Flight: The Flight Identification of North American Migrant Raptors.* Boston: Houghton Mifflin, 1988.

Eastman, John. *Birds of Forest, Yard, and Thicket.* Mechanicsburg, PA: Stackpole Books, 1997.

Ehrlich, Paul R., David S. Dobkin, and Darryl Wheye. *The Birder's Handbook: A Field Guide to the Natural History of North American Birds.* New York: Simon & Schuster, 1988.

Gerrard, Jon M., and Gary R. Bortolotti. *The Bald Eagle: Haunts and Habits of a Wilderness Monarch.* Washington, DC: Smithsonian Institution, 1988.

Greenberg, Russell, and Jamie Reaser. *Bring Back the Birds: What You Can Do to Save Threatened Species.* Mechanicsburg, PA: Stackpole Books, 1995.

Gruson, Edward S. *Words for Birds: A Lexicon of North American Birds with Biographical Notes.* New York: Quadrangle Books, 1972.

Hamerstrom, Frances. *Harrier, Hawk of the Marshes: The Hawk That Is Ruled by a Mouse.* Washington, DC: Smithsonian Institution, 1986.

Hancock, James, and Hugh Elliott. *The Herons of the World.* New York: Harper & Row, 1978.

Hanson, Harold C. *The Giant Canada Goose.* Carbondale, IL: Southern Illinois University Press, 1965.

Harrison, Hal H. *A Field Guide to the Birds' Nests: United States East of the Mississippi River.* Boston: Houghton Mifflin, 1975.

Headstrom, Richard. *A Complete Field Guide to Nests in the United States.* New York: Ives Washburn, 1970.

Hines, Bob. *Ducks at a Distance: A Waterfowl Identification Guide.* Washington, DC: U.S. Department of the Interior, 1963.

Hochbaum, H. Albert. *The Canvasback on a Prairie Marsh.* Harrisburg, PA: Stackpole Books, 1959.

Johnsgard, Paul A., and Montserrat Carbonell. *Ruddy Ducks and Other Stifftails.* Norman, OK: University of Oklahoma Press, 1996.

Kaufman, Kenn. *A Field Guide to Advanced Birding.* Boston: Houghton Mifflin, 1990.

Klein, Tom. *Loon Magic.* Ashland, WI: Paper Birch Press, 1985.

Leahy, Christopher. *The Birdwatcher's Companion: An Encyclopedic Handbook of North American Birdlife.* New York: Hill and Wang, 1982.

LeMaster, Richard. *Waterfowl Identification: The LeMaster Method.* Mechanicsburg, PA: Stackpole Books, 1986.

Martin, Alexander C., Herbert S. Zim, and Arnold L. Nelson. *American Wildlife and Plants.* New York: Dover, 1961.

Martin, Laura C. *The Folklore of Birds.* Old Saybrook, CT: Globe Pequot Press, 1993.

McCabe, Richard E. *The Unique Wood Duck.* Mechanicsburg, PA: Stackpole Books, 1993.

McIntyre, Judith W. *The Common Loon: Spirit of Northern Lakes.* Minneapolis: University of Minnesota Press, 1988.

McPeek, Gail A., ed. *The Birds of Michigan.* Bloomington, IN: Indiana University Press, 1994.

Monroe, Burt L., Jr., and Charles G. Sibley. *A World Checklist of Birds.* New Haven, CT: Yale University Press, 1993.

Nero, Robert W. *Redwings.* Washington, DC: Smithsonian Institution Press, 1984.

Peterson, Roger Tory. *A Field Guide to the Birds.* 4th ed. Boston: Houghton Mifflin, 1980.

Peterson, Roger Tory, Guy Mountfort, and P. A. D. Hollom. *A Field Guide to Birds of Britain and Europe.* 5th ed. Boston: Houghton Mifflin, 1993.

Poole, Alan F. *Ospreys: A Natural and Unnatural History.* Cambridge: Cambridge University Press, 1989.

Pough, Richard H. *Audubon Bird Guide: Small Land Birds.* Garden City, NY: Doubleday, 1949.

_____. *Audubon Water Bird Guide.* Garden City, NY: Doubleday, 1951.

Robbins, Chandler S., Bertel Bruun, and Herbert S. Zim. *Birds of North America.* Racine, WI: Western Publishing Company, 1966.

Root, Terry. *Atlas of Wintering North American Birds: An Analysis of Christmas Bird Count Data.* Chicago: University of Chicago Press, 1988.

Scott, Peter, and The Wildfowl Trust. *The Swans.* Boston: Houghton Mifflin, 1972.

Stokes, Donald W. *A Guide to the Behavior of Common Birds.* Boston: Little, Brown, 1979,

Stokes, Donald W., and Lillian Q. Stokes. *A Guide to Bird Behavior.* Vol. II. Boston: Little, Brown, 1983.

_____. *A Guide to Bird Behavior.* Vol. III. Boston: Little, Brown, 1989.

Terres, John K. *The Audubon Society Encyclopedia of North American Birds.* New York: Alfred A. Knopf, 1982.

Tucker, Priscilla. *The Return of the Bald Eagle.* Mechanicsburg, PA: Stackpole Books, 1994.

Van Wormer, Joe. *The World of the Canada Goose.* Philadelphia: J. B. Lippincott, 1968.

_____. *The World of the Swan.* Philadelphia: J. B. Lippincott, 1972.

Walkinshaw, Lawrence H. *The Sandhill Cranes.* Bulletin no. 29. Bloomfield Hills, MI: Cranbrook Institute of Science, 1949.

Wright, Bruce S. *High Tide and an East Wind.* Harrisburg, PA: Stackpole Books, 1954.

Index

page numbers in italics indicate illustrations

Also by John Eastman
with illustrations by Amelia Hansen

The Book of Forest and Thicket
Trees, Shrubs, and Wildflowers
of Eastern North America

The Book of Swamp and Bog
Trees, Shrubs, and Wildflowers
of Eastern Freshwater Wetlands

Birds of Forest, Yard, and Thicket

Unique ecological guides to common plants and birds of
Eastern North America, featuring each species as a community
member that affects other organisms and processes.

"The amount of detail is impressive. . . presented in a readable,
easy to follow narrative."
—Eirik Blom, Bird Watcher's Digest

"Recommended for all libraries."
—Booklist

"A very useful reference for both amateur and professional field
biologists."
—John D. Mitchell, New York Botanical Garden

Available in bookstores
or directly from Stackpole Books (800) 732-3669
e-mail: sales@stackpolebooks.com